D1596556

WARRIOR

A Champion's Incredible Search
for His Identity

WARRIOR

MATTHEW SAAD MUHAMMAD

TRIS DIXON

Foreword by
Frank Stallone

First published by Pitch Publishing, 2022

Pitch Publishing
9 Donnington Park,
85 Birdham Road,
Chichester,
West Sussex,
PO20 7AJ
www.pitchpublishing.co.uk
info@pitchpublishing.co.uk

ISBN 978 1 80150 070 8

Typesetting and origination by Pitch Publishing
Printed and bound in Great Britain by TJ Books Limited, Padstow

CONTENTS

FOREWORD by FRANK STALLONE

THE FIRST time I met Matthew Saad Muhammad, he was still Matthew Franklin. I tapped him on his back. It was like concrete. Inside his sharp white suit was a physique of solid muscle and on his face was that great, unforgettable smile. He was such a handsome guy and always so well-dressed. But he was never a bragger and had such a nice way about him.

He was about 6ft tall, a good-sized light-heavyweight and very strong. I would go to his fights at the Spectrum in Philadelphia. I'd sit at ringside, and watch Matthew Franklin go to work.

His best defence was his offence. I used to yell at his corner, 'Keep your fucking right hand up,' because he was getting hit by left hooks all the time. He'd look over at me and I'd say, 'Don't look at me, look at the guy punching you!'

But if Matthew caught you, he'd *really* hurt you. His chin was incredible, too, and his recuperative powers were as amazing as his will to win. He was a real warrior. You couldn't hurt him and Matthew got hit by the best of them. They'd think they had him but he'd catch them with a shot and that was it. For a time, he was unstoppable.

Matthew fought Marvin Johnson twice and Marvin was a tough bastard. He could punch, he was left-handed, an Olympic bronze medallist. You had two young guys in their twenties, hard as nails. Marvin had skills, then it turned into a war. Matthew won both of those fights.

I was at the first John Conteh fight in Atlantic City, and I thought Conteh was an excellent fighter. A good boxer and a good puncher.

It was another great bout. Conteh was winning but Matthew, like he always used to, started getting to him later and John just couldn't keep him off. Saad was so damn strong. He was a tough, tough guy.

I knew Nick and Joe Belfiore, his first trainers. I went backstage after the Conteh fight to say hello to Matt, who had recently changed his name, and he's surrounded by people with sunglasses and bow ties. They were giving me some attitude before Nick told them I was okay. Who were these guys? Nick explained that Matthew had joined the Nation of Islam. He said, 'You know what the sad thing is, Frank? He's going to end up broke and punchy.' And that's how he ended up.

Nick and Joe loved Matt. They treated him like he was a son. When the Nation of Islam took over, he put those guys on the back shelf. I think it broke their hearts, because they thought of him so highly.

Back in the day, Matthew had it all. He had a white Steinway piano, a Rolls-Royce, all the bullshit. He had a really nice life yet ended up living in a hostel, which was terrible because he made good money.

By the time he fought Dwight Braxton, who would later be known as Dwight Muhammad Qawi, Matthew had taken too many shots and he'd taken a lot of punishment. He went for the Clubber Lang part in *Rocky III*. I remember me and Sly talked about him, but I was only there when Earnie Shavers and Joe Frazier came down and read. I knew they weren't going to get the part.

Many years later, he was on the *Rocky Balboa* set and Sly said, 'Saad's here'. I could tell Matthew was 'shot'. He was a little heavier, maybe 205lbs, and when I talked to him, he sounded a little slurry. But that great smile was still there. He should have retired after that first Qawi fight and he might have been okay. It's always after they lose the title that the downside comes, when the accumulated punches take hold.

People talked about his life story becoming a movie and I don't know why it didn't happen. Boxing movies are a really hard sell. I think *Rocky* was big because it's more of a love story and *Rocky* just happens to be a boxer. In boxing, there are a lot of tragic stories but

Matthew was always Matt, this nice guy with a great heart. I saw him at a reunion with Yaqui Lopez and they were getting on so well but Matthew was friends with everyone he fought.

Back in the day, he was always trying to better himself. One time I tried to get him to come out with me and he said he couldn't come because he had elocution lessons.

He was my man. I loved him.

PROLOGUE

ABANDONED
15-16 JUNE, 1959

'STAY CLOSE together.'

The youngest boy was almost out of the front door when the older child spun around and nodded subtly to the woman.

The door slammed behind the boys and they were off and running down the street.

They laughed and joked, pushed one another and played and then, with time passing by, the older boy vanished.

The younger child, only four or five, grinned happily and began to search for his brother.

They had gone from 'tag' to 'hide and seek', clearly. The boy looked excitedly behind parked cars, then started checking beneath them.

He ran down one end of a bustling street and investigated heaving avenues. No luck. He ran back to where he last saw his brother but the older boy hadn't returned.

The youngster's enthusiasm wasn't dampened. He crossed the street and went the other way, peering through doorways, running in front of slow walkers and shoppers to try and catch up with his brother.

Was he somewhere out of sight, watching the little boy's every move?

Was he about to jump out and start laughing again?

Time started to get on and the young lad's excitement and optimism were starting to transform in to a panic.

His legs were growing tired, his feet were getting sore.

He ran and ran, not knowing where he was going and before long, he didn't know how to get back to where he had started, either.

It started to get dark. The boy was so shy he couldn't bring himself to ask for help and as the sun started to shrink and the night air began to bite, he thought he might get in trouble when he got home for catching a cold.

Distress and desperation replaced expectation. If it had been a game, he was losing badly.

He tried to talk to several strangers but couldn't form words, let alone sentences and then he'd run off, terrified. Sometimes he would run up to a person but be so scared he would just run again. He muttered, panicked, a shocked look across his face and then he'd sprint on, hoping to catch his brother.

Time ticked by, minutes turned into hours, and he had no idea where he was and the busy period when no one stopped to talk was replaced by a still, urban quiet.

That despair gave way to a lonely, silent acceptance that he could do no more.

His legs betrayed him so he found some steps to perch on.

Lit glumly by streetlights, he soon curled into a ball and rested. Rarely someone would walk by, the echoes of sirens blared in the distance, but soon the noise faded and his only memory years later was of lying down there, thinking he could do nothing and no one could help him.

Then his eyes closed.

* * *

The morning traffic brought him round.

The boy stirred, hearing busy commuters and the sound of leather shoes on tarmac, horns tooting and engines revving. He had no idea where he was but in the bright sun, he saw a police officer directing traffic.

Hungry and lost, he made his way towards her, eventually stood next to her and froze.

'Hello,' she said, ushering him to the pavement.

He looked at her.

She repeated herself. 'Hello.'

Nothing.

'What's your name?'

'Where are your parents?'

Nothing.

She looked around, over his shoulders and across the street, half expecting a mother or father to be frenetically running around looking for the boy, but there was no one.

She asked the same questions again. The boy didn't say anything but he didn't take his gaze off her.

A few minutes went by and the police officer started to realise that the little boy was lost.

She led him to her police car, letting him sit up front, and they made their way through busy Philadelphia.

The boy stared anxiously out of the car window, hoping to see his brother or recognise another relative, but there were strangers everywhere.

At the police station he waited.

Occasionally someone would ask him his name but he couldn't get any words out. Hours dragged by. Every time a door opened, he looked up, expecting a family member to come and pick him up.

'No one came to claim me,' he would say mournfully, shaking his head decades later.

He spent a night at the police station anxiously waiting, managing little sleep but the next morning two women came to collect him. They talked in soothing tones, spoke about food, a bed, other children. But really it was all a blur.

He had been turned over to an orphanage.

The following day, the child's picture appeared in a Philadelphia newspaper with the caption, 'Found on highway.'

No one responded.

The boy had been abandoned.

CHAPTER 1

NO GOING BACK

NOW IN the orphanage, routine became the young boy's friend and, as the days turned into weeks, he learned to adapt.

The hope that someone would come to collect him gave way to the resignation that no one ever would.

No one in Philadelphia had even reported him missing.

He had come under the care of the Catholic Social Services at 222 North 17th Street and was being looked after by nuns in the orphanage.

When they asked the boy what he was called, he could scarcely say, 'Maaa, Maaa, Maaa,' so one of the first things they had to do was give him a name.

Partly because Matthew was the name of one of the nun's favourite saints, legend has it, and partly because Matthew is what the nuns thought the boy was attempting to say, they chose to call him Matthew.

And because he had been found on the Benjamin Franklin Parkway, they decided his surname would be Franklin.

Matthew later recalled seeing 'a whole room of kids' when he first arrived. The lessons started with simple things, like using manners and being courteous to each other.

'None of us knew where our parents were,' he said. 'They trained us to be good kids.'

He slowly added to his vocabulary and built up some of his fragmented confidence, but that was well-hidden by a stammer that he may have had before but that certainly had not been aided by his traumatic upheaval.

Sometimes he'd allow himself to think of home. He wondered if his parents had been embarrassed of him because he couldn't talk properly or if they had found him too difficult to deal with because he struggled to communicate.

Whatever he thought, it always came back to him. He thought it was all his fault. He tried to understand, saying he thought 'they struggled' because he had been so slow to pick up talking.

But he no longer felt it had been just a terrible accident. He realised that he'd been ditched, cast out never to return.

Now, he was part of a new community. He was in a dormitory of 15 boys. He had to go to mass, to church, to lessons. Everything was based around him becoming a good child. And he was.

New kids would arrive and old ones would leave. Some seemed to have been in the orphanage forever. He made friends, only for them to be taken away.

He did as he was told. He wasn't any trouble. His social skills improved. He was not a quick learner, but he was learning.

The idea of the orphanage was never to have children for the entirety of their childhoods. The idea was to raise the children until they could be added to households as foster children. After almost two years, the nuns thought it was time Matthew lived with a family.

They matched him with one in South Philadelphia.

John 'Pops' and Bertha Santos were an older couple, Portuguese immigrants who had adopted several children.

They lived in a small terraced house at 1314 Catherine Street. Neighbours wondered how so many people could live together in such a small house, but they made it work.

One of Matthew's earliest memories was going to City Hall with John and Bertha as they went through the required paperwork for his adoption.

The nuns had used their best guess and came up with 16 June 1954 as his birth date.

And life with the Santos family was good.

'I probably couldn't love this family more had I been born into it,' Matthew said.

He had brothers of all ages. John and Bertha had four of their own children and six foster kids. They were not South Philadelphia's wealthiest family, but they found a way.

'They always made a meal,' said Matthew. 'At times, it was hard. Some days we didn't eat lots but then when we did, we had so much. We were always taken care of and they would always freeze the food, so there was always a meal. We didn't live in the ghetto, but it was an area I guess you'd call lower class.'

The Santos family were Christians, so they celebrated Christmas. Matthew went to Bible school and his overwhelming recollection was that 'it was a nice, comfortable atmosphere with them.'

The family would always celebrate Matthew's birthday, and through those formative years he paid little mind to the trauma of his past. He would not think about his family.

'I got into the mind that they gave up on me so they don't care about me,' Matthew explained. 'I couldn't feel bad for them'.

Besides, Matthew grew in confidence. Although his speech still faltered at times, he formed close bonds with several of the other boys, including Joe Johnson.

Matthew tried sports in school, too. 'I played football, I loved the roughness, the contact and I think the roughness and toughness helped prepare me for getting hit.'

When Matthew turned 10 or 11 years old, though, his routine was regularly interrupted.

John Santos had told Matthew the fastest way to walk to school, not knowing it would take Matthew through tough neighbourhoods and active gang grounds.

Street kids, focusing on Matthew's inability to talk the way they talked, picked on him, and he was subjected to beating after beating.

'Where you from, kid?' the biggest of the crew would yell.

Matthew would look at the ground and try to walk on but his route would be blocked.

'Where you from?' he was asked again, this time with a shove to his chest.

'I'm from No Street,' Matthew shakily replied, not wanting to let on where he lived.

'Oh yeah? You're from No Street?'

Bang. Matthew would be punched in the face and then the others would beat him, too, leaving him bloodied on the ground.

'Sometimes they'd use body punches and they'd try to break me up,' Matthew recalled years later. 'There might have been 14 of them, maybe 25 on bad days.'

He remembered many beatings.

'They would beat me up every time they caught me and at that time a lot of gang war was going on,' he said. 'I was a kid, only about 11 or 12. Come on.'

Occasionally he would see them first and be able to outrun them, but that didn't happen as often as he hoped it would. If anything, having to work for their prey antagonised them. But Matthew knew no other route to school apart the one his step-parents had shown him.

Stephen Chandler was a part of it all as a kid growing up in South Philadelphia.

'People had gangs because it was about survival back then and only the strong survived,' Chandler said. 'A lot of the time you had to be from a gang because another gang would come to your neighbourhood and then when they would hear you're not from a gang ...'

The stakes were high. Clinton Barnes was from those same rough Philadelphia streets with Matthew.

'It could be serious,' said Barnes. 'Mostly it was fist fights but there were stabbings and shootings that could happen and we would carry knives or guns, whether you could fight or not. Mostly it was the high schools that brought all these different neighbourhoods together.'

Often rows would erupt over girls and blood would be spilt.

Philadelphia music legend Teddy Pendergrass, coming through the city at the same time and familiar with the gang culture, once said going to serve in Vietnam was a more attractive option for young men in Philly than growing up on the wrong side of the tracks.

Boxing great Bernard Hopkins was born in Philadelphia in 1965, and his mother knew the city was catching fire with gang wars, so they moved into a suburb to escape.

'In the sixties, it was terrible,' Hopkins later said.

The Santos family felt powerless to put a stop to the bullying.

'I know what was happening to me was upsetting to them,' Matthew said. 'They were upset for me. Trouble wouldn't stay away from me. I got tired of trying to be good. Being good only got me beaten up by every bad kid in the neighbourhood.'

Things needed to change.

'I wanted to protect myself,' he explained. 'That was the whole thing. I wanted to learn how to box and keep these guys from beating me up all the time. That's all. I remember, when I first got in a gang I was scared. But once I got on the road toward being a really bad kid, I lost my fear.'

Matthew's view on what he might be able to do changed, too, when he first saw a Muhammad Ali fight, in the late 1960s, having watched Ali with his step-dad and his brothers.

'And I was looking at this man who was saying he was the best in the world and he was "The Greatest", and with that he was getting better and better and bigger and bigger,' said Matthew. 'I started looking up to Muhammad Ali because he could move and dance, he was a colourful fighter and he could punch and not get hit and I wanted to be like him. And I loved Philadelphia's Joe Frazier, his power and his heart – I loved his heart – and he was one of the best fighters back then.'

There was another early Ali memory, too, and it stuck with Matthew. In a Philly gym one day, the great heavyweight – who lived nearby in Cherry Hill – was sparring a local tough guy known simply as 'Cheese'. 'Cheese' took the liberty of punching Ali in the mouth but Muhammad lit him up in response. Matthew was amazed. 'I saw that and I said, "Oh man. I want to be like that guy."'

Matthew knew a Philly boxer called Alfonso Evans, a super-featherweight nicknamed 'Bubby', and he told Matthew about Nick Belfiore's Juniper Boxing Gym in South Philadelphia. With the blessing of his step-parents, Matthew set about sharpening his own physical tools.

Outside the gym was a sign that read, 'No Women Allowed' and each day young Matthew would climb the steep, narrow staircase in the mid-terrace gym not far from his home and he'd tread the old wooden floorboards, learning to skip, move left and right and throw punches.

'These are kids obviously with troubled backgrounds, most of them, and it was a clean, safe place and it was close to where they were living, so they were more or less driven there by street life,' said veteran Philly boxing writer Nigel Collins. 'It was a place you could go where you were given respect, treated as men, so I think that was the attraction. Nick was pretty good on the basics, always yelling at guys, "Jab and move around. Jab and move around."'

Among fight posters of Philly's big nights yellowing on the walls, Matthew studiously listened to Nick Belfiore, who was there with his brother Joe, an ex-pro fighter who had had some 60 fights through the 1940s, mostly in Philadelphia and New York with the odd outing in Atlantic City and a few further afield in Chicago and New Haven.

'Nick was a crusty old guy, heart of gold,' continued Collins, who was reporting on the Philly fight scene at the time. 'I think maybe there was some money behind him, but I'm not really sure. It was a very small, immaculate gym.'

Matthew soon realised that it wasn't easy being a fighter and that the road ahead to safety and self-defence was not going to be easy.

'That was the secret,' Matthew would smile years later. 'I didn't realise how hard it was going to be. That was a shock. You had to be mentally and physically prepared and so determined.'

But he respected the Belfiore way and set about improving as quickly as he could.

'He was a good man and I will always admire him,' Matthew said of Belfiore, who would wear a fedora but take it off to work with his fighters. 'He showed me the little things in training and he was an expert – like his brother Joe. Nick was heavy-set, he would always say, "You cocksucker this, you cocksucker that …" and he would curse. He was aggressive and he made me do things and I would just do it because he was so grouchy.'

Philadelphia promoter and historian Russell Peltz used the same adjective to describe Belfiore.

'A loveable old grouch whose bark was louder than his bite,' opined Peltz. 'Nick began training his brother Joe in the '40s and Joe fought guys like Joe Miceli but a lot of good fighters passed through his gym.

'He was a great guy. He was too emotional to be a great trainer but he had the good fortune of having all of these talented guys come through his gym.'

Nick would threaten to crack the head of one of his boys for not listening, but in the same breath would drive him home to make sure he got an ice pack on the wound!

'Nick was miserable, but he took care of us and showed us the right way,' said Mike Everett. 'We started with him and he took us places that we wouldn't have gone without him. Nick was a loving person …'

Stephen Chandler agreed. 'He'd bawl you out, but he never treated you wrong.'

Over the years, Jeff Chandler (no relation to Stephen), Obe English, Alfonso Evans, Kevin Curry and Tyrone Everett all took the steps up to the two rings in the gym.

Outside the Juniper, everything changed for Matthew with a punch.

Once again surrounded by bullies, the largest teenager started to get in Matthew's face.

Tired of running, Matthew planted his feet, swung his right hand and that was that.

Everyone else backed off and Matthew, fired up and invigorated, called for more challengers. Months of torment came spilling out but there were no volunteers.

Instead, an offer to join the 13th Street and South gang was extended and Matthew became one of them. Gang members called him 'Iceman'.

'He was blessed with power,' stated childhood friend Salim El-Amin. 'He could knock a man dead.'

Matthew's naivety was replaced by ambition, his fear with confidence and his trepidation with power.

He was at the top of the food chain and he enjoyed it. It was far more preferable than what had gone before.

He felt he had to become 'a bad kid'.

'Those guys were robbing and sticking places up but I was strictly a gang member, I was fighting and I would just fight to control my turf,' he explained. 'I didn't understand. "What am I controlling?"'

'13th Street was one of the most vicious gangs in the city at that time,' said Eddie Everett, who like his brothers Tyrone and Mike would become a professional prize-fighter. 'Me, Mike and Tyrone joined Cartman Street [20th and Cartman] for a minute, and that became the most vicious gang in South Philly and we got right out, because we realised we weren't gangsters, we were boxers. We're not going to stab you, we're not going to shoot you, we just fight with our hands, so we just got out of the gang right away. Matthew wasn't really a gangster. Matthew was like us. Matthew was a fighter, too. There was a difference. The gangs back in the day had respect for boxers, and if you were a fighter, you got respect all over the city from gangs.'

The Santos family didn't know how deep Matthew was in.

Tony, one of their birth sons, was also involved. Matthew had wanted to be like him, too. Like any kid at that age, Matthew wanted respect.

'It was very rough in that gang,' he recalled later. 'I was lucky I wasn't found dead somewhere. How would I describe my childhood? Dangerous.'

El-Amin continued: 'They called us the black gangstas, we weren't no gangstas, man. We were struggling, man, so we'd swim with anything that would help us get on track. In South Philly, these Italians would be shooting at each other, up in New York and then down here in Philly there were killings ... People dealing with positions and trying to be in control of narcotics, gambling and liquor.'

'There was two kinds of gang down there, the white mafia and the black mafia,' El-Amin went on. 'But they did their thing and everyone did what they could to make money. Everybody had to learn how to fight and you had big guys and you had small guys.'

Blood was shed on a regular basis and the violence was extraordinary.

And Matthew and young Mike Everett were caught up in it for a while.

'You had a lot of gangs back in the day,' Mike added. 'Gangs would get together and start fighting and that's how I knew Matt, down there on 13th Street. We became close but I wouldn't mess with them guys down there.'

Matthew was regularly in scrapes and became known to the cops. They could never put anything on him but he was a marked man and there were several near misses.

'There was this one cop who was always after me,' Matthew recalled. 'But he could never catch me. One day, I was walking along and he came up behind me ...'

Perhaps thinking he'd have his hands full, the policeman pulled a gun and forced Matthew to the ground, frisking the teenager to discover a 10-inch blade.

The cop didn't need to find anything else. Matthew's luck ran out and he was sent to a juvenile facility. The justice system was trying to make examples out of kids involved in gang culture as it swept through the city and Matthew was on the receiving end, losing three teenage years to institutions.

Initially, he fought back inside and rebelled. He was moved from one place to the next for fighting and acting out. Having been in the Daniel Boone School and the Glen Mills School for Boys, Matthew sparked a riot at the Youth Study Center and was sent to Camp Hill. 'Camp Hell,' he would call it. There, he was sent to Ward E and then to Ward H, as his behaviour deteriorated and he spent time isolated from the rest of the population. 'Quarantine,' he said. 'I couldn't get along with anybody. Some tough guy would shove me or yell at me or order me around and I'd pop him.'

He was angry. He didn't know where he'd come from, who he was and he certainly didn't know where he was going.

Trouble followed trouble.

'I beat up a guard, knocked him cold,' Matthew said. 'That brought about nine other guards running and I was giving them pretty good action for a while … but man, they eventually did a number on me. Afterwards, they put me upstairs in a special room and locked the door. What I remember most about that experience is that there was no light in the room, and that after it got dark you could hear the rats and the mice running around. I'd sleep with the blanket pulled over my head, hoping they couldn't get to me.'

Realising his life was spiralling out of control rather than progressing, he decided to turn things around. He was handed a copy of the influential Muslim newspaper *Muhammad Speaks* and read it with interest, particularly because Ali was often featured inside.

'I read certain literature but I was confused,' he said, explaining the information he was trying to absorb. 'There was a lot of prejudice and racial stuff between all religions, it had nothing to do with colour. They were talking against each other but I just liked Muhammad Ali because he was one of the best fighters. It wasn't because of religion at the time.'

Matthew also took classes to become an electrician. And then there was boxing.

A man named Edgar Carlis, who taught English behind the walls, had heard about Matthew's reputation for punching and recommended he focus on his boxing. Matthew would later credit Carlis with turning him from a troubled kid into a boxing hopeful.

There was no boxing programme inside, and only limited gym use, but Matthew would wrap his hands in his bedsheets and pound the cell walls, firing combinations to the body and head of would-be opponents. He waged war on the wall as though he was Frazier and would dance around the small room thinking he was Ali. He tied old rags together to make a skipping rope.

His friend El-Amin joined him in Camp Hill. El-Amin was facing a minimum of ten years in prison 'after someone got shot' on the streets.

'I couldn't believe it that he was there,' El-Amin said. 'Matthew used to come to my cell and ask me about boxing, because he didn't know how to fight. He was hitting tied up pillows when he was in the cell, trying to learn how to do things.'

Another inmate who was locked up with Matthew remembered Matthew sticking his mattress up against the cell wall and punching it. 'He'd wrap towels around his hands and punch that mattress.'

'That was because I wanted to see how hard I could punch,' Matthew remembered. 'You always heard about fighters like Oscar Bonavena, Rocky Marciano, Joe Frazier ... these guys were excellent punchers, strong men and I wanted to be like them, so I worked on my power and I'd sometimes punch concrete walls, making sure I had enough padding that would protect my hands from cracking or breaking.'

Upon his release, Matthew stepped out of Camp Hill in the fresh suit given to all inmates at the end of their stay, tasting free air.

'I walked out of there and said I'm never coming back.'

CHAPTER 2

NOTHING ELSE BUT TO BOX

AS A teenager, Matthew Franklin tried to make the best of his fresh start. He got a job 'hacking chickens' and in 1973 he won the Trenton Golden Gloves.

'I'm going to be a fighter and a champion,' he told his step-father, John Santos, unflinchingly.

'Hey, I know who you are,' Santos replied.

Matthew was training out of Nick Belfiore's gym in South Philly and there were no problems with street gangs any longer, or with the cops.

But his career as an amateur boxer was relatively short. He reckoned he had around 30 fights. He even lost his first contest.

'The kid needs a lot of work,' sighed Belfiore.

Matthew won his second fight, however, then won four on the spin, got a draw, lost and was victorious in his next 23.

He lost to Coatesville's Jimmy Clark, but there was no disgrace in that, because Clark had beaten future heavyweight pro champions like John Tate and Greg Page.

Belfiore wasn't sure about Matthew's potential but he did see something.

'At times he wouldn't listen,' Nick said. 'He was a little thick-headed. But I knew he had something all along because he was always a good puncher and he took a good punch.'

For Matthew, whatever Belfiore told him was matched by another influence. He still adored Muhammad Ali. He admired his anti-Vietnam stance and he loved to watch him box.

'I continued doing what Muhammad Ali was doing,' Matthew said. 'He did a lot of dancing. He did a lot of movement. He showed me movement, you don't just fight, you have to know how to box, you have to move your head, even though I was more like Rocky Balboa.'

That was also true. Whether it was a typo or not, one local newspaper captioned an image of Matthew winning an amateur fight by calling him 'Mayhem' Franklin. It was prophetic, even if it was done in error.

At 18, Matthew had a job for a while loading trailers as a dock worker for about $300 a week which helped develop his shoulders and back, as did his stint operating a jackhammer on a construction site.

He might not have been born to box like Ali, but boxing gave him hope and aspirations and he'd never had either. It also gave him an identity, and that had also been lacking. And while he might have been an orphan, at the gym he fitted in. He made friends. He won fights. He was more popular than he had ever been at any point of his life.

'I didn't know anything else but to box,' Matthew said. 'I fought all the way up to the Golden Gloves. I won some and I lost some. I didn't make it all the way to the nationals but I just thought, "I can't eat trophies," so I turned professional.'

* * *

Pat Duffy had a saltwater taffy shop in Atlantic City but was also a czar of amateur boxing on the East Coast. He could spot talent and would syphon off promising amateurs into the clutches of certain managers, including Pinny Shafer, a well-known Philadelphia fight figure who had fingers in many pies. Shafer was the head of the local bartenders' union and had managed heavyweight contender Leotis Martin, former Olympian Sammy Goss and middleweight Jimmy Soo. Pinny knew everyone. Everyone could hear Pinny.

'Pinny was bombastic and loud. If he said "hello", you could hear it down the street,' recalled Philadelphia boxing promoter Russell Peltz. 'He was a colourful character. He managed [Bennie] Briscoe for a while until he sold him to Jimmy Island and Pearce Management and he was a good man.'

Belfiore was the man charged with improving the fighter, while Shafer was steering the ship.

Philadelphia had long had a history of being involved with the shadier side of boxing. Back in the 1940s and into 1950s the sport was being run, for all intents and purposes, by a pair of gangsters called Blinky Palermo and Frankie Carbo. Hiding behind the front of the International Boxing Commission, they made the big fights and worked with many significant fighters across North America.

Bad decisions and corruption were accepted as part of the sport and in 1947, they fixed Billy Fox's four-round upset win over Jake LaMotta, which LaMotta 'threw' in exchange for a title shot later.

Carbo – a gunman and killer in the infamous Murder Inc as part of the Lucchese crime family – was the boss and Palermo his Philadelphia lieutenant. They owned a piece of heavyweight champion Sonny Liston for starters.

In 1960, there was an investigation into Mob influence in boxing by Senator Estes Kefauver. Carbo wound up in prison on a charge of managing fighters without a licence and in 1961 Palermo was charged with conspiracy and extortion of former contender Don Jordan. They were sentenced to 25 years.

But boxing had not been able to move beyond its shady past and would always have some link to a criminal element.

Still, Philadelphia was not just on the boxing map through the 1970s, it was a crown jewel.

As a fight town, Philly was becoming the centre of the universe. 'Smokin' Joe Frazier was one of the world's leading heavyweights and, with the careers of the talented Harold Johnson, Stanley 'Kitten' Hayward and Gypsy Joe Harris winding down, middleweights Eugene 'Cyclone' Hart, 'Bad' Bennie Briscoe, Bobby 'Boogaloo' Watts and Willie 'The Worm' Monroe fought for supremacy in the city.

The gyms were packed. Heavyweight contender Jimmy Young was on the scene, there were the talented Everett brothers, Tyrone and Mike, and an emerging South Philly bantamweight named Jeff Chandler, whom Matthew was friendly with.

'You had the Cloverlay Gym in North Philly, you had the 23rd PAL in North Philly, Champs Gym in North Philly, the Blue Horizon and in South Philly you had the Passyunk Gym, the Juniper Gym, gyms in West Philly,' explained Peltz. 'Boxing was big then. You had fights at the Arena, the Convention Hall, the Spectrum, the Blue Horizon ...'

And Matthew quickly learned there were significant differences between the amateur and professional codes in the sport.

The professional side of boxing is a hard world. You fight in the gyms trying to get noticed. You fight for your life in the ring trying to give yourself a better future.

Fight tactics and strategies are different. They're generally more measured and deliberate while amateur fights are sprints over shorter periods.

'As a professional, I had three minutes to do whatever I could do, whereas when I had two minutes in the amateurs, I had less time to do what I needed to do,' Matthew explained. 'In some ways it helped me. If I had to run, I'd run. If I had to take punches to wear a guy out, I would do that. For a person to be able to do a thing like that is special.'

Matthew realised, as Belfiore had, that he had a rare gift – the ability to take a heavy punch without blinking or flinching. Sure, he accepted that it was not in his best interests to do so, but it wasn't a bad thing to have in his arsenal.

Away from the ring, Matthew made money in construction and working on the docks and Belfiore didn't charge him gym subs so Matthew saw that as a free upside.

He also got a small place of his own, a simple apartment with a kitchen, bathroom and living room. It wasn't much but he didn't need a lot. Besides, it was certainly an upgrade from Camp Hill.

Veteran boxing writer Nigel Collins – who would go on to have an International Boxing Hall of Fame career as editor of *The Ring* – met Matthew in the early- mid-1970s, either late in his amateur career or when he was boxing a preliminary fighter.

Collins would see Matthew every time he visited the Juniper.

'In the gym, Matthew was like a bubbly kid,' recalled Collins. 'He was that way a lot of the time. He had a great smile, nice laugh, good looking guy. He was very down to earth.'

Behind closed doors, Franklin learned the hard way. Philadelphia has a reputation for gym wars. Educations were rough. Some fighters were ruined in the gyms and some never graduated from being excellent gym fighters to true greats.

Matthew was sparring the likes of Hayward, Hart, Watts and Briscoe, not just crafty veterans but tough men against whom he had to pay his dues. He said he learned defence by having to spar heavyweights like Jimmy Young and Roy Williams.

It is not an insult to say Matthew was sparring better boxers than he would fight in his early paid bouts and on a cold Monday night on 14 January 1974, he made his debut against Scranton's Billy Early in Philadelphia at the Spectrum over six rounds. Early had won one and lost four of his first five career bouts and in his next fight was stopped by Bob Stewart, who would go on to uncover the potential of a young detention centre inmate named Mike Tyson.

Matthew beat Early in two, earning brief mentions in the *Philadelphia Inquirer* and the *Philadelphia Daily News*.

'He could punch,' Matthew said of Early, trying to recall that first fight. 'I was just getting into the boxing game and I didn't really know how to throw punches and combinations but I knew that when I did, I did good. I wanted to keep that up. He had more experience than me. [It] was a rough fight and he rocked my clock and I rocked his but I didn't want to get embarrassed at the Spectrum, which was like Madison Square Garden to me. He was orthodox but I was new and I didn't really know much. All I knew was to hold my hands up and not get hit.'

Six weeks later Matthew was abroad for the first time in his life when boxing took him to France. While he did manage to get matched in the Palais des Sports in Paris, his primary reason for going to Europe was not to notch his second career victory but to serve as a chief sparring partner to Bennie Briscoe, who fought in the main event.

'Matthew was just a young kid with a handful of fights,' remembered Peltz of the trip. 'When we went to Paris to fight [Tony] Mundine – who was tall – we took Matthew with us and I remember they [had] boxed in the gym in Philly and Bennie drilled him and knocked him down with a straight right hand, but Bennie knew how to work with those guys. Matthew had only had one fight at the time but they were not what you'd consider gym wars.'

'When Bennie clubs you in the body, it feels like someone is hitting you with a sack of wheat,' Matthew would smile.

That was because the gap in class between a one-fight novice like Matthew and a world-class middleweight contender like Briscoe was too great.

'What are you going to tell Briscoe? To take it easy?' continued Peltz. 'These guys don't know how to take it easy.'

It worked both ways. Matthew's ambition, size and strength meant Briscoe was getting good work, too, sharpening his tools.

'I was hitting so hard they wanted me to go and be with Bennie,' Matthew explained. 'He was beating everybody up and they said I was similar to his opponent so they let me go and train with Bennie in Paris. And while I was there, I knocked the guy out in the second round. Bennie and I would throw hundreds of punches at each other every round.'

On the night, Matthew outscored Mukeba 'Bele' Apolosa in a four-rounder and Briscoe stopped Australia's Mundine. A couple of weeks later, back in Philly at the Spectrum, South Philly's Matthew beat North Philly's blown-up middleweight Roy Ingram on points over four in the show opener on a bill that featured 1968 Olympian Sammy Goss and Matthew's friend Tyrone Everett. Two months later, Franklin beat 'Smokey' Joe Middleton, winning in the fifth and in July, on a big Spectrum bill that saw Boogaloo Watts stop Cyclone Hart in a round, Matthew knocked out the slightly heavier Joe Jones after two minutes and 19 seconds of round two.

Matthew wasn't facing world-beaters. He was learning his trade against fighters who could give him rounds and confidence.

'Those were guys who would keep me busy,' Matthew said. 'But it was good that they kept me busy because you don't want to take long lay-offs between fights. You don't want six months or a year between fights – that's too long for a fighter to wait. I was getting better each fight.'

Buffalo's Lloyd Richardson had won two and lost one fight when they met on a Tuesday night at the Spectrum on 10 September 1974. Matthew halted him in four rounds. He stopped Joe Middleton in two in a rematch in October of that year when Middleton suffered a cut eye and couldn't continue. That was at a roller rink on a club show in Virginia.

It had been a big year for Matthew. The *Inquirer* said the 7-0 prospect had been one of the most active fighters in the city in 1974. He was still only 19 but his next opponent, 25-year-old Wayne McGee, was billed as a three-time New York Golden Gloves champion who had moved to Philly to progress his boxing career. He did just that when he handed Franklin his first loss, on points over six rounds at the Blue Horizon. It was McGee's second pro fight and his second win.

'Wayne McGee was a big fighter,' Matthew recalled. 'I was skinny and he was stocky like a bull and, when I looked at him, I wanted to shit my pants. He was so ugly, I said to myself, "I want to beat the ugliness off him" but I didn't. I was a young kid. He was stronger than me, he was a man.'

Things were slower for Matthew in 1975 with just three fights, spread out in February, July and October with inside-the-distance victories over New Jersey's 3-1 Vandell 'Big Boy' Woods in front of 500 patrons at the Blue Horizon. He then gave away 7lbs in weight to stop Boston's Roosevelt Brown, who had won 15 and lost just twice. Franklin tried to avenge the McGee loss in October, ten months after their first meeting, but had to settle for a draw.

'Wayne McGee was a lot better than his record,' recalled promoter Peltz. 'He'd beaten Angel Oquendo, who was a fringe contender, he had those two fights with Matthew, which always led me to believe Matthew had trouble with people shorter than him, like [Dwight]

Qawi, and yet Marvin Johnson came to Philly in 1976 and blew McGee away in a round – but it was a hell of a round.'

Matthew was building his experience and growing as a fighter. The scared, bullied kid was becoming a solid local pro and his confidence was increasing. Sure, he suffered pre-fight fear and nerves in the dressing room before his bouts but he was learning to control those emotions.

'Sometimes a person might be macho and say they're not going to get nervous, but a lot of times he tells himself, and he must tell himself, that he's a champion, that he's a man, regardless of what comes into his mind that tries to scare him,' Matthew explained. 'You get these unwanted questions coming to you but you have to psych yourself up to be strong. I was always nervous but after I got hit, I was okay. You go from being scared to being brave. Sometimes I'd say, "I want to see how well you hit to be able to absorb that and not let that punch affect me."'

Early in February 1976, Matthew went ten rounds for the first time when he was drafted in as a late substitute for New Jersey's Jerry Judge.

Franklin fought Cleveland, Ohio heavyweight Harold Carter at the Painters Mill Theatre in Owings Mill in Maryland. Matthew was said to be 21 years of age, experienced Carter was 28, had lost 34 of 54 fights but he went the full ten before Franklin took a points decision. Stiffer challenges would lie ahead, but the orphan from Philadelphia had now won ten fights, lost one and had drawn another.

He had sparred some of the city's finest fighters, getting used to brawlers, technicians, punchers and movers. He was learning and improving, still just a young man gaining experience in the ring and in the world but the learning curve was about to get a lot steeper, and very quickly. Still, he remained optimistic.

'I knew I would make money anyway,' Matthew said. 'I was on the right path, man.'

CHAPTER 3

THE SHAFT

'I REMEMBER, he was an outstanding European fighter who threw a lot of punches and I was sure I was going to beat him,' Matthew recalled. He found himself back in Europe as the opponent, as cannon fodder, against Mate Parlov. The brilliant left-hander from what was then Yugoslavia was a decorated amateur who had lost only a handful of his 310 amateur fights and had captured a gold medal at the 1972 Munich Olympics, defeating top Cuban Gilberto Carrillo in the final. Parlov had also won the World Amateur Championships in Havana in 1974. By the time he fought Matthew in an eight-rounder in Milan, Parlov was an unbeaten pro – 12-0, ranked No. 8 in the world by the World Boxing Council (WBC) – and ready to put on a show.

Behind the scenes, things were changing for Matthew. He was being managed by Frank Gelb, a Norristown, Pennsylvania, businessman who had his own stable of fighters. Gelb worked with Jimmy Young, who had recently lost a close and contentious decision to Muhammad Ali. He was also managing two of Matthew's friends, Mike and Tyrone Everett, a pair of talented Philly up-and-comers.

Gelb's father, Maurice – also known as 'Mo' – had also been a promoter and they had a furniture business.

'I was a promoter and well-known manager in those days and people would come to me to represent them,' recalled Frank Gelb. 'Matthew was with some other gentlemen for a few fights and in the gym he was working out of, his workout opponents [Mike Everett et al] were managed by me and he decided that he may be better off going with me. We started partway into his career and made very well of it.'

It was a good transition for both parties. Gelb was getting deeper into the boxing business and Pinny Shafer was in his late sixties and trying to do less.

'Pinny was a great, great manager and had a whole list of great fighters,' Gelb reflected. 'But he was aging and I was the young guy and we made a pretty good deal between each other and I inherited many boxers from him.'

This was how the deal went down, according to Russell Peltz. 'Gelb managed Tyrone Everett and he thought it would be cool to have the Everett brothers together, so he made a deal with Pinny to buy Mike's contract and have Mike come along in the Gelb stable, along with a stablemate called Alfonso Evans. Well, Matthew Franklin didn't want to be left alone, they were all friendly, so he called Pinny up and said, "I want to go with them, too," and they threw him in as part of the deal. Gelb didn't know what he had. None of us knew. I think he'd already fought a draw with Wayne McGee and so he threw him in as part of it.'

A few fighters went in the same direction. After Young lost to Ali, Shafer and his partner Pat Duffy turned his management over to Gelb for $5,000.

As part of the Gelb gamble, nothing was expected of Matthew, and he soon found himself on his way to Milan to fight Parlov.

What Parlov had not anticipated from the unknown American was his hunger, his work rate or his right hand. Matthew matched 27-year-old Parlov punch for punch in an exciting fight that saw Franklin spring an upset over eight rounds, silencing the European fans.

'I couldn't think about being a loser,' Matthew said. 'They brought me over to lose but people who knew me knew I was an okay fighter and it would be pretty tough for Mate Parlov and it was a huge win for me. The whole city of Milan was flabbergasted. It felt good.'

The contest made a paragraph in Britain's *Boxing News* magazine, which said Parlov 'suffered a shock points defeat against black American Matthew Franklin in their ten-rounder'.

In the same issue, WBA light-heavyweight champion Victor Galindez defended his title against New Jersey's Richie Kates in, according to *Boxing News*, 'one of the most savage and sensational fights ever seen in South Africa'.

On 10 July two months later, Parlov defeated Italian Domenico Adinolfi for the European crown in front of 30,000 fans at a Belgrade football stadium and, a week later, Matthew was back on away soil against another unbeaten fighter.

Marvin Camel, a southpaw, was 14-0 and a Native American from Missoula, Montana. Camel boxed Matthew in Stockton, California in front of a crowd of just over 1,000 spectators.

Camel had been involved in a car crash two weeks beforehand, which resulted in him needing 20 stitches and losing around a pint of blood, but he refused to use that as an excuse for a flat performance.

Franklin and Camel's ten-round bout was on a card that also showcased Marvin's middleweight brother, Ken, but Matthew doled out what the *Scranton Times-Tribune* called 'a sound thrashing' to Camel, winning on points.

Matthew was knocked down in round four and lost some of the early rounds, but he dominated the rest of the way, flooring Camel in the ninth and coming on strong in the tenth as Camel tired.

The show also saw Stockton light-heavyweight contender Yaqui Lopez (30-3) moving into title contention with a victory over Larry Castaneda. Channel 5 – WNEW-TV, had been due to screen the bill, but it was beset by technical issues that meant the main event featured 'schmaltzy music interludes' before it was replaced, accidentally, by a short on the hobbies of doctors, from model railways to kite-flying. Then, the sound from the boxing came on but there was no picture. Finally, producers managed to sync some fighting with commentary. Still, it was too little too late. As one observer put it, 'This was the first time a televised boxing show had to be cancelled on account of audio and visual gremlins.'

Matthew was now ninth in the world rankings and had scalped two excellent undefeated contenders. He kept busy by sweeping through an overmatched Bobby Walker ('Just an up-and-coming fighter who wanted to make his name off me,' Matthew said) in Scranton, Pennsylvania, in four rounds but then he was matched with Camel again.

A proposed fight with Adinolfi back in Italy had been in the works but Matthew was bullish about the Camel return and predicted an eighth-round stoppage win with the caveat that it was in Camel's hometown.

'I hope the people don't rob me,' Matthew said, but there was controversy. Franklin–Camel II took place in front of a measly 854 paying customers at the Adams Field House (which could hold 10,000 fans) in Missoula, Montana. Matthew was the aggressor but ringsiders contended that Camel's counterpunching was clever and that he'd troubled Matthew in the second round. Still, Camel was shaken in the third and forced to retreat in a more-even fight than the first time they'd met.

Camel won by margins of 100-91 (for referee Bob Foster, the former light-heavyweight champion), 98-96 (Billy McFarland) while one judge (Joe Antonetti) saw it quite differently, scoring 96-96 after ten hard-fought rounds.

Franklin's manager Frank Gelb called Foster's verdict 'ridiculous' and demanded to see the scorecards only to be informed that commission members Sonny O'Day and Bob Blome had left so they wouldn't miss the bus back to their homes in Montana. To appease the irate Philadelphians, Board secretary Mary Lou Crawford altered the verdict to a no decision, which she did not have the authority to do.

Gelb made an official complaint and was told, 'The merits of the protest will be judged and a decision made on the matter.'

Said Gelb: 'Matthew won eight out of ten rounds. He forced the fight all the way and outpunched Camel two to one.'

Two days later, and with the Philadelphia crew back in Pennsylvania, the commission awarded Camel the win and moved swiftly on.

'I never knew when or where they were going to hold the hearing,' fumed Gelb, who said he'd get his lawyer involved. 'I was told that we would definitely be notified.'

The *Philadelphia Inquirer*'s Gene Courtney felt sure a fix of sorts was in and looked at the situation a different way, with Gelb's assistance.

Gelb told him: 'I knew from the minute we set foot in that place we were going to get the shaft …. The referee, Bob Foster, voted all ten rounds to Camel and that stuck in my throat. Now listen to this: Camel's chief second is Billy Edwards, who is also the manager of Foster, who was the referee. And furthermore, the promoter Elmer Boyce is also Camel's manager … But that isn't all. Camel also works in Boyce's music store in Missoula. From now on we're going to stay away from those cowboys. We felt just like Indians at a massacre out there.'

It was also a one-sided loss for Boyce, who took a reported $15,000 hit on hosting such a poorly attended show.

It would be easy to put the verdict down to a hometown decision – or even something more sinister – but even Camel's press in Montana shook their heads at what had happened. One writer in *The Missoulian* said it had been a terrific and close fight but that the controversy had left a stain. 'As a referee, he stinks,' wrote John Blanchette of Foster, concluding, 'His scorecard only topped his transgressions.' Blanchette also hammered Blome and O'Day for leaving early, writing, 'It doesn't matter if they live in eastern Montana or in Latvia – at least one of them should have been there at the end of the fight. If the state has to pay their overnight lodging, so be it. But make certain a board member is there.'

He didn't let up, either, insisting, 'So all the post-fight brouhaha did was cast a cloud over boxing in Missoula and Montana – a cloud that cheapens the sport, the town and the state.'

No one in Montana came out of it with any credit and boxing people simply thought that Camel, a very capable fighter, had been given a gift.

'I beat him the first time and I knew going back to his hometown it would be very difficult,' Matthew remembered, years on. 'I thought that they might take the fight from me and they did. That was controversial. I won the fight but I was more concerned with not making it out of there! They were trying to bring him [Camel] up. He was the hometown guy, that's all it was.'

Boxing News ranked Camel at eight in the world, Franklin ninth and Parlov tenth.

Britain's John Conteh held the WBC title, which he had recently defended against Stockton's Yaqui Lopez in Copenhagen, and Galindez had the WBA belt in a weight class that was starting to get crowded. Eddie Gregory, an up-and-coming New Yorker, and Mike Rossman, based in Philly, were also making waves. But Matthew was doing just fine and he was featured in *Boxing News* for the first time under the headline, 'Matthew nears top after 16 bouts.'

The article was written by Nigel Collins, who would visit Franklin at the 'spotlessly clean yet brimming with atmosphere' Juniper Gym in November of 1976.

Matthew was listed as 22 years of age, even if no one knew when the orphan had been born. It was all guesswork. Still, Collins wrote about how Belfiore's 'humanity' had rubbed off on the likeable Matthew and he'd seen him improve upon his many trips to the Juniper.

'I have had the opportunity to watch Franklin develop from an awkward preliminary fighter to smooth and confident contender in a relatively short period of time,' wrote Collins.

Nigel felt that Matthew wasn't a true power puncher and that he wasn't blessed with the ability to fight in close, speculating that an East Coast contest with former world title challenger Richie Kates 'would be intriguing'.

Meanwhile, Parlov wanted revenge and apparently said he'd chase Matthew out of the ring if they fought again. He had a chance in December of 1976, and Matthew travelled back to Europe to fight the Yugoslavian in Trieste.

These were hard fights, against good fighters and on the road every time, but there was much to gain in terms of learning the ropes as a professional and equipping himself well against boxers who had good amateur careers. After the fight, reporters said Parlov was lucky to be awarded a draw having been on the defensive throughout.

Matthew went back to America knowing he had not lost, but knowing he should have won.

'Gelb would put his fighters in,' asserted Peltz. 'He didn't care. He put him in in Italy, in with Marvin Camel, then he went to where Marvin was from and fought him over there, he fought Parlov but he [Matthew] wasn't getting anywhere locally. Frank Gelb believed, like me … He put you in … Out of town … And guess what, it didn't hurt Matthew at all because right away he found out what he had. He had a good fighter. You don't go over to Italy and beat and draw with Mate Parlov and then fight Camel twice and the second fight with Camel was a joke … But it didn't hurt him.'

Did Gelb start to realise what he had with the Camel and Parlov fights?

'Absolutely,' Gelb smiled.

And Franklin's reputation was on the rise. As a learning pro, he had just had an important and priceless four-fight education – in the space of just seven months – with two future world champions, in Camel and Parlov.

CHAPTER 4

SWAPPING THUNDERBOLTS

IT WAS time to see if the wanderer could draw on his return to Philadelphia. Matthew's recent fights had received cursory mentions in the North American newspaper sports sections and the overwhelming sentiment after the Marvin Camel rematch was that Matthew had paid his dues on the road and now it was time to have the deck stacked in his favour.

West Coast promoter Don Elbaum had teamed up with video producer Hank Schwartz to stage a TV tournament featuring some of the sport's best emerging talent. The idea was to stage 25 consecutive weekends of boxing and names on the starting grid of the World Television Championship Series included Matthew and his light-heavyweight contemporary Eddie Gregory, super-lightweight Bruce Curry, middleweights Vito Antufermo and Cyclone Hart and welterweight Billy Backus.

Promoter Don King apparently liked the idea so much he sold a similar concept to ABC, but neither undertaking would be heralded a success.

In keeping with his 1976 bouts, Matthew was in tough again and he had to lose a little over a pound having come in heavy on the day to face Gregory.

They boxed on the tournament's opening night on Friday, 11 March 1977 at the Spectrum in Philadelphia.

Gregory had seamlessly moved up from middleweight to light-heavyweight and knew all about Philly fighters, having stopped

Cyclone Hart in four rounds in New York in 1974 before losing a split decision to Bennie Briscoe in Philadelphia a year later. Gregory argued the defeat was contentious at best.

'The Flame', as he was known – because his manager Jack Singer had a couple of steakhouses in New York by the same name – had 20 wins against two losses and a draw. Matthew's record was 13-2-2.

Tournament rules stipulated that there would be no draws, so if a fight was even after ten rounds an extra round would decide the winner.

Gregory and Matthew had been friendly in the build-up. They posed happily for pictures during fight week and hit it off but Gregory would later say he wasn't taking the fight or his career seriously. He said he had only trained for two days and that he'd had sex just hours before he was due in the ring. Even as the fighters talked smack to one another through the referee's pre-fight instructions it looked like either one could burst into laughter.

Interestingly, *The Ring* magazine commented on that head-to-head saying, 'Gregory and Franklin imitated two love-struck Eskimos by rubbing noses and SMILING.'

'We were talking about how, "You better be ready because I'm Eddie Gregory,"' Matthew remembered. 'I was saying, "So what if you're Eddie Gregory, you're going down." We knew each other and we gave each other respect.'

Commentator Don Dunphy introduced Matthew as a good boxer and Gregory as a hard hitter but in the opening round Matthew landed a crisp lead right hand and Gregory tumbled on to his backside. Shaken, Gregory found that his trunks were split up the back and needed to be changed. The Brooklyn man came out for round three with some green shorts over his blue pair. They were borrowed from fellow New Yorker Antufermo, who had fought Cylone Hart earlier in the evening.

One ringside journalist took great delight in seeing it all unfold, writing, 'The rear of Eddie Gregory's trunks were almost totally split down the seam and for one full round TV cameras had their finest moon shot since Neil Armstrong.'

Still, the Spectrum buzzed throughout an enthralling fight. 1976 Montreal Olympic boxing stars Michael and Leon Spinks watched intently from ringside.

It was engrossing with both prospects having their moments. Gregory scored with some strong right hands, but Matthew's chin didn't betray him and he controlled the bout in parts to the extent that Dunphy announced, 'Franklin is really giving Gregory a boxing lesson.'

Conversely Nigel Collins, reporting for *Boxing News*, wrote that there were periods when Matthew was doing 'next to nothing'.

That proved to be costly: Matthew lost a split decision.

The fight received mixed reviews although the crowd of around 2,500 had enjoyed it. Collins referred to it as a 'classy ten-rounder' while *The Ring* called it 'a dull fight' but said Gregory's aggression was the decisive factor.

The *Philadelphia Daily News* reckoned Matthew's 'backing up' had cost him, although they still thought he'd done enough to win.

They credited the fighter with using a good jab and good defence and reckoned judge Herb Rhodes, who scored 47-45 in Matthew's favour, was the 'voice of sanity', swept aside by referee Tom Reid (47-44) and judge Tom Cross (46-45). The newspaper believed Matthew had won by 47-44.

'Even Philadelphians can't win in Philadelphia anymore,' read their report, with a nod to the now-infamous Alfredo Escalera–Tyrone Everett bout four months earlier when skilful Philadelphian Everett, Matthew's friend, seemed to have won the WBC super-featherweight title only to be denied by a corrupt scorecard. Philadelphia judge Lou Tress voted for Escalera, ensuring he kept his title. Everett's team had been so concerned by the Mexican judge and the Puerto Rican referee that they hadn't thought to check on Tress who, one boxing insider said, 'Could be bought for a cup of coffee.'

Of his own fight, Matthew charged: 'I was robbed. I dropped him in the first, outboxed him in each round, and took it to him in the tenth.'

Collins felt Gregory, trained by veteran Chickie Ferrera, had nicked it by a point, but conceded he was in the minority on press row and Gregory, of course, always contended that he'd done enough to win.

'It was a close fight, no doubt,' Gregory admitted. 'He knocked me down in the first round, but after that, I went right to him. He had the biggest heart in the world. And I kept hitting him. I was a good combination puncher and I would catch Matthew with combinations and step around instead of moving back and I outboxed him. That's all I did. I knew after that we were both world class.'

Years later, Matthew remembered, 'I laid back. He was a puncher but I fought smart and sat back a bit. I knocked Eddie Gregory down, he was a New York boy. He was from Brooklyn and when I fought him people really liked it because he could really fight, but everybody knew after that that this guy Franklin could take a good punch but they didn't know I could hang in there with Eddie Gregory. That was an unanswered question.'

Gregory thought the fight made them two of the best light-heavyweights in the world but Matthew still needed answers. Yes, the fans had found out he could take a punch but he vowed that he had to do more to win bouts, trying to make the judges redundant. He felt he'd deserved to win all three of the blemishes caused by Parlov, Camel and now Gregory.

'After fighting Eddie, I became a puncher,' Matthew recalled. 'I was more aggressive. Instead of dancing and being Muhammad Ali I stopped that and changed my whole style. Now it was seek and destroy.'

Eddie Everett saw the change, with Matthew saying he wasn't going to depend upon skills anymore, he was going to slug:

'Matthew was a beautiful boxer at one time,' said Everett. 'He changed his style into a complete slugger. He had strength, and I guess he realised, "Why am I boxing when I've got this awesome strength?" He threw away the boxing, the dancing around, and he just turned into a beast. Those losses wouldn't have happened if he'd done it sooner but that's when he said he was done with boxing and he knew his strength and willpower was better than the guys' he was fighting. He won fights on raw power and strength. He had skills, but his willpower and strength were absolutely amazing.'

Matthew maintained in the press that he wanted a rematch – Gregory claimed they offered it, and back in Philly – but for now the friends were on different paths, working towards the same goal.

In fact, Eddie had his first attempt at a world title just eight months later, losing to Victor Galindez in Italy narrowly on points, and although Matthew's 13-3-2 record was far better than it looked on paper, he no longer was sure he would get a fair shake – even boxing at home.

'The Philadelphia judges want blood,' Matthew claimed a few weeks later, citing his defeat, Everett–Escalera and super-featherweight Alfonso Evans's majority decision loss to Trenton's William Berry. 'They don't respect boxers. They gotta learn to respect skill, endurance and boxing ability. That's why I've been going overseas. It doesn't make sense to fight in your hometown and get robbed.'

As for the Elbaum–Schwartz TV tournament, that fell by the wayside. King's ABC version saw *The Ring* falsify fight records to make matches more attractive for TV and heavyweight contender Scott LeDoux cried fix after losing to Johnny Boudreaux at the Naval Academy in Annapolis, Maryland. LeDoux kicked off commentator Howard Cosell's hairpiece in a melee, and a national investigation not only killed King's tournament, but the negative publicity killed the World Television Boxing Series as advertisers ran a mile. It was over less than two months after it began.

* * *

Matthew was due to fight Baltimore's 'Wild' Bill Hardney, who'd fought light-heavyweight champion Bob Foster, but Hardney – inactive and stopped inside three rounds in his five most recent bouts – never made it to the first bell in Wilmington, Delaware. At the last minute, promoter Gus Parodi thought Hardney would have been battered, and quickly, so Parodi drafted in heavyweight journeyman Joe Maye to at least go some rounds.

Maye, who was 2-20, soaked up a lot of abuse and Matthew was satisfied to go the ten-round distance, building his engine for the stiffer tests that would lie ahead.

'I think I'm ready for anyone in the top ten,' he said.

Maye would make his own list when *The Ring* unkindly ranked him as one of the ten Worst Heavyweights.

A month later, on 26 May a dark cloud fell on Philadelphia boxing when Tyrone Everett was shot and killed by his girlfriend, Carolyn McKendrick.

A tribute event was held at the Philadelphia Arena, with ticket proceeds going to the Tyrone Everett Scholarship Memorial Fund. Tyrone's brother Mike and Matthew appeared in ten-rounders, with Matthew facing Orlando's Ed 'Savage' Turner, who'd lost three of his last four going in.

Turner was vanquished in the sixth; the fight had become so one-sided that State Athletic Commissioner Howard McCall leaned through the ropes and told referee Bob Polis to stop it.

'Ed Turner was a big, big, tall kid and I figured if I hit him it would be a case of tiiiiimber, but I couldn't get anywhere near him,' recalled Matthew. 'My arms were nowhere near as long as his. His were like giraffe's legs.'

Tyrone Everett had been tipped for superstardom and South Philly had pinned a lot of hopes on his skills. He should have won the world title against Escalera but was robbed and he never got another chance. The city needed another hero.

'After Tyrone passed, there was a void as to who's going to be the face now,' said South Philly boxing historian Stephen Chandler. 'You'd already had your Briscoes and all of those guys, but Matthew took it like, "I'm stepping up." He improved, trained harder and started shining because he wanted that spot that Tyrone left. And the world saw him.'

* * *

In one of the great opening paragraphs in a report from an all-action fight, Bill Livingstone for the *Philadelphia Inquirer* wrote, 'This one came right out of the blood-plasma unit, the same folks who brought you Ali–Frazier reddening the dawn skies in Manila. The same script that gave the world Graziano–Zale and, before that, Christians and Lions. Loser gets a thumbs down ... This fight had it all over everything but the neutron bomb.'

Livingstone was writing about the brutality Matthew Franklin shared with Indianapolis star Marvin Johnson on 26 July 1977.

One ringside reporter said the fighters 'were swapping thunderbolts' and another called it 'a truly epic fight'.

It was a Tuesday night at the Spectrum and 6,459 were glued to the violence. The vacant North American Boxing Federation title was on the line and Johnson was an undefeated left-hander, tipped for big things after an Olympic bronze at the 1972 Munich Olympics. Johnson raced to 15-0 as a pro, halting 12 opponents and the East Coast press warmed to the softly spoken contender after a couple of fights in Philadelphia.

'Marvin Johnson is a typical Philadelphia fighter,' wrote Don Benevento in New Jersey's *Courier-Post*, seemingly keen to adopt the young hopeful for the city. 'You know the type. They look hard, jab with surgical precision, and would rather die honourably than surrender to an out-of-town opponent.'

Johnson and Matthew had a couple of mutual opponents but Wayne McGee stood out. McGee had given Matthew everything he could cope with and more by handing him his first loss and a draw. Johnson, meanwhile, had beaten McGee in a round.

But this was not a fight of stats or science, it was vicious, gruelling, draining and, for many, the best fight they would ever see.

Nigel Collins, who was becoming hardened to the Philly fight scene, watched in amazement and awe.

'It's the only fight I ever saw where I thought both guys might die,' Collins recalled, years on. 'You often get a funny feeling in a fight when you know it should be stopped because something bad might happen, before it happens. It was crazy. It never happened before or since. It was horrific and both guys could punch. Matthew could punch harder but Marvin was no joke.'

No one was laughing but the crowd was shocked – and deeply satisfied.

The action was breathtaking and unrelenting. Both knew they were on the cusp of a world title fight and were aware how high the stakes were.

'I know I have to win, but I don't expect Franklin to cause me any undue concern,' said Johnson beforehand. 'The way I look at it, each of my fights has taken me one step closer to Victor Galindez [the WBA champion].'

'I think I'm championship material,' contended Matthew. 'And I think you'll see that against Johnson … If we get past the fifth [round] Tuesday, he'll start to tire and then I'll have him. I'll just keep on coming.'

By the time the 12th round started, the judges couldn't split them. One had Johnson ahead, one favoured Matthew and the other was scoring it a draw.

They had been roared on by a disbelieving audience for almost 50 minutes.

Matthew's nose pumped blood from the second round and the fighters took turns hammering away at one another in a non-stop affair punctuated by hundreds of heavy, clean headshots.

Johnson was nearly 'gone' at the end of round four when Matthew whacked the southpaw's mouthpiece out with a right hand. The crowd cheered so loudly it took a while to split the fighters as referee Ozzie Sadler couldn't hear the gong above the frenzied fans.

Johnson was struggling at the end of the ninth. By the close of the tenth, TV analysts speculated that the fight could finish in a draw. There was further carnage at the end of that session when Sadler stopped the fight with seconds left thinking he heard the bell, only to have to restart it and let the fighters go at each other for a few seconds more.

The crowd was so invested, no one could hear anything but the screams.

'That happened a couple of times,' remembered Matthew. 'The people got so loud and the fight was so exciting that was just something that happened. I didn't even hear the bell was ringing. He was a very hard man.'

The 12th was wild, violent and, ultimately, definitive.

It became clear that Johnson had nothing left. Matthew piled in with both hands, not allowing Johnson any reprieve. Hard shots thudded in, Johnson's legs betrayed him and his arms hung by his sides. His left glove reached desperately for the middle rope but his faint grip couldn't keep him up. He sagged, slowly on to the seat of his trunks and then lay prone, flat on his back.

The raucous crowd popped loudly, arms were thrown deliriously into the air. Matthew was held aloft by his team.

Well after the count had finished, Johnson tried to roll into a recovery position of sorts and was helped by concerned team members and officials for several minutes. Matthew collapsed, too. He dropped on to his stool, and had to be brought round with smelling salts.

'I fought the fight I had planned,' he managed to say afterwards, through cracked lips with a bumpy face, swollen features and bloodshot eyes while lying flat on a treatment table fighting off the pain from the adrenaline dump. He said he would happily defend his new North American title against local rival Mike Rossman or Gregory but he was also hungry for a world title chance.

'Now I'm rated, so they have to give me a shot,' he said.

The *Daily News* observed Matthew's change in style from the Gregory contest, saying he'd 'abandoned his crotchet needles and reached for a billy club'.

Johnson reckoned his trainer, Colin 'Champ' Chaney, had lost track of the rounds and told Marvin the 11th was the 12th and final round and Marvin left everything he had in that session. 'He told me to throw a lot of punches because my right eye was closed,' recalled Johnson. 'I was exhausted in the last round.'

Old school as ever, Johnson felt three months of inactivity had cost him as he had been due to fight in the aborted World Television Championships.

'I think the 90-day lay-off made the difference,' he said.

Peltz didn't say on the night what either fighter had been paid, just that 'They didn't get enough.'

After all the blood and violence, they made around $2,500 each.

'I don't think we made much money on the show, maybe the Spectrum made $1,500,' said Peltz.

No one could believe that Matthew had stood up to so much abuse. For the *Inquirer*, Livingstone was stunned. 'That the Philadelphian did not falter throughout the siege, that never once was he knocked off his feet, was absolutely incredible,' he wrote.

'Some fighters can, some can't take it,' shrugged a disconsolate Johnson. 'That's what proves he's a good fighter ... staying in there.'

Johnson had been ranked No. 3 by the WBA and was due to fight Galindez on 17 September in Copenhagen had he won.

'You'd hate to have the headaches Matthew Franklin and Marvin Johnson have today,' wrote Bill Fleischman in the *Philadelphia Daily News*, saying that fans had left 'awed' having witnessed 'the best fight seen in Philadelphia in years'.

For the record, Paul Harris's scorecard was level at 51-51 going into the last, judge Harold Lederman had Matthew ahead 51-48 but referee Sadler had Johnson up 53-49.

'I didn't think I was ahead,' admitted Matthew. 'I thought I needed a knockout to win.'

Within an hour of the biggest win of his career, Matthew was being challenged. Johnson wanted a rematch and as the swelling ballooned on Matthew's face, Richie Kates went into the new champ's locker room and said, 'I won that title in '74. I haven't lost to anybody but they took it away from me.'

Kates had beaten Jimmy Dupree in the Philly Arena but his career had taken a different road, and he'd fought four of his next seven contests in South Africa, leaving the title on the shelf.

Regardless of Kates's stance on Matthew's newly acquired hardware, the Johnson battle had endeared him to the city.

The damage might have taken years off the back end of Matthew's career but it meant he was no longer an anonymous filler on fight cards. It was also unlikely he'd have to box abroad any time soon.

Life was changing for the orphan who'd learned so much from winning, losing and drawing against top fighters on the road.

'People are coming up to me now and saying, "Hey, Matthew Franklin," and I don't even know 'em,' he smiled. 'People are coming up and telling me my fight with Johnson was the greatest one they've seen in 20 years. It makes me know I'm finally beginning to be somebody.'

Then, thinking back to the fight, he said, 'I looked like I had went through a meat-grinder. I felt pain all over my face. It felt like someone had thrown hot water on my face. That was the first time I ever looked like that. One time out of 21 fights, that ain't bad. I don't like to slug. I know the fans want to see that over again. But it won't be like that. That was once in a lifetime.'

Matthew's stock had never been higher and it became obvious to his South Philly friends, who were delighted to see him getting the recognition such a magnificent fight warranted.

'When he took the shots that Marvin hit him with in that particular fight in 12 rounds, getting really hit but giving it back too, when he beat Marvin until Marvin dropped, that was it, he was made,' smiled Stephen Chandler. 'You took that and you came out on top? And he was still strong … That was when he was made.'

'Oh, he blew up,' agreed Eddie Everett.

'He wasn't an attraction until we made the fight with him and Marvin Johnson … and I was fortunate enough to have promoted the greatest fight I ever saw in person,' remembered Peltz, who said that after more than 50 years in the sport. 'There's no doubt that was it.'

Peltz, however, also witnessed the darker side of boxing that night. Long after the crowd stopped whooping and hollering at the feast of ferocity they'd dined out on, things almost took a tragic turn.

'I remember he [Marvin] had a white suit on and we were putting fighters in the Penn Center Inn, 20th and Market in Center City, and I went back there to see Marvin [after the fight],' Peltz said.

'When I went up to his room he was sprawled out in the hallway, unconscious. He was laying in front of his room, and we [along with Indiana Boxing Commission chairman Kelse McClure] carried him in to his hotel room.'

They tended to Johnson and put him to bed.

It was a once in a lifetime fight. Nigel Collins certainly thought that. He wrote that week in 1977, 'It was the sort of terribly punishing fight that may leave a permanent scar on the career of both fighters. Their battered and bruised faces will heal but I have to wonder if either will ever be the same again.'

'I still get a headache from talking about that fight,' Matthew would say years later. 'Marvin Johnson ... I can still hear bells and see shadows.'

* * *

Seven weeks later, Matthew Franklin was back in the ring defending his NABF title against one of the division's most dangerous punchers.

Frank Gelb wasn't in favour of Matthew fighting Billy 'Dynamite' Douglas, but Matthew assured his manager he'd box and move and wouldn't give Gelb the palpitations he'd had to endure against Johnson.

Philly heavyweight Jimmy Hayes ran with Matthew daily at 5am, helping keep him in shape. Hayes also didn't think it was smart fighting Douglas so soon after the war with Johnson.

Eddie Gregory watched the Douglas fight at the Spectrum from ringside. 'I'll be rooting very hard for Franklin to win,' said Gregory, who'd had to make do with a fight against little-known Eddie Phillips as he waited for a title fight of his own. 'I want him to win. It'll increase the gate when we fight again. I got $10,000 for fighting him last time. I'm looking for a much fatter payday when we meet again.'

Franklin–Douglas was the co-feature on the bill with Roberto Duran headlining against Edwin Viruet, in what turned out to be a drab 15-round slog for Duran's WBA lightweight title.

Step up Matthew Franklin to give the crowd their money's worth.

The promise to box and move was gone after two so-so rounds as he and Douglas entertained one another with warfare.

'The fourth round was murder,' wrote Nigel Collins. 'Both men hammered home enough clean headshots to kayo a horse, but they somehow kept their feet.'

In front of 7,910 fans, it came down to two moments of impossible drama.

The first came in the fifth when Matthew was decked for an eight count by a big right hand having shipped several clean shots during a desperate period that lasted about a minute and a half. As Douglas steamed into Matthew when the fight resumed, around a dozen more blows had Matthew in dire straits before Douglas tired and Matthew returned fire. Collins would later write it was 'one of the most punishing rounds this reporter has ever witnessed'.

Despite a good start to round six from Douglas, Matthew soon roared back and referee Hank Cisco almost immediately intervened and the fight was over.

Cisco had let Franklin fight back from the brink when hurt in round five, but with Douglas shaken momentarily in round six, Cisco didn't afford the 37-year-old Ohioan the same courtesy and many felt the referee's intervention was premature.

Douglas's team complained loudly and booing fans weren't satisfied with the climax.

'You should never be allowed to referee a fight in which Frank Gelb has an interest,' Peltz screamed at Cisco, overheard by Bob Wright at the *Bulletin*.

Cisco and Gelb were from Norristown and they were, according to the paper, friends.

'He's got a helluva nerve,' charged Cisco afterwards, saying he'd been told by the doctor that, at the end of round five, both fighters were in such bad shape that he should stop it the next chance he got.

The doctor, Alfred Ayaiila, said he had told Cisco the fighters were in a bad way but claimed he had not recommended the stoppage.

Cisco then cited their respective ages, that Douglas was 37 and Franklin was just 23. He said Franklin rallied when he was hurt but Douglas 'went' in the sixth. 'His arms were by his sides and his facial muscles started to relax. He could have gotten brain damage if I'd let that kid keep poundin' on him,' opined Cisco.

Matthew didn't mind and even took a few minutes to joke after. 'I do that all the time,' he smiled. 'Look like I'm dyin' so the guy will come to me … then bang.'

'I want that sucker again,' charged Douglas about a rematch, but he was the only one who wanted it.

Gelb said: 'I didn't want to fight this guy the first time. I only took it because Matthew talked me into it. After this, I sure as hell don't want Douglas again.'

Belfiore, trainer and co-manager with Gelb, felt the same. 'Rematch? What the hell for? We don't need it. We're already ranked higher than him.'

The *Times-Tribune* in Scranton called the contest 'sensational'. The same newspaper reported how 'a few months ago Franklin was virtually unknown in his hometown' but had become an 'overnight hero' with the Marvin Johnson knockout.

Don Benevento wrote about how Matthew had developed 'into one of the hottest draws in the city', adding, 'Say what you want about Matthew Franklin, but never say that he can't take a punch …. He takes more punches than an entire corps of NFL cornerbacks can throw.'

'I get hit,' Matthew agreed. 'But I don't get hurt.'

'I would have been in deep trouble if I had met Douglas in his younger days.'

Decades later, Peltz remembered the night Matthew was dropped and hurt by Douglas.

'They say the last thing a fighter loses is his punch,' Peltz explained. 'Douglas was getting his ass kicked for four rounds and then he drilled Matthew with that right hand of his and he went down. They could have stopped that fight, and today they would have.'

The Matthew Franklin train steamed onward, with the crowds growing and his legend enhanced once more.

'Billy Douglas was another beast,' said Eddie Everett. 'Matthew was destroying some awesome fighters.'

'It can be safely stated that Franklin has the hardest head in Philadelphia boxing since the early days of Bennie Briscoe and Joe Frazier,' wrote Nigel Collins, who had again been ringside. 'Whether he continues his current crowd-pleasing, give and take tactics or reverts to skilful boxing remains to be seen.'

That was in an article that featured Matthew for the first time in *The Ring*.

'Two of the most vicious and thrilling ring wars in local boxing history have catapulted Matthew Franklin from relative obscurity to the heady status of hometown hero,' said the magazine.

Collins continued to be impressed with the young fighter's mentality and warm personality.

'Matthew has a big smile and a kind word for everyone,' wrote Collins.

'He's a good kid but sometimes he gets stubborn and won't listen,' contended Belfiore.

Matthew could be painfully modest or, at times, he could try to bring part of his personality to life that replicated his braggadocio idol, Muhammad Ali. Looking back on the fight with Douglas, father of future world heavyweight champion James 'Buster' Douglas, Matthew said: 'He could punch. He was strong. He was a heavy hitter and he brought it to me. I tried to stay in there with him and he punched so hard. Every time he hit me it was like being hit with something made of metal. I overlooked him. It might have been a combination of a left hook and right hand [that knocked Douglas down], that was my hardest punch. Set them up with the left, knock them out with the right. And it worked.'

The fans didn't care that Duran and Viruet stunk the joint out because they had seen another Matthew Franklin war.

That was Matthew's fifth fight in 1977, having boxed Gregory, Johnson and Douglas. He was finally a star in Philly.

'Philadelphia needs a new hero,' wrote Collins. 'Bennie Briscoe can't top every card. Tyrone Everett is dead. His brother Mike failed in a recent bid for Shengsak Muangsurin's junior welterweight title, while Jimmy Young has priced himself out of the local market. Matthew Franklin is the man to fill the void.'

* * *

About six weeks later, Matthew Franklin was back.

With another training camp under Matthew's belt and a secondary title, the North American Boxing Federation crown around his waist, he knew he was getting close to the top of the sport. He hoped his activity would be a reminder to authorities that he was closing in on a world title fight.

His NABF title wasn't on the line against Florida's Dave Lee Royster at the Spectrum in November and both men came in three pounds over the light-heavyweight limit but it didn't matter.

Royster, 15-8-2, was a tough journeyman who'd beaten Wayne McGee and, in his most recent fights, defeated Australian contender Tony Mundine in a round before losing a return on points over ten. His career was on a decline but Matthew's was ascending and more than 6,000 paid to watch.

Royster talked a good fight, too.

'I've never known a guy who can share punches with me,' he said ahead of their fight. 'I hear how he can take a punch, but there's no man that can get up after I hit him.'

Matthew boxed and banged, he out-fought and out-thought Royster, putting him on the floor six times in total, twice in the third round, twice in the sixth and twice in the tenth. One reporter wrote, 'Royster absorbed volumes of punishment, the likes of which has not been seen since the Allies landed at Normandy.'

Through the fight, fans chanted 'Big Matt attack' and aside from an eighth-round right hand, Royster had little success and later blamed a cold he'd picked up during fight week. Belfiore and Matthew said the idea had been to trade less after the Johnson and Douglas battles.

'I don't want any fighter to get hit with too many punches,' explained Belfiore. 'I think he realises that he's got to turn into a different type of fighter. He knows he can't go walking in.'

In the co-feature, Franklin's two most recent victims, Billy Douglas and Marvin Johnson were paired in what was always going to be a bloodbath, with Johnson prevailing in five rounds.

Having cut up and stopped Douglas, Marvin said he didn't have to fight Matthew again and hadn't taken the loss to Matthew personally. When asked whether he wanted to avenge the defeat, he said simply: 'I'm not in this business to get revenge against people who beat me. I'm here to make money.'

For him, it was a race to the title. 'Matthew Franklin is getting close to a title shot, too,' contended Gelb, who thought the winner of a mooted Franklin–Kates bout would be bound to get a title shot. 'Matthew won't be fighting Johnson again. Not right away, anyhow. He has greener pastures.'

Matthew was rated fourth by the WBA and ninth by the WBC and the Philly fight connoisseurs wanted to pair him with two-time world title challenger Richie Kates, a New Jersey man who'd made many of his bones in Philly.

Unsurprisingly, the Johnson epic won the Spectrum's 1977 Fight of the Year and all the way up to Christmas the Franklin–Kates fight was rumoured before it was finally signed and announced in the newspapers on Christmas Day.

It would be in February and it was heading to Philly.

CHAPTER 5

A MATT FRANKLIN SPECIAL

'HE'S THEIR boy now,' conceded Richie Kates, knowing Matthew Franklin's popularity in Philadelphia was gaining momentum ahead of their 7 February 1978 fight. 'And I'm the underdog. I'll just have to focus the crowd out of my mind and fight a little harder. This could lead to big things for either one of us. [He's a] good fighter. I think I'm better.'

Kates had lost twice to Victor Galindez in shots at the world title and had beaten Ohio journeyman Harold Carter five months earlier while Matthew had stayed in the gym after defeating Royster. Despite the frequently gruelling outings, it was never long before he was back in the Juniper in South Philly.

'He was the most dedicated fighter I ever saw,' growled Belfiore. 'He'd be back in the gym two days after a fight working for the next one.'

By now, however, there were pockets of resentment towards Matthew from some areas of the city. Was he getting too big for his boots, or were others just jealous?

In the build-up to the fight, Kates, a recreation director at Leesburg Prison in New Jersey, said of Matthew: 'I think his head is getting a little big.'

That sentiment was echoed by Matthew's North Philly rival, Mike 'Youngblood' Williams. He was bitter about his purse to box on the undercard, and took it out on Matthew ahead of his contest with Alfonso Haymon.

'This fight's not gonna draw a thing because they're all pricing themselves out of the market,' spat Williams, a welterweight, about the Franklin–Kates card. 'This is not a $15 [price of best seats] fight. These guys are not worth that. Everybody on the card is making a bundle but me. I didn't demand that much because it's not fair to the public.'

Then, getting more specific, he focused his ire on Matthew.

'He's become too wrapped up in himself,' Williams snapped. 'His hat size has gotten too big. If he bothers to speak to you now, it's like he's doing you a favour.'

Kates went further still. 'He's putting himself next to God since he beat Johnson.'

Those who were around Matthew saw no difference. He was the same as he ever was: happy, friendly and with that winning smile that could light up a room.

He was simply focused on winning. He wanted to fight Parlov – who now held the WBC title – again, box WBA champion Galindez for his belt and, in four years, when he reached about 27, retire. He had it all mapped out. Get in, get rich, win titles, get out.

'I would like to be the one champion – like Muhammad Ali,' he said. 'Make a big hit, then get right out.'

Gelb was just back from South Africa where he'd been fielding offers for a Parlov fight. Peltz, meanwhile, hoped the Franklin–Kates winner would face Rossman in another derby, but Rossman's team weren't keen. Rossman's father and manager Jimmy DePiano told them to forget that idea. 'We were training at Franklin's gym before Mike's second fight with [Mike] Quarry, and they threw us out,' DePiano fumed. 'Then [they] spread the word that we hadn't paid our gym dues. I never welched on anything in my life, and I sure as hell didn't begin with a gym rental. I told them at the time, "Someday you're gonna need Mike Rossman and he won't be available." That's a promise I'm gonna keep. Mike can make good paydays fighting anywhere in the country. We don't need Matthew Franklin.'

There were hostilities between the Kates and Franklin camps, too, because Richie claimed he should have still held the NABF belt following that 1974 one-round knockout of Jimmy Dupree, but it was four years later and he'd not defended it once. It was such a minor quarrel that the *Inquirer*'s Gene Courtney thought the belt was 'as important as winning a Boy Scout merit badge for cooking.'

That wasn't necessarily unfair, but the NABF title was a stepping stone to world championship rankings and fights.

Interestingly, when Matthew was asked about his background and childhood ahead of the Kates contest, all he said was, 'I really don't want to get into my past because it's something I've put out of my mind. Let's just say I always loved to fight and I finally met Nick Belfiore and he taught me to fight for money. Training helps me erase what I used to be from my mind. Now I feel like I can be somebody. I feel like my destiny is to win the world title … I want to block out my past.'

Joe Gramby, Kates's co-manager, could tell Matthew liked to fight, and said, 'Franklin has a lot of enthusiasm but he also fights with his face.'

The hotly anticipated clash had been scheduled for Tuesday, 7 February, but when Philadelphia came to a halt because of a snowstorm – 'the worst blizzard to dump on the city in a decade' – just 30 hours before the first bell, quick-thinking Peltz saw an opening at the Spectrum on the Friday night and postponed it.

Both fighters were stuck in town, but they approached the delay differently.

Kates grumbled through the boredom while Matthew had energy to burn, telling the *Daily News*, 'On Tuesday morning, I grabbed a shovel and went out into the neighbourhood. I walked around looking for houses where there were old people who couldn't clear their own walks. Quite a few of them said "Hey, I know you, you're the fighter." And I'd say, "You want your pavement done?" I didn't charge. I did it for the exercise, and because there are a lot of fine people in South Philly. I loved it. I was out at 7am, ran all the way up Broad Street from Ellsworth to City Hall … shadowboxing, waving to people. I felt real good, just like *Rocky*.'

The fight talk between the camps was respectful in those remaining days and the strategy Matthew had used to outbox Royster seemed to be all-but forgotten as he talked up the impending battle.

'If a fighter makes me fight extra hard, he's in trouble,' Matthew said, readying himself for war. 'When I have to fight extra hard, I'm like a cornered animal. I have nowhere to go but straight ahead and as hard as possible.'

Kates was more experienced aged 24, with 33 wins against three losses. Eighteen of his victories had come early.

Matthew's record was slowly improving but he was still having trouble hitting 175lbs and had to lose 3lbs at the noon weigh-in.

He made weight by chewing bubble gum and taking hot showers.

It wasn't ideal preparation, but ultimately the fight was what the 6,500 fans hoped it would be and more, another gruelling Matthew Franklin fight and one that Nigel Collins called in that week's *Boxing News*, 'a brutally thrilling struggle'.

The *Inquirer* charged, 'It was the most savage fight in Philadelphia in more than a decade,' and the report continued with the line, 'They fought like Neanderthals throwing rocks at each other.' *International Boxing* magazine called it 'a pier 6 brawl'.

Compared to the rest of the fight, the first round was uneventful. It got hard from the second, however. Kates was put over by a tremendous right hand but referee Charlie Sgrillo ruled it a push and didn't score the knockdown. Kates *had* been hurt and when he was back on his feet, he retreated to the ropes where Matthew hacked away with a number of long right hands, scoring often. By the end of the round, Kates had to be shepherded back to his corner by his team. He was groggy and walking through quicksand.

Kates was nailed by a right so cleanly in the third that it was all he could do to shake his gloves in a bid to show people it hadn't hurt him. But in the fourth Kates was in charge, landing a crisp left hook that rocked Matthew. With seconds remaining in the round, he launched a long right hand that put Franklin face down and out in the middle of the ring.

It was a shot for the ages. Matthew's lights were out and he pitched forwards dramatically like a statue toppling over, his hands still cupping his head.

Kates hurried to his corner to hear the count, excitedly bouncing up and down, then he slowed and took a moment to realise what was happening in front of him.

Matthew was clambering back to his feet.

Matthew's body swayed like a sapling in a strong wind. Referee Sgrillo held him by the gloves, assessing his ability to continue. The bell sounded and Matthew had a minute to recover.

As Matthew stumbled to his corner, Belfiore scooped him on to his stool for emergency attention.

Kates's team thought he'd won and hoisted Richie into the air. Matthew looked to Belfiore to explain what had happened.

The Spectrum crowd buzzed in anticipation of the fireworks that might lie ahead, but Matthew was tired coming out for the fifth. Kates stalked in to apply the finishing touches.

'Hang in there,' screamed Belfiore at Matthew.

Matthew stopped moving, planted his feet and let Kates come at him. Kates fought hard, becoming increasingly arm-weary. Matthew not only battled back, but he started to take control.

With seconds left in round five, Matthew landed a replica of the right hand that had floored him at the close of the fourth – with the same result. Kates pitched forwards on to his face, seemingly out.

This time it was Matthew's chance to celebrate his miraculous victory. He threw his arms into the air but it was his turn to be stunned by his opponent's recuperative powers as Kates wobbled to his feet.

As with the previous round, the bell sounded. This time Kates's team sped into the ring, desperately trying to revive their man.

Two rounds back-to-back, and both fighters had been saved by the bell.

Matthew had bled from the nose. Kates, trying to get his legs back under him in the sixth, was cut above his right eye.

After 30 seconds of round six, the ending was a formality. Matthew went through the gears and Kates couldn't match him. Matthew crashed home a series of left hooks and right hands and Kates, off balance and with nowhere to go, fell to the floor.

He stood up, but with his legs drained, his heart pumping and his mind fuzzy, he was a sitting duck.

Matthew marched in confidently and lined him up. He threw a couple of short, quick jabs trying to measure his man and then looped over a terrifying right that landed flush in Kates's face.

Describing the finishing punch, Tom Cushman wrote, 'The building shuddered. Cars in the parking lot trembled.'

The effect was devastating.

Kates lost control of his body and senses.

His hands dropped by his sides, he bent at the waist and his rudderless legs caused him to lurch from one side of the ring to the other.

His brain went blank, even though he was still on his feet. Sgrillo had no option but to stop it there and then.

Finally, Matthew could celebrate while Kates was tended to by his team.

It was one of the most dramatic light-heavyweight fights of all time.

Peltz, describing the best bouts he promoted, said, 'If [Marvin] Johnson is No. 1, Kates is 1A.'

Not long after the contest, Matthew, who thanked Belfiore, Gelb and Frank's father, Mo, called from the ring, 'I want Galindez, I've gotta have Galindez, or even Mate Parlov. Kates is a good fighter. I can't take nothing from him. He's good.'

The crowd still hummed noisily, basking in the mayhem they had seen, but backstage things were getting serious.

Kates had been conscious in his dressing room but was soon seen 'nodding off'. One camp member said, 'He was kind of coming and going.'

When ice to his neck failed to bring him back, an ambulance was summoned. He was concussed, as was Matthew, but Kates was rushed to the Metropolitan Hospital.

Matthew was interviewed, knowing Kates had been taken away for treatment and he apologised to his fallen foe. But even in victory Matthew couldn't comprehend the chaos he had come through.

'I did go down?' the confused winner asked writers afterwards. 'I know he hurt me seriously. I don't even remember going down. If I did, I must have gone down very fast because the next thing I remember, I was up.'

A day later, the *Daily Journal* in Kates's hometown of Vineland, New Jersey, reported doctors' speculation that Kates could be brain damaged. The fighter had been released, and in a statement said he had fought a tactically naive fight.

'It was the stupidest fight I ever fought,' admitted Kates, who said he'd taken Matthew lightly because of his fights with Wayne McGee, who Kates had regularly used for sparring. Decades on, Kates laughed at recollections of that week and the night itself.

'He [Matthew] did a lot of talking about how good he was and everything,' Kates smiled. 'I had a conversation with him afterwards about that and he was a very good fighter. I thought it was a good fight. In fact, some people said it was the Fight of the Year.'

He had come so close to having Matthew down and out in round four. He'd had a couple of world title fights with Galindez by that point, but Matthew was the one that got away.

'It was something,' he said, of Matthew's miraculous rise from obliteration. 'You remember those things. I thought he was gone, yes. I certainly did. I didn't think he'd get up from that but he did. He had a lot of heart and a lot of drive. He pitched face first and I thought he was gone. Maybe I should have fought a little harder. It was a very exciting fight. I went to the hospital for a little while but I came back out and I still won quite a few fights. And when I retired, it was just time for me.'

Kates said that whatever animosity there had been before the fight was superficial. It was just promoting the show.

'He was in Pennsylvania and I'm from South Jersey but whenever I saw him, we spoke,' Kates said of Matthew. 'We were very cordial. I liked him. Even when we fought, I had no problem with him.'

For Matthew, the fight was a defining contest, a crucial step towards world title fights but it might have knocked years off his career. The mileage was rising. Still young and learning, he'd gone the distance with Parlov and Camel twice and gone into the trenches against Johnson, Douglas and now Kates.

'The Lord brought me back,' he said, while smiling and recalling the end of the fourth round.

'He [Kates] knocked me down. Unbelievable. I don't know how I made it [back up] but I did. It was a bad fall. I fell like a tree. It didn't just look like I was out cold, I was. I looked so stupid going down. Richie hit me so hard. It was testament to my body and my conditioning that I rose up. The referee said next time I go down that's it. These guys I was boxing prepared me for great fights. I didn't mean to put him in hospital.'

Tom Cushman accurately explained: 'As you may have gathered by now, this was no ordinary prize fight. It was, in fact, another example of what is rapidly coming to be known as a Matthew Franklin special.'

CHAPTER 6

UNCROWNED CHAMPIONS

'PARLOV'S 23-1,' a promoter told a top TV executive during a late 1978 contract negotiation.

'Who beat him?' replied the television exec.

'Matthew Franklin,' was the promoter's answer.

'How about [Marvin] Johnson?' the executive went on.

'He's 20-1,' came the response.

'Who beat him?'

'Matthew Franklin.'

'Franklin? How come he's not fighting for the title?'

Matthew wanted answers to the same question.

After four months of inactivity, the fighter went through the motions against Seattle's Dale Grant on 19 June 1978, to the backdrop of the story that Matthew wanted to sever ties with his co-manager Frank Gelb.

Matthew claimed he wasn't getting enough attention, saying that Gelb was spreading himself too thin with too many fighters on his books. Their contract was due to expire on 25 October but Gelb reckoned Matthew had signed a two-year extension. Matthew argued otherwise. He had been offered the chance to fight Victor Galindez for the Argentine's WBA world title on the undercard of the Muhammad Ali–Leon Spinks rematch in New Orleans. It was a huge opportunity against a man he felt he could beat, but Matthew turned it down because, had he won, he would have had to sign over options on his next three fights. The deal, with promoters Top Rank, would have been signed while Gelb was still manager. Gelb would have had his share from each of the three fights, and Matthew didn't want that.

'I wasn't ready to be king under those circumstances,' he said.

Instead, he fought Grant, the half-brother of 1972 Olympic gold medallist Sugar Ray Seales. Grant was said to have an amateur record of 303-16 – beating Marvin Hagler in the unpaid code – and had amassed an 18-3-1 record as a pro.

The native Virgin Islander had started out as a middleweight but, after some managerial problems of his own, he suffered a year of inactivity and returned at 175lbs.

He'd managed a draw with Marvin Camel and had won ten consecutively since.

Matthew was putting a lot on the line in the main event at the Spectrum, risking his No. 2 spot with the WBC and his No. 3 spot with the WBA but he said he'd been in the gym, building up his stamina, and that he needed the activity having been 'unable to get the right fights at the right prices'.

He shed rust against Grant in front of 4,707 fans.

Grant winced when Franklin let hard shots go to the body and head. Matthew carelessly shipped blows here and there, and the fight was all but over when a terrific right hand caused Grant's legs to buckle and sway before he collapsed into the ropes in the fifth round. Yes, Grant – who benefited from the wisdom of Philadelphia legend George Benton in his corner – made it back to his feet and yes, he was allowed to fight on. But he was in no fit state, took another right, sprawled forward on to his face and referee Frank Cappuccino called it off.

Asked what he hoped would happen next, Matthew said, 'I keep telling Mate Parlov I want him but it seems like he keeps ducking me so I've got to go on with Victor Galindez. I believe I'm the uncrowned champion and they better give me a championship [shot] or I'm going to have to see Mr Galindez personally.'

But Matthew's fight in the ring with Grant wasn't the one people were talking about, it was about Franklin vs. Gelb. Even on the day of the Grant contest, the headline in the *Philadelphia Daily News* set the scene for the battle outside the ropes. It read: 'Franklin plans bout with co-manager.'

Matthew told the press he hoped that he, Gelb and Belfiore – who was being dragged into dispute – might patch up their differences. 'I don't really want to say more about it because we need good feelings on all sides during the negotiating,' Matthew said.

It was starting to get messy. Gelb admitted that he and Belfiore did take 50 per cent between them [25 each], but they paid the trainer – Belfiore – five per cent out of their end. Gelb said he was going to hold talks with Matthew to try to remedy the situation, but the sides were becoming distant, and Gelb felt their bond weakening.

Matthew's head had been turned by a group of Newark businessmen, led by Murad Muhammad, who had found an opening into boxing back in 1967 when he began working as part of Muhammad Ali's security detail.

Then, in 1976, five Muhammads – Abdula, Akbar, Bahar, Bilal and Murad – created Cornerstone Promotions.

The organisation's first show saw Pedro Agosto take on Ernie Lassiter at the Newark School Stadium on a bill that featured the young, future middleweight title challenger Mustafa Hamsho. Soon, the five men went their separate ways, and Murad and Bahar started Triangle Promotions with Ben Muhammad in 1978. Abdula left boxing, but the others wanted to stay involved, and Bilal and Matthew were talking.

Matthew was following Islam, something he had taken an interest in while he was locked up, and he liked what the Muhammads were offering.

Consequently, Gelb felt his relationship with Matthew suffered and that he was starting to lose influence as Matthew's focus shifted.

'That is correct,' Gelb admitted. 'That is when we had a big overflow [of too many people being involved].'

Two months after the Dale Grant fight, Matthew boxed Freddie Bright on a Murad Muhammad-promoted show in Newark and

Muhammad Ali, along with his heavyweight rival Joe Frazier, were part of a crowd of almost 3,000 inside a New Jersey ice rink. Eddie Gregory, Matthew's friend and former rival, was also on the bill.

Ali had broken camp from nearby Deer Lake, his training HQ in rural Pennsylvania, as he completed preparations for the September rematch with Spinks in New Orleans. Meanwhile, Galindez was getting ready to defend his title against Mike Rossman. 'The Jewish Bomber' had answered the call after Matthew turned the Superdome fight down.

Matthew beat Freddie Bright in round eight.

'He wasn't bright that night,' said Matthew, perhaps with a nod to the special guest ringside.

* * *

As the weeks went by, things were becoming increasingly fraught behind the scenes. Matthew didn't fight Galindez in New Orleans. Instead, he watched from ringside as Rossman stunned the favoured Argentine to capture the WBA light-heavyweight title, stopping Galindez in the 13th round in front of 65,000 fans. It was a shock, and Matthew was left to lament what might have been. He thought Galindez was ready for the taking, but he didn't think Rossman would be the one to do it.

Matthew spent some time in New Orleans ahead of Spinks–Ali and was making new connections. One night, as Matthew drove near Bourbon Street, he stopped at a light and saw two smartly dressed men who seemed to recognise him.

'Hey, you know who I am?' Matthew asked.

'Yeah, sure. You're Matthew Franklin,' came a reply.

'You got it. I'm going to be champ someday.'

'You sound like you believe it,' said the other man.

'I do. I do,' Matthew said.

The two men were colleagues of an up-and-coming promoter named Harold Smith, who was getting close to Ali and starting to wield significant influence. Within a year, Smith would feature highly in lists of the most powerful people in the sport.

Meanwhile, there was a new threat emerging at light-heavyweight.

Behind the walls from Rahway Prison in New Jersey, James Scott had miraculously been able to continue his boxing career. After years spent in the prison system as a young adult, Scott had moved to Florida where he trained out of Angelo Dundee's 5th Street Gym, Muhammad Ali's old training HQ. Scott quickly built up an impressive record. Managed by Chris Dundee and with popular publicist Hank Kaplan behind him, he raced to 10-0-1 with wins over Jesse Burnett, Baby Boy Rolle and Ray Anderson.

Then, however, Scott had gone back to New Jersey, returned to the streets and got into trouble.

He was involved in a drug robbery that resulted in a murder. Scott was sent back to jail.

He was serving time for the robbery and would have to stand trial for the homicide at a later date.

However, the industrious warden at Rahway, Bob Hatrak, used Scott to create a programme to help inmates transition into a career in boxing when they got out. Whether they wanted to promote boxing, train fighters, manage them, treat cuts on fight night or compete in the ring, the Boxing Authority would give them experience. Hatrak had known Scott for years. Their paths had crossed several times previously as Hatrak rose through the system ranks in various correctional facilities where Scott was often an inmate. In fact, one of Hatrak's first memories was of an underage Scott having to carry a lead pipe with him in Trenton prison to keep the predators away.

Still, in 1978, Scott not only resurrected his career in prison, with fans paying to go and watch televised fights behind bars, he started to work his way up the rankings. A month after Rossman defeated Galindez, Scott stunned Eddie Gregory in the jail's sports hall, live on HBO, to become – in Scott's words – the No. 1 contender. As he screamed for a world title fight, Scott regularly wrote to boxing publications around the world calling himself 'The Uncrowned Champion'.

He did it all under the promotional umbrella of Triangle Productions, headed by Murad Muhammad.

Muhammad was the exclusive promoter in Rahway, a place described by one writer as 'the dregs of the Eastern penal system'. But Hatrak had put it on the map with the boxing programme and it was getting rave reviews nationwide.

The WBA, however, believed the winner of Matthew's upcoming fight with tough Yaqui Lopez would be the No. 1 contender for Rossman's belt. But with backstage boxing politics being what they were, Matthew couldn't expect a Rossman fight any time soon, even though it could have filled a stadium in Philadelphia.

Jimmy DePiano still seethed about being tossed out of the Juniper years earlier but with speculation about a possible Rossman-Franklin fight intensifying, Belfiore countered the claims Rossman's father had made.

'He [DePiano] came in to my gym like he owned the joint,' steamed the permanently crotchety Belfiore. 'He and Mike were welcome, but all of a sudden he was bringing along four or five guys to train, and ten or twelve to watch. I told him, "This is a small place, I don't have room for all these people." I asked him why he didn't go around to Passyunk Gym, where they could accommodate him.'

DePiano, according to Belfiore, said nothing. But then Belfiore read about their 'feud' in the paper.

'Next thing I know,' Belfiore continued, 'He [DePiano] said I couldn't train a mouse to go up a cuckoo clock. We haven't talked since, and I'm not about to apologise to him for something I never did. But if he wants to bury the hatchet, I'm willing.'

With Rossman as the champion, DePiano held the cards and doubled down on his stance.

Meanwhile, promoter Russell Peltz knew how bad the ill-feeling was, and thought Rossman's team would rather hand back the WBA belt than give Matthew a shot.

'The real truth is, he knows Matthew could be champion tomorrow,' Belfiore continued of DePiano. 'He don't want his kid hurt, and I don't blame him for that. Matthew and Michael used to spar, and at the start Matthew had trouble with Michael's jab. Later, it was obvious Mike couldn't handle Matthew anymore. That's the real reason they left the gym.'

Matthew's approach to making the fight was far more amicable. He respected Rossman for what he'd done to Galindez and even tried to go and see Rossman in his dressing room before he fought for the title, only to have the door shut in his face.

Then, Matthew said he went to pick Rossman's brains about Yaqui Lopez at the Passyunk Gym because Rossman had already fought and lost to Yaqui. Rossman, Matthew alleged, simply shrugged his shoulders as if to say, 'You figure it out.'

Still only around 24, Matthew looked at the bigger picture.

'I'm sure there's gonna come a time where we're gonna fight each other,' Matthew insisted. 'And someday, after it's all over, I can see us sitting down, talking about the days when there was so much money hanging out there and we couldn't get to it because our managers were quarrelling.'

Instead, Matthew was stuck with grizzled California-based Mexican Yaqui Lopez. The Stockton warrior was one of the toughest men around, one of the division's many dangermen. Lopez had won 43 and lost seven. Two of those losses had been again Galindez in Italy, where many felt Lopez had been robbed. A third was to the British fighter John Conteh, a former WBC champion who was still a threat in the division after a disputed split-decision loss to Mate Parlov in Belgrade.

Lopez was rated No. 4 in the world by the WBA and the WBC, and he had that emphatic six-round win over Rossman to his name. In fact, he was so good that *The Ring* showcased him in a feature calling him The Uncrowned Champion, a title being used by Matthew – based on Matthew having a win over WBC champ Parlov – and by James Scott.

The talent pool at light-heavyweight was so deep, there just weren't enough belts to go around. Only the very best made it, but if you did, you had to look over your shoulder because the queue of top fighters was growing by the month.

Lopez was 27, and his manager and father-in-law Jack Cruz reckoned he was entering his prime. He felt Franklin and Lopez, for the NABF title, was a bout between the two best light-heavyweights in the world.

There was, however, more in-fighting on Matthew's team. Matthew was at occasional odds with Belfiore which meant he alternated his training sessions, spending a week at the Juniper and a week at the Passyunk with Jimmy Arthur.

Matthew said, as the fight neared, that he and Belfiore had resolved their problems and called it 'petty stuff', but it was not ideal preparation for such an important fight.

'I have a written contract in my lawyer's office with Bob Arum of Top Rank,' Matthew said. 'It says I will fight the winner of the Mate Parlov–Marvin Johnson fight within five months, providing I beat Lopez.'

But the managerial situation was still a contentious issue.

Peltz was promoting the fight but had lost his previously open lines of communication with Matthew.

'The Yaqui Lopez fight was the first fight where I started dealing with his attorney because he and Frank Gelb were on the outs and that's when the Muslims were taking over his career,' said Peltz. 'Even if it was not officially – because Gelb's contract was upheld through 1980 – he wasn't quite the nice Matthew he had been before. He was like a little kid, but when he got involved with them all – and I knew them all, Bilal Muhammad, Akbar Muhammad, Murad Muhammad – he did get a little surly. I know he regretted it later in life that he got involved with them, certainly financially.'

Gelb added, 'How can I explain it to you other than to say, they wanted, and had, an inside hand everywhere.'

But the New Jersey group were giving Matthew something he had not experienced before. While he had enjoyed life in the Juniper with Belfiore, Mike Everett and the others, the Muslims and their beliefs and values appealed to him. After all, he was still the lost boy from Philly, occasionally asked about the trauma of his childhood.

'He found an identity,' explained Mustafa Ameen, a friend and part of the group. 'He just navigated to us as brothers.'

Matthew fought Lopez at the Spectrum in Philly ten days after Scott's shocking triumph over Gregory.

Matthew knew Lopez was susceptible to cuts and the strategy was to split the skin around the veteran challenger's eyes to force a stoppage. 'By the time it's over, there could be blood all over the ring,' Matthew predicted. He had developed a punch Lopez would not be able to avoid, 'the loop-a-doop', a crashing overhand right that he predicted would butcher his challenger.

'You heard Muhammad Ali talk about the rope-a-dope, so I developed the loop-a-doop,' he announced. 'It was like an overhand right that came down very hard on the chin. A lot of people experienced that punch and they knew it was a good punch, that's why people started copying my right hand.'

Behind closed doors, however, Matthew figured this would be his toughest fight. Lopez was battle-tested and came with a terrific reputation. He was respected throughout the sport.

'I remember my nerves getting all tensed up because I knew he was a warrior who'd fought guys like Galindez and [Jesse] Burnett and he was older than me,' Matthew said. 'But I knew I had the heart, I was younger and I thought that would make the difference.'

Rossman was among 8,877 fans ringside at Franklin–Lopez, having recently spent time with President Jimmy Carter at the White House amid speculation fuelled by promoter Bob Arum that Rossman could move up in weight for a mega money fight with Muhammad Ali, who had regained his title from Spinks.

'The thing is,' Rossman said when asked for a prediction at the Spectrum, 'Matthew's been sticking his chin out a lot lately. It makes for exciting fights, I guess, but it ain't necessarily the best way to make a living in this business.'

Once again, Matthew had to lose some poundage on the afternoon of the fight, but remained confident of making Lopez his seventh consecutive stoppage victim.

In the early going, both attempted to establish dominance behind their jabs and were unafraid to throw combinations.

The first breakthrough came in round three.

An overhand right from Matthew seemed to stun Lopez and instantly his legs looked heavy. The Mexican tried to fight back but when a left hook crashed into the side of his head, Lopez lost control of his legs altogether. He staggered into the ropes as Matthew wheeled away to celebrate, his hands overhead in triumph.

'That was so stupid of me,' Matthew recalled. 'That was me doing an Ali thing. I thought I was The Greatest. I thought he was going down. He was getting ready to fall but he caught his feet and he did like an Indian dance across the ring.'

Lopez reached out with his right glove to hold himself up as his legs buckled beneath him. It looked as though it was all over. It certainly seemed Lopez was about to touch down.

Referee Frank Cappuccino allowed it to continue and Matthew surged forwards to finish the job, but Lopez hung tough, slumping on to his stool at the bell, relieved, exhausted and damaged.

The crowd sensed a surprise early night, but Matthew felt it was a sign of the opposite.

'I thought, "Well, I'm going to be around for a little while,"' he said.

Throughout the fight, Rossman's trainer and father DePiano was used as an expert summariser on TV, and he was often acidic towards Matthew. (That was to be expected, given the frosty relations between the camps.)

DePiano thought Matthew should have finished Lopez in the third, felt he was tiring in the fifth, and said he was flat-footed in the sixth …

But, in the seventh, Matthew broke through with a series of right hands and blood started to cascade down Lopez's face. It was exactly what Matthew hoped might happen with his 'loop-a-doop' – and the last thing Lopez needed.

Then, in round eight, came the excitement.

Lopez, moving to his right, got Matthew to move with him and he trapped the Philadelphian with a right hand that sent Franklin stumbling backwards. On the ropes, Matthew tucked up, chin down behind his gloves, elbows by his sides to protect his ribs, but Lopez smashed away with both hands. Matthew was pinned back. Barrage after barrage came his way, as Lopez maintained a relentless pursuit.

Matthew, perhaps sensing Lopez's power reducing with each bit of energy he expended, came off the ropes and beamed a smile through his bloody mouthpiece.

'Look at him laugh,' screamed Jack McKinney in commentary.

Then Matthew roared back, opening Lopez's cut further still and bringing the crowd to their collective feet.

It was sensational stuff. Lopez had won the round but paid a heavy price.

'Mr Excitement', as the fans and media members addressed Matthew, was doing his thing again.

The session was so enthralling, Nigel Collins wrote, 'It was the sort of glorious round that makes boxing the most exciting of all sports.'

'I was covered up and getting myself straightened out while he was throwin' all them punches,' Matthew said, having admitted he had been hurt.

In the ninth, Lopez's right eye was slammed almost completely shut from Matthew's battering ram jab. Lopez knew it was bad and stamped his feet when he went back to his corner.

DePiano commented that Belfiore's tactics of urging Matthew to aim for the body were wrong because he needed to be working the cut eye. Before the 11th, DePiano reckoned Matthew was struggling to get off his stool between rounds.

'You seem to be rooting for Lopez,' DePiano was told by co-commentator McKinney. Then, cards on the table, DePiano said he hoped Rossman would get the Lopez rematch.

Lopez was blind in one eye, could hardly see out of the other, yet still he ploughed on. Backward steps were few and far between. If this fight was the bout that could earn him one last title shot, he wasn't going to go quietly. Lopez's right eye was purple and had closed; his left looked as though someone had been hacking it with a knife. He was cut in three places and blood poured into his eye after another sickening 'loop-a-doop'.

At the bell, referee Frank Cappuccino called it off. He didn't think Lopez should be injured further and believed there was no way he could overturn the deficit. Lopez's moment had come and gone in the eighth round.

'The last one did it,' Cappuccino explained. 'He [Lopez] was blind on both sides then. I would have stopped it earlier, if he'd been missing a lot, but he wasn't. I didn't want to see the dude get hurt.'

Even before the result was announced, Matthew was on the ring apron shouting, 'Number 1, I'm the greatest. I'm the greatest.'

The influence of Ali on Matthew was obvious, and after the decision was announced Matthew had more to say.

'I think he's a good fighter,' Matthew added, giving Lopez his props. 'I was taking my time, he was a very smart fighter ... He's one helluva fighter. If me and Mike Rossman ever get in there, I think it will be a helluva fight. I think they should have it in Philadelphia, it's surely a million-dollar gate.'

Belfiore corrected reports that Matthew had to lose 3lbs beforehand saying it was 2lbs, and when asked whether he was concerned during the eighth-round crisis, Belfiore said, 'No, nobody takes a punch like Matthew. He takes a helluva punch. He works with heavyweights, [he] hurts them, they don't hurt him. A lot of people don't know Matthew, he stays like this [Belfiore held his hands up by his cheeks], he wants the guy to get tired and then he opens up. You've seen it.'

Matthew credited a beef broth made for him by manager Becky O'Neil for helping him replenish after struggling with his weight. Lopez said he'd twisted his ankle in round three and had been unable to plant his feet to get purchase in his shots from there on.

But he was gracious in defeat. He puffed out his warrior's heart proudly and said, 'No excuses. I did think they could have let it go one more round [it was scheduled for 12], but ... Ah, I hit the guy pretty good. He can take a punch and I couldn't see. He beat me.'

Some 40 years later, Yaqui remembered, 'I was stopped on a cut in the 11th round and that was a good fight. That one in

Philadelphia was the Fight of the Year and round eight was round of the year.'

As Stan Hochman wrote in the *Daily News*, Lopez left Philly with a face 'that has more lumps than a bag of walnuts'.

'If you come to Philadelphia to fight Matthew Franklin,' he continued, 'you are liable to leave town looking like the Liberty Bell.'

Another writer said of Lopez, 'It looked like he'd run into a brick wall,' and the Philadelphia press teased a world title fight between Rossman and Franklin.

It was certainly the one they wanted.

Matthew didn't mind. Rossman (WBA) or Parlov (WBC), it didn't matter.

Rossman was allowed to defend against Aldo Traversaro and the winner would have to fight Galindez within 120 days. Bob Arum was now the promoter going in to bat for Matthew. He contended that his win over Lopez put him at the front of the queue for a title.

But because Conteh had been hard done by on the scorecards against Parlov on the road, the WBC had seen fit to reinstall the Englishman at No. 1.

'That's a damn disgrace,' charged Arum, who said his 'greatest ambition' at the time was to stage a unification world title fight between Rossman and Matthew in Philadelphia. 'Matthew Franklin should get the fight,' Arum continued. 'Matthew Franklin deserves a shot.'

After vanquishing Lopez, Matthew said he didn't try to finish Lopez after he was hurt in round three because he wasn't sure if Lopez was faking an injury to lure him in. As Matthew swaggered down the corridor to his changing room, he said, 'Go beep all the horns. Look at me. No cuts, no bruises. I am the uncrowned champion.'

CHAPTER 7

THE CHAMP

ON 4 JANUARY 1979, it was announced the orphan from South Philly would get his chance. Matthew Franklin still did not know who his family was, or who he really was, but the identity he craved was that of world light-heavyweight champion.

Franklin travelled to Indianapolis to box a rematch with newly minted WBC champion Marvin Johnson on 17 February at the Market Square Arena in the champion's hometown.

Johnson had won the title on 2 December with a tenth-round stoppage of Mate Parlov in Italy.

Johnson–Franklin II was part of a two-day boxing programme with the heavyweight attraction between Duane Bobrick and John Tate scheduled a day earlier.

Top Rank, Russell Peltz and Johnson's promoter Fred Berns were working together on the event. ABC was broadcasting both nights. Johnson was set to earn $150,000 and Matthew would make $50,000. That was a fair increase from the first fight, for which Matthew made $2,500 and Johnson $1,875. The *Indianapolis News* predicted that a total audience of 200 million would tune in to watch the fights.

'I could have picked an easier opponent,' admitted Johnson, discussing his first defence. 'However, I chose him because I wanted my friends in Indianapolis to see me fight the best competition available. This fight could have been in New York or Philadelphia, but I insisted it be held here.'

Sportingly, he called Matthew 'the most outstanding light-heavyweight challenger in the world' and he had a second title defence already penned in, with England's former WBC title-holder John Conteh ready to challenge him in Monte Carlo in May.

Promoter Bob Arum thought the winner could fight Conteh almost straight away, unify the titles against Mike Rossman and then go in to a lucrative clash with Sugar Ray Leonard at the Superdome in New Orleans.

The Johnson–Franklin rematch was due to take place on a Sunday but there was a problem: an old Indiana law forbade fighting on Sundays.

Arum, a lawyer before he became a promoter, claimed the Indiana law was unconstitutional, threatened to change the venue and prompted local headlines such as 'Sock it to the Sabbath'. Arum argued other sports, from tennis and hockey to auto-racing and basketball, could take place, and a motion in the senate resulted in a 41-6 vote in favour of the law being changed and the show going on.

Johnson said he'd actually thirsted for vengeance after his first bout with Matthew, and that he had spent time studying it to correct his mistakes.

Following that first loss, Johnson went home to Indianapolis, hid behind dark glasses and said, 'I feel a little bit ashamed.'

Johnson was a proud man, which factored in to his decision to fight Matthew once more.

Only a few weeks after winning the world title, he was back in camp with Champ Chaney in the Indianapolis PAL, sparring with the likes of national amateur champion Frankie Williams, fellow Indianapolis pro Sammy NeSmith and an ambitious JB Williamson. But disaster struck when one of Johnson's sparring partners damaged his jaw. X-rays were taken and Johnson was originally cleared to fight, but when doctors and commissioners checked the scans, they revealed a hairline fracture and an impacted wisdom tooth that had to come out and the fight was postponed until 22 April.

Johnson then went to Philly to get some hard rounds under his belt.

He worked out at Joe Frazier's Gym in North Philly and sparred with contender Jerry 'The Bull' Martin, among others.

'You had to hold your breath watching Jerry and Marvin spar,' said Peltz. 'You didn't know who was the better fighter. You knew he was the real deal.'

Back home in Indianapolis, community-spirited Johnson attended the assembly at Crispus Attucks High School for Marvin Johnson Day but those within the sport knew it was going to be another war and there would be no time for niceties.

Nigel Collins wrote of Johnson and Franklin that, 'Together, they possess enough guts and determination to stock the division.'

Veteran Philly trainer Leon Tabbs had even called the first fight 'the war to end all wars'.

'Believe me,' promised Matthew. 'This will be one of the best fights in history.'

'This is not a mandatory fight for me,' asserted Johnson. 'I picked Matthew Franklin because he deserves it. I live with the night he stopped me. I'm a proud fighter and I have to settle this thing. I have to know I can beat him, and I will.'

Business in the light-heavyweight division was booming.

James Scott was trying to work out how he could get out of prison to fight Rossman at the Meadowlands on day release, and Rahway warden Bob Hatrak was hoping to facilitate it, but Matthew knew the money was the all-Philly duel with 'The Jewish Bomber'.

However, a week before Franklin–Johnson II, the prospective Rossman payday went down in flames when Rossman lost a return to Galindez back at the Superdome. He'd been a champion for about six months and the dreams of seven-figure purses were gone.

Rossman and Galindez had been due to fight in February at Caesars Palace in Las Vegas, but with Rossman waiting in the ring, Galindez baulked at the appointment of three Nevada judges and fled. Promoter Bob Arum couldn't win him round so the fight was eventually held in Louisiana. It included a South African referee and officials from Puerto Rico and Venezuela.

Galindez, who in February had complained of personal problems, marital issues, not training properly and a savage weight cut, did not make the same mistake twice.

Matthew hoped to topple Johnson, beat Conteh and then the money would have been so big for a Rossman tear-up that the camps would have no choice but to put their differences to one side. He felt it was his Ali–Frazier fight.

To make matters worse for him and Johnson, a bout with Conteh had lost its appeal after the former champion was dropped twice and thought to be a faded force following his London fight against Jesse Burnett that resulted in a draw. Burnett could fight, but many thought it was an indication that the Englishman's days were numbered.

But even as his biggest night neared, Matthew knew his boxing days were shortening due to the wars he was having.

'Everybody looks for the biggest pile of money he can make,' Matthew explained. 'But my main thing in boxing is not to come out of it on my heels.'

He was referring to what was once called punch drunk syndrome but later became dementia pugilistica and would, many decades on, become known as chronic traumatic encephalopathy (CTE), where those who have taken too many blows to the head can wind up with short-term memory loss, slurred speech and mood swings, sometimes suffering from depression and walking unsteadily.

But boxing being boxing, things were not as simple as who was fighting who on 22 April and who was going to win. Boxing politics was in full effect. Matthew was disappointed that the officials were going to be appointed from the local commission and was concerned the deck was stacked in Johnson's favour. And there were problems closer to home. Matthew was still at odds with Gelb, and the dispute was being played out in the fight week media.

Three days before the championship bout, Indianapolis Athletic Commission members met to investigate the disagreement as it related to Matthew's purse.

A meeting in the Indiana State Office Building included Peltz; Johnson's promoter Fred Berns; promoter Bob Arum; Arnold Weiss;

Gelb; Bilal Muhammad – who claimed to be an advisor to Franklin – chair of the commission Richard Bossung and Kelse McClure II, who was the administrator for the commission, along with a few lawyers and reporters.

Gelb, meanwhile, showed up with a bagful of legal documents including, he contended, proof that Matthew had signed a two-year contract extension with him that meant they were together until September 1980. Matthew alleged Gelb had him sign autographs and that he'd filled the legal-speak in around the signatures.

'I asked Gelb for $200 and he had me sign on the back of a cheque, then he asked me to sign about six autographs,' Matthew claimed.

Belfiore sided with his fighter. 'Franklin signed a plain piece of paper when Gelb asked Franklin for an autograph and everything else was put on paper later,' he contended. 'Gelb knew we were getting ready to dump him and he used this sneaky way to get Matthew's signature.'

The quarrel meant that the commission would withhold Matthew's purse until after the event so the situation could be resolved. Matthew had also taken a $10,000 advance from his $50,000 purse against commission rules, so that further complicated matters, but McClure said he wouldn't cancel the fight. 'I'd be dead by morning,' he joked. 'There are financial problems with the Franklin people, but I've told them that the fight will go on and those can be cleared up afterwards.'

Despite how good the first Johnson–Franklin battle had been, ticket sales were disappointing. Although Johnson had promised his fans he would make his first title defence in front of them, they seemed nonplussed at best, and Peltz was fuming as a consequence. He thought the rematch could have sold 16,000 tickets in Philadelphia without TV, 10,000 if the fight was screened.

The Market Square Arena had sold about 5,000 seats.

'We're not coming back,' vented Peltz, despite prices being on sale from $6 in the cheap seats to $25 at ringside. 'This is a disgrace … Indianapolis has to prove it can support big-league professional boxing.'

Berns said the earlier postponement hadn't helped sales.

As the countdown continued, Matthew was often surrounded by his lawyer, trainer and what the media called 'members of the Muslim faith', who were repeatedly addressed with suspicion by the press.

Johnson stayed at his parents' house, just a few minutes from the venue. It was fair to say he had far fewer distractions.

A couple of weeks before the fight, Matthew did some rounds with future champion Thomas Hearns, then a gangly power-punching welterweight, but that sparring session told Hearns's trainer, Emanuel Steward, that his frame could take him up to 175 in the future.

'Tommy didn't have the strength, but he could outhit him [Matthew] with his speed,' recalled Steward. 'He did well against him.'

Journalist Nigel Collins was disappointed to miss it. He showed up at the gym as the fighters were taking their hand wraps off.

* * *

Talking later to Collins, who visited Matthew as he had prepared for the fight of his life at the Montgomery County Boys Club, Matthew said he found Islam in 1973 after being given a copy of the paper *Muhammad Speaks* while he was locked up. He planned on changing his name to Matthew Saad Muhammad following the fight.

'I must make a public announcement on this eventually,' Matthew told Collins. 'I think that everybody should have a name that is part of their culture and race. Something that they can identify with. I will keep the first name Matthew because it is a good name, a Bible name. But Franklin is more-or-less a slave name and not fitting for me. Saad means good fortune and I will fight under the name Matthew Saad Muhammad.'

He was backing himself to win, too, and said he'd destroyed sparring partners Anthony Jones and Bernard McClain, a former sparring partner of Johnson's.

'If he stands up to me, he will have to put up a great fight,' said the fired-up challenger. Belfiore predicted it wouldn't go beyond ten rounds.

* * *

The newspapers had started to pay close attention to Matthew's backstory. The media was running with the tale of the orphan making good and it was a significant part of the build-up on ABC.

When asked who his parents were, Matthew could only mournfully say, 'I really don't care. They don't worry about me, so why should I worry about them?'

But he did.

Sister Bernadine, one of the nuns at the orphanage where Matthew spent time, was interviewed and remembered how Matthew couldn't say his name because of a speech impediment. 'He was, in a way, saying something that sounded like Matthew so that name stayed with him,' she said.

The story continued with how he got involved with gang activity, serving his time in lock-up before going to the Juniper and finding Belfiore.

'Winning the championship means more to me than anything,' Matthew said, in some of his final thoughts. 'I was an orphan, and there aren't too many orphans who make it. They think that once you become an orphan, you're through, but I can show that you can be one out of a thousand or one out of a million and really be a good product.'

It was moving stuff. He could have been written off, condemned to the streets or to a life in jail, but here he was, staring down his destiny against a man he had already beaten.

Conversely, Johnson spoke about how he'd become disillusioned with the sport. It was a business to him now. The fun of the amateur days had been replaced by deals, decisions and the darker side of boxing.

'I don't love it like I used to,' Johnson tried to explain. 'Now I'm champion of the world, I can make the paydays I've always dreamed about … I'd like to retire, spend more time with my wife [Delores] …'

He would talk about growing up poor and how one of his goals was to buy his mother a 'big, beautiful home' and to 'have a family with the love he had' as a child but with the financial stability they did not have.

* * *

Disaster nearly struck Matthew two nights before the bout. As he jogged off the last few pounds, he picked up an injury to his right knee that caused him to go to hospital for some of the evening and then spend part of the next day resting it in a whirlpool bath. It was not ideal, but he had waited too long and wasn't going to let it deter him.

Those around him thought he was confident and relaxed. The morning before the fight, Nigel Collins was having breakfast in an Indianapolis restaurant with a colleague when Matthew walked by and waved cheerfully.

The fighters weighed in at 7.30am on the day and would reconvene for hostilities at 2.15pm.

'My intention is to knock you out,' was one of the last things Johnson told Matthew.

As Johnson had his hands wrapped, Matthew's advisor Bilal Muhammad said to the champion, 'Matthew loves death more than he loves life.'

That might have rattled Johnson, but Matthew was dancing to 'Ain't No Stopping Us Now' in his dressing room, relaxed and carefree.

Ticket sales had picked up in the final few days and it was reported that 8,395 fans, paying a gate of $103,000, were in the Market Square Arena, watching the hometown boy defend his title against the Philly thrillseeker.

Matthew, 22-3-2, wore royal blue trunks and waited in the ring for his fate. Johnson walked second and the crowd screamed their approval.

Marvin, 22-2 (17), with white trunks, walked second.

The champion's long chin straps, moustache and receding hairline made him look far more advanced than his 25 years but he was an excellent fighter, an experienced crashing, banging southpaw with a chest full of pride and determination.

Violence erupted from the start. As expected, the fighters picked up from where they had left off. The champion lowered the boom with several hard lefts in the first round, and Matthew struck him with some stiff rights in return. Neither prioritised defence, and the crowd roared every success Johnson had and gasped every time Matthew landed a bomb.

At the close of the opening session, Arum leaned back in his chair and said, 'This fight isn't going the distance.'

By the start of the third round, the atmosphere was bubbling.

'I can't conceive that these two men could go at this pace for 15 rounds,' said ABC commentator Keith Jackson.

The third was wild. Matthew dug ferocious shots into Johnson's body but he was paying a price, taking violent left uppercuts and straight shots that jarred his head back. One uppercut seemed to daze Matthew.

Johnson took a quieter fourth. The crowd lapped it up and roundly booed referee George DeFabis, who asked both fighters to keep their punches higher as they slugged away throughout the fifth round, which was a better session for the challenger.

However, Matthew was cut in the next and his eyes were puffy.

Johnson, typically relentless, kept coming but he was marked by his right eye, too. The wound deteriorated and the sixth became a bloody affair. Matthew's nose pumped claret while blood poured out of Johnson's right eye, turning his white shorts pink.

To close round seven, Matthew thudded home a right hand that would have turned out 1,000 lights. Johnson sagged, retreating involuntarily. Matthew set about him only to be denied by the bell.

There was blood everywhere. Matthew's face had been smashed open at his right eyelid, he spat blood from his mouth and his nose was a torrent. The skin had been split on Johnson's right cheekbone and above both eyes, and both fighters' faces were covered in welts.

The emotion of it all was getting too much for Nick Belfiore, who was within touching distance of his first world title but also with his man at risk of being pulled out because of the cuts.

'I hated to see him beat up so badly,' Belfiore said afterwards.

'Nick was cryin' and sayin', "Do it Matthew. Do it,"' Matthew remembered. 'I kissed him on the head and went out to do it.'

Both fighter and trainer knew Matthew was hanging on by his fingertips. The cuts were so bad that officials wouldn't need to see much more before they waved it off in the champion's favour. Now the question was whether the one-minute interval had given Johnson enough time to recuperate ahead of the impending storm?

Initially, the answer was yes. Johnson landed a desperate left hook that buoyed his crowd and carved Matthew open by his left eye. Blood was smeared across Matthew's face from his nose. He was all but blinded, working from instinct, experience, feel and hope.

'I just kept swinging,' Matthew said. 'As long as I was throwing punches, I felt the referee wouldn't stop it.'

It was a gory spectacle. Matthew kept throwing and Johnson, trying not to drown in the sea of leather, was waiting to be able to plant his feet and fire back. Matthew bit down, unrelenting, applying unimaginable pressure, forcing the tiring champion back before Johnson finally wilted. Marvin buckled from three huge, booming right hands. The champion wanted to rise but his tank was empty.

Johnson was face down in his corner; Matthew went back to his to watch the count.

Johnson eventually managed to stand, but referee DeFabis waved it off.

Even in victory, Matthew could hardly stand. There was a moment when the old guard, Nick and Joe Belfiore, went to celebrate, but Matthew was already being held aloft by Jimmy Hayes and Akbar Muhammad.

Johnson, trying to regain his senses, teetered unsteadily as his corner team attempted to stem the bleeding.

Matthew closed his eyes and seemed on the verge of exhaustion, but he walked slowly over to console the ex-champion before being held aloft by his friend, Salim El-Amin, and shouting, 'Allahu Akbar'.

Moments later, Matthew was having his wounds tended to on his stool. 'I'm the champ,' he said, letting it sink in. He made his way over to Keith Jackson for the post-fight interview and asked Nick Belfiore, 'How do I look?'

'Messed up,' Belfiore replied, grouchy as ever.

'Every time I fight Johnson, it's going to be a hard fight,' said the new WBC champion. 'I think that he's the best light-heavyweight I've ever fought. All you light-heavyweights out there, watch out for Marvin Johnson, because he's bad. I'm just glad I'm the champion of the world.'

He went on: 'I could hardly see. Blood was draining down both my eyes but something kept saying, "Go on, go on, go on." I remember Steve Traitz at Montgomery County said, "Don't stop it, if you're in trouble, just keep on fighting."'

Matthew again said he needed to go back to the gym and work on his boxing. He knew the wars weren't good for him in the long run. This one had been so violent that he declined to watch the brutal climax back for analysis.

The *New York Times* called it 'one of the best title fights in recent years', and Nigel Collins, ringside, described it as 'stirring and savage'.

Decades later, Collins recalled being ringside for both Franklin–Johnson encounters.

'Cuts were a lot more a part of it [in the rematch],' said the writer. 'It was a damn good fight and if you hadn't seen the first one … it didn't go as long …'

A cub reporter named Al Bernstein – who would become an International Boxing Hall of Fame inductee years later as a broadcaster – covered the fight as his first boxing assignment for *Boxing Illustrated*.

He was amazed that both boxers had survived, calling it 'one of the most amazing brawls any light-heavyweights have ever staged'.

Johnson's nose and the cuts by his right eye were still bleeding a full 45 minutes after the fight, as he continued to protest the stoppage.

In his changing room afterwards, the new champion announced that he would be known as Matthew Saad Muhammad and again praised Johnson.

Matthew was taken to hospital but Johnson, initially defiant, stood his ground in the dressing room.

'He didn't have me unconscious at all,' Johnson argued. 'The referee didn't speak to me or anything. I think it was very obvious I could have gone on. Anytime I don't want to fight, I'll stop it myself. I feel I was treated very unjustly.'

Johnson thought that being the hometown fighter would have strengthened his case for the war to go on. Unlike many, he had thought he was winning.

'The problem with Indianapolis is that they try to be too honest to the point where they favour the other fighter,' the former champion claimed.

Matthew had been ahead on two of the three scorecards, so there wasn't much in it.

'His eyes were glazed,' confirmed referee George DeFabis, who said he'd stopped the count at nine because Johnson couldn't tell him where he was. 'I was afraid he'd be seriously hurt if I allowed the fight to continue. His right eye was badly slashed inside and he was spurting blood. He couldn't focus his eyes and could not put his arms up.'

Johnson's manager, Weiss, had conceded his man was 'out on his feet'.

Johnson reluctantly joined Matthew in hospital, calling for a third fight, and one local headline unkindly read, 'Both looked like losers' such was the damage.

Matthew told reporters there had been so much blood in his eyes that he could barely see, he could just feel Johnson on his chest. He kept throwing leather and stayed close to Johnson so DeFabis wouldn't take a closer look at his wounds.

Years later, Matthew could not recall the intricate details of his fights with Johnson, and neither could Marvin. A lot of time had passed and two fights became one.

'He [Matthew] was very good,' Johnson recalled. 'He was a strong fighter and I've got nothing but respect for him. I beat him up and he beat me up. Then he came to my hometown but I did better in Philadelphia than I did in Indianapolis. It was a war. They were both wars. I tried to put aside the hard feelings that I had for him [after both contests]. I just wanted to win the fight but once the fight was over, I tried to put that away but he was a winner and I thought he was a good fighter. I didn't like him because he beat me, but I thought he was a good guy besides that.'

'I'd be cut so bad, blood splashed all over the place,' Matthew remembered of their battles. 'Those Marvin Johnson fights! Oh my goodness. Let me tell you about them … That was one of the first that showed me how it was going to be. He really rung my bell. I had no idea I was going to fight him again. I would have fought him a third time if the money was right.'

Matthew was paid $27,300 a few days after the fight, but the issue of who managed him was unresolved. That was caught up in the Philly courts and the commission decided to pay out and leave them all to it. His remaining purse was held in escrow. Gelb was due $11,250, or 25 per cent, but the court needed to make it official.

'Last week in Indianapolis, a man named Bilal Muhammad from Newark was identifying himself as Muhammad's adviser,' wrote Martin Ralbovsky in the *Philadelphia Inquirer*.

Gelb was on the outs, but he had been at the fight even though he hadn't been involved. Now, Matthew had Philadelphia lawyer Harry A. Rubin as his counsel, saying his client was 'ready to go to trial' to break free from Gelb.

Matthew told one journalist of his manager, 'The man hasn't been around for my last six fights. He just comes around to collect his money.'

The *Daily News* would call Bilal, 'A fascinating fellow.'

'He says he owns two apartment houses in Newark,' claimed the paper.

Belfiore, filled with disdain, sneered, 'He don't have two dimes to rub together.'

One newspaper said Bilal represented a New England insurance firm and he insisted, 'I'm just an advisor. Matthew doesn't need a manager. He's his own manager.'

Bilal had previously worked for Arum and for Don King as a consultant. He was a high-school dropout who said he was an entrepreneur when asked about his background. 'I sat there in King's office, with Hank Schwartz, 18 hours a day, heard all the deals being made, got a firm knowledge of how they're made, the logistics. I spent time in Arum's office. I learned,' he said.

Until 1965, Bilal Muhammad was known as Norman Barrett. 'I registered with Islam because it became evident that Islam was where I had to be. Now I relate with all my brothers. It's a wonderful feeling.'

'They eventually bought the management from me,' Gelb explained. 'Once they got in, I had the contract, I was his manager, but I had no influence because Matthew leaned to the Muslims, considering he wanted to become one and was one, so I just sat back, they made the fights, I collected the money, I went on.'

'They were still getting a cut of his purse,' said light-heavyweight contender Tony Green, who had started sparring with Matthew ahead of the Marvin Johnson fight. 'You just had a poor, illiterate guy who didn't have the knowledge of finances and then you had bloodsuckers coming in from all angles getting his money, taking advantage of a good situation and Matthew was soft-hearted anyway. Someone would come up to him with a sad story saying their mum was in hospital or they needed a dollar for this or a dollar for that and Matthew would give it up. He was too soft-hearted. If I loaned someone $1,000, I'd expect it back with some interest on it. He didn't even ask for it back.'

* * *

After changing his name, Matthew told the press, 'It will take my fans a while to get used to my new name, but didn't it take a while to get used to Cassius Clay changing his name to Muhammad Ali? A few more fights and everyone will know the name Saad Muhammad.'

But at the time, his choices were being questioned in some quarters. In a letter to *The Ring* in 1979, one reader from New Mexico wrote in offering Matthew praise for his victory over Johnson and then discussed Franklin's decision to change his name and join the Nation of Islam.

'The new champion will now allow his boxing skills to be exploited and used by a bunch of lunatics whose repertoire of black magic includes race hatred,' wrote Dick Templeton. 'I suppose in a few years we'll be hearing about bogus assassination attempts on this great black champion as he prepares to do battle with perhaps Mike Rossman – who is both white and Jewish.'

On 29 May 1979, notice was served in the local papers that Matthew had filed to legally change his name. Rubin was 'attorney for the petitioner'.

'I was in a Catholic orphanage and that was the first religion but what converted me to Islam is I went through a lot and I was just confused", Matthew reflected in around 2004. 'I think I just went with the flow. I can't say what I was thinking at that time … Racism … But no, I thought I'd go with the flow, everybody seemed to be doing it who was black. I did it because that's what was happening at the time.'

Matthew's friend, Mustafa Ameen, formerly Gary Ross from Allentown, Pennsylvania, explained why they were changing their names. 'Most of us urban black men began to learn about Islam and the history of our ancestors being brought over here and made slaves and given the names basically of the slave owner. We rejected that, went back to our roots and for those of us who accepted Islam, we took on Islamic names.'

Matthew Saad Muhammad was now the WBC light-heavyweight champion of the world. The orphan from Philly had done it. He might not have known his family or his true identity but to be known as a world champion was something else. That was just fine for now.

'I always knew I would get the championship,' he said years later. 'It was just a matter of time and how I was going to get it. That's all I wanted. And I got it.'

CHAPTER 8

PICKING THE LOCK

MATTHEW DIDN'T have to walk through arrivals when he got back to a wet and dreary Philadelphia a few days after becoming world champion. He was carried on the shoulders of supporters and escorted through security, greeted off Allegheny Flight 131 by around 50 fans, including old friends from South Philly and even a mayoral candidate. Matthew was followed by TV cameras and the press through the terminal building, with signs reading, 'Welcome home, Matthew Saad Muhammad' being waved. There were cries of 'Congrats, King' and 'Well done, Champ' and Matthew signed autographs.

He still signed Matthew Franklin, even though the transition to Matthew Saad Muhammad was almost complete.

The grand arrival was great news bulletin fodder, but the champion's mind raced. His face was still lumpy, the cuts had not healed, but now he had two names, a new title, a manager he had but didn't want and another he wanted but who he referred to as an advisor. Newspapers said he was engaged to a woman, Sandra Alexander, but there had been no engagement, and for the first-time reporters wrote about the daughter Matthew had when he was 18.

It seemed that, already, life as the champ wasn't all it was cracked up to be. 'I won the title and look what's happened to me already, I got half my money held up,' the new champ explained. 'I got the Indiana commission saying that Frank Gelb is my manager and I'm saying that he's not. Just shows you what kind of snakes are out there waiting for you whenever you do something.'

* * *

A few days later, Matthew met the press at the top of the *Rocky* steps at the art museum in Philadelphia. He took a moment to reflect. Looking out over his city, the one that had abandoned him and then taken him in, he said, 'I'm the champion of the world, the whole wide world. If this is all a dream, I don't want to wake up. It's all too beautiful to be true ... especially after all I've been through.'

The story of Matthew being abandoned on the streets as a child was becoming big news, picked up all over the media. Matthew was abandoned outside the orphanage ... Nuns found him wandering the Franklin Parkway ... He had been left on a doorstep ... He was found on a park bench ... He had been given to an aunt who got rid of him ...

The truth was, a kid a little older than him was with him one moment and then wasn't the next. Abandoned, Matthew had looked for help but couldn't talk. When he found a police officer, which might well have been the next day as he remembered years later – he couldn't say his name. She took him to the station where he waited to be claimed but no one came. After a few hours, nuns from the Catholic orphanage came and he lived there until he was adopted by the Santos family.

It was the stuff of Hollywood, to now be on top of the world after such a disastrous and traumatic start.

Comparing it to *Rocky*, one journalist wrote, 'There is one big difference between the two stories. *Rocky* is a movie with a carefully conceived and orchestrated plot to provide entertainment and drama. The drama in the Matthew Franklin story is real. The saga is not a conceived celluloid projection.'

But Matthew wasn't just turning his life around, and he wasn't merely content with being the WBC champion now, either. He wanted to unify the two titles and become an all-time great.

He knew former champion John Conteh was next in line, but he was looking ahead and wanted more in life than the tatty Dodge Diplomat he was driving around in.

'I'll fight all the top guys,' he promised. 'I'd fight Victor Galindez next if the fight could be arranged. But right now, John Conteh is next on my list. After him, maybe Eddie Gregory. I don't intend to slack off now, just because I'm on top. If anything, I've got to work even harder. I want to become the greatest light-heavyweight champion in history. I'm serious! I want to be greater than Archie Moore, Bob Foster, Billy Conn and all the rest.'

There was scope for greatness, too. He sat atop a powder keg of a weight class that was as deep as any division in history, with Galindez, Marvin Johnson, Mike Rossman, James Scott, Eddie Gregory, Conteh, Mate Parlov, Lottie Mwale, Yaqui Lopez and many others.

'With Muhammad Ali out of the way now,' Matthew said of the recently retired king, 'people will be looking for someone new to create excitement, and I think that's me.'

He told one writer, 'I always wanted an identity.' Now he had one; he was the champ.

Nick Belfiore, celebrating his first world titlist at the gym after opening its doors 11 years earlier, had hung a banner in the Juniper that read 'Welcome home, Champ!'

It was more upbeat than the one that said, 'All dues must be paid, or else ...'

Life was good for them both. It was a long way from Belfiore's days pushing heavy machinery for the City of Philadelphia.

Matthew moved to an apartment in North Philly, out of the ghetto. He was as popular as any of the other light-heavyweights, too, if not more so, and boxing magazines were filled with complimentary letters about the Philly orphan.

One Aaron Mosely, from Detroit, wrote to *World Boxing*, 'I like Matthew Franklin. He has the potential to become the greatest storybook hero since Joe Louis and Jackie Robinson ... The only thing that bothers me is that he takes too much punishment. Franklin is a fine defensive boxer with an excellent left jab. He should use his skills more often. After all, even storybook heroes are made of flesh and blood.'

Still, Matthew had the new start he had wanted and the identity he had craved.

To remember how far he had come, he went back to the Daniel Boone School, the North Philly School for children with disciplinary problems, and Camp Hill.

Dressed in a black velvet tuxedo, the new champ talked to inmates, took tapes of his fights and hosted Q-and-A sessions about how he had turned his life around.

Speaking in front of some 400 kids at Daniel Boone, he said, 'When they sent me here in the fall of 1968, I was the baddest guy you ever saw. I was in a gang and I was getting in deeper. Well, it was here at Boone that I started to realise I had to get myself together, to be somebody.'

'Hey Champ,' came one reply. 'We can't all be boxers.'

'Right,' Matthew agreed, thinking on his feet. 'But you can all be somebody. Get your heads on straight and you'll make it.'

One inmate asked him about a possible fight with James Scott, the Rahway prisoner who was ranked in the top ten and who was calling out Matthew from behind the walls of the maximum-security prison he resided in.

'I couldn't bring my people in there,' Matthew said. 'Is that a good place for small children to look up to? To have a world title fight in prison? He would have to come out of that prison for me to fight him.'

Matthew was well-received by those he spoke in front of. One 16-year-old said, 'He hasn't forgotten that a lot of his roots are here at Boone.'

There were, however, some who felt Matthew was forgetting where he came from.

'There was a time when Matthew got big and he changed his name, I think he lost touch with his friends,' said his old associate Stephen Chandler. 'The people that put that banner across Christian Street when he won the title and they were waiting to hug him ... Yeah, you're being pulled in a different direction with everyone wanting to know you and you're the champ now and other people want to be around you and maybe they're people that wouldn't want to be around you if you weren't champ ... Now you've got these new people around you wanting to pat you on the back and that's intoxicating. And he went that way.'

Eddie Everett agreed. 'You were with people who were there on your way to the top, now you're with people who are there once you got to the top ... So he kind of lost touch with the people where he came from.'

It wasn't as much Matthew altering his outlook as much as his circle being adjusted, and he wanted to be a role model.

'I'll go to some orphan homes, some schools, and talk to kids,' he said. 'I want to be known as an individual who respects people. You know, a swell guy. I'd like people to look toward me, not up to me.'

* * *

It wasn't lost on some observers that Matthew's success was coming at a physical cost. Tom Cushman, of the *Philadelphia Daily News*, questioned Matthew about the mounting list of wars. Cushman wrote, 'There is a cloud drifting across this horizon, however, and Matthew Muhammad is not unaware of it. There is a terrible price exacted for the kind of excitement he creates, and his conversation is sprinkled with references to that fact.'

'I want to come out of this business walking on my toes, not on my heels,' Matthew told him.

He'd needed plastic surgery to repair the wounds from the Johnson rematch so the 22 July date in Monte Carlo for Conteh was switched to 18 August in Atlantic City, New Jersey.

Conteh had been more than ready but was okay to wait.

Matthew started an early war of words with the English veteran, insisting he needed to make sure cuts would not be a factor because Conteh was a dirty fighter who used his head. He admired Conteh as a boxer but charged, 'He's a butt man. He is an extremely dangerous butter.'

'I'll have a good cutman,' Matthew continued, referring to the Johnson damage. 'I don't think they'll be much of a problem. I hope they don't open.'

As Conteh tapered his preparations in England, Matthew was given the keys to Muhammad Ali's Deer Lake training camp in

Pennsylvania to get ready for his first defence of the WBC title. Matthew used Ali's cabin, and some saw him as the successor to Ali's throne of popularity.

One day, Ali dropped by to visit while Matthew trained and the heavyweight legend was interviewed by ABC's Howard Cosell. Ali and Matthew looked at an old picture of them together from a few years earlier.

'Ain't this something,' said Ali. 'Damn. I didn't know you'd be light-heavyweight champion.'

Then Matthew read a poem to Ali. It wasn't the best, but Matthew was trying to be like Ali while being blocked by modesty, introversion and a lack of the over-confidence Ali had.

'We all know that one day Muhammad Ali will go,' read Matthew's poem.

'And that there's this new light-heavyweight, I've been told, that will put boxing back on its toes.

'And that new man and that great fighter is Matthew Saad Muhammad, the light-heavyweight champion of the world.'

Ali could only say, 'You're just as crazy as I am.'

Matthew was a lovely guy, hugely well-liked, and his beaming, contagious smile was mentioned at almost every opportunity, but he wasn't Ali, even though he wanted to follow in his footsteps. That said, the *Philadelphia Daily News* thought he or Sugar Ray Leonard *might* be the heir apparent.

As the years wore on, Matthew fondly recalled the time spent with Ali at Deer Lake.

'We were chopping wood,' he remembered. 'It was beautiful up there ... the trees, the log cabins, we had big humungous beds, Muhammad Ali was up there and he was still training. We'd do everything together.'

'He was starstruck but also amazed at Ali, his mannerisms and dealing with people,' said Mustafa Ameen, a regular in the camp. 'Ali was like the Pied Piper. He could sit here and 50 people could gravitate towards him and he had a way that he'd never put people down. He wasn't mean to anybody ... We were all in awe of Ali's personality and Saad may have been awestruck but Ali's stature was so great, just for him to know you and call you on the phone … it was like a circus around Ali and it was a lot of fun.'

Matthew would be up daily at 6am, running four miles on the hilly and windy roads around the camp.

Then he'd chop wood, have breakfast and train in the gym at 2.30pm.

He would skip rope and do seven or eight rounds of sparring with between one and four sparring partners.

A young heavyweight called Tim Witherspoon, a few months away from his professional debut, was one.

'He was a tough guy to spar with,' recalled Witherspoon, who went on to hold the WBA heavyweight title and who would do as many as four rounds at a time with Matthew.

Some sparring partners survived, but plenty didn't. 'Man, I've been rolling them out of here,' Matthew laughed as the Conteh date neared.

Sandra was up there, too, and the *Daily News* wrote of their plans to marry, but Matthew said his focus was on Conteh. 'Believe me, IT'S not allowed,' Matthew smiled.

Still, at times he found Deer Lake boring. He had wanted to go on vacation after the first Johnson war, then after Lopez, but the contests kept coming and now he was disclosing his three- to five-year plan, which involved unifying the light-heavyweight titles and then moving up in weight.

'I also plan to capture the heavyweight championship,' he explained. 'I am confident I will.'

Ali believed Matthew could do it and planned on having Matthew's name hand-painted on one of the camp's famous boulders that paid homage to old champions and some of Ali's rivals, including Sonny Liston, Rocky Marciano, Kid Gavilan and Sugar Ray Robinson.

Matthew was flattered.

'He's a very good man,' Matthew said of Ali. 'Smart, a great champion and I just thank him for letting me use his facility. Ali picked the rock out for me. It says *Matthew Saad Muhammad, the light-heavyweight champion of all time.*

Bilal Muhammad spoke about how he planned on making Matthew more marketable, as did Akbar Muhammad, who was being described as Matthew's business manager.

'Look at his story,' said Akbar. 'It's the American Dream.'

Matthew might have idolised Ali, but he also had no intention of being a clone and scoffed at the notion that he was an Ali-lite.

'I'm coming up in my own style,' he insisted. 'I want to be my own man. I want to set an example for those who are orphans and for those who have had a hard life.'

And his self-confidence was growing. His stutter was receding and while he wasn't Ali or anywhere near as bombastic, he was becoming a better interview. Those in the press who knew him acknowledged that part of his journey, too.

'Matthew is quiet, solemn and has trouble, especially in front of a crowd, translating his thoughts into correct grammar,' wrote Tommy West in the *Inquirer*. 'But he always apologizes for that weakness, in such a manner that it no longer seems a weakness.'

* * *

With Matthew in Deer Lake, there were changes afoot. Nigel Collins visited, noticing a lot of new faces. Nick Belfiore took him to one side.

'They're stealing him away from me,' Belfiore told the young reporter.

Bilal Muhammad was there with his friend Mustafa Ameen, whom Bilal had known from New Jersey. Amen was often in Deer Lake and he'd been there in the Ali years.

Ameen, who was in financial planning and insurance, would go back to his offices with stories of Ali and the celebrities who came by. Mustafa discovered Matthew did not have insurance or financial protection and sold him a million-dollar policy.

And even though Matthew was Bilal's only client, Ameen would see the manager struggling under the weight of phone calls in his office and would help. They talked about Ameen taking on a role as 'gopher' and 'facilitating stuff' following a 30-day trial.

'I was employed by Bilal and Bilal paid me,' Ameen explained. 'He wanted me to be with Saad so I started going to Philly, staying at his house, accompanying him to events, co-ordinating appearances and I was loving my life.'

Matthew's old friend Salim El-Amin had been released after ten years in prison and was brought into the fold. Inside, he'd been on a barber's course and he cut Matthew's hair and worked in camp as a training assistant.

But the changes were coming at a financial cost. Matthew's partnership with Gelb was at an end and Saad spent a bundle on litigation. He didn't think Gelb had a case, but Gelb's argument was upheld in court and Matthew had to pay him a percentage of his earnings for at least another year.

Apparently, however, the new champion was not worried by the cost or the changes.

'He believed we were all family and it was "Hey, you're the fighter and we're going to take care of all of the other stuff,"' said Ameen. 'He trusted Bilal, he trusted those who said we need to make this break. This was all part of the transition. A new regime comes in, like presidential elections. Out with the old, in with the new. And Nick [Belfiore] had more allegiance to the old manager.'

Despite the acrimony, Gelb insisted years later there had been no hard feelings on his side.

'There wasn't a big argument,' Gelb contended. 'I never counted him as being active in wanting to split. They really knew how to … Firstly, I didn't want to argue with anybody. I never did. They were going to pay me off or use me and pay me my amount of money until the contract expired – one or the other, and I was perfectly happy.'

* * *

Big-time boxing was headed to Atlantic City. There hadn't been a world championship fight at the seaside resort since middleweight Joey Giardello beat Dick Tiger over 15 rounds in 1964. Howard Davis, one of the touted 1976 Olympic stars from a decorated team that included Sugar Ray Leonard and Michael and Leon Spinks, had fought there in 1978, two years after gambling had been legalised in New Jersey, but Matthew's fight with Conteh was a big Boardwalk attraction. For Matthew, from Philly, it was a little more than an hour away if the roads were clear.

The casinos were also stumping up hefty site fees hoping to lure high-rolling gamblers to the coast for an expensive weekend. They would comp the tickets to try and get customers to the tables and the slots. The fighters liked it, too.

As Nigel Collins wrote of the emerging city at the time, 'Who wants to slug it out in some dingy, smoke-filled club, when you can do battle in the posh surroundings of a glittering casino, and get paid twice as much in the process? No longer is it a promoters' market; now it belongs to the fighters, and A.C., N.J. was the ingredient that changed the equation.'

There was the Tropicana, Resorts, Bally's Park Place, the Sands, the Playboy, the Claridge and Harrah's. Caesars Boardwalk Regency hosted some cards at the Convention Hall and then there was the Golden Nugget. Some casinos would comp up to 75 per cent of their tickets to their highest rollers. It was about what they could offer rather than what they could make.

There had been just seven boxing shows in Atlantic City in 1975. But there were 79 in 1981 and all nine casinos had tried it.

'Boxing is our featured invitational event,' explained Bucky Howard, the Playboy's vice president in charge of casino operations. 'Every time we have a boxing event, we send out over 2,000 invitations to our top customers to come as guests. We don't expect to make any ticket money.'

Saad Muhammad–Conteh was on ABC, promoted by the Resorts and was due to take place in the small arena on the rickety Steel Pier, but it was moved into the Resorts Superstar Theater in fight week. That only happened once organisers had been given the all-clear by Diana Ross, who agreed to move the time of her show back to allow ABC cameras enough time to pack up. Ross was ringside for that fight, as was Frank Stallone,

Sylvester's brother, who sat next to the aforementioned Giardello, and the Rat Pack's Joey Bishop. Only a handful of the 1,600 tickets were unsold.

Gelb was working for Resorts and had been given licence to head up promotions in Atlantic City, so anyone wanting to stage fights there needed to go through him.

'In the next two or three years, that will be the major battle,' Gelb said of talk about where boxing's capital would be, Las Vegas or Atlantic City. 'I don't see how Vegas can compete once we have a new arena. I foresee a bidding war.'

Robert Lee, then New Jersey commissioner, saw the battle lines drawn between the two destinations, but things needed to change. 'One is getting people into the city. They have to fly to Philadelphia and drive the rest of the way,' said Lee. 'The second drawback is the tax structure. Rectify those two things and we'll be No. 1 in the world.'

The tax issue was significant. Promoters had to pay more to stage a successful card in Atlantic City, which, depending on the profit margin, could be as much as 50 per cent higher.

But that didn't dampen the ambition or enthusiasm of many who thought they were entering a new golden era of boxing.

* * *

Matthew was due to earn $150,000 and Conteh $50,000. Bob Arum, with his three options on the champion, hoped the winner would fight Rossman – particularly if Matthew retained the title – or the victor of a proposed WBA title fight between champion Victor Galindez and Marvin Johnson.

Conteh was a considerable underdog. The Liverpool hero, son of a Sierra Leone immigrant, had won the WBC championship with a superb 1974 performance against Argentine Jorge Ahumada and had never lost the belt in the ring. The WBC stripped him when he refused to defend against Miguel Cuello, but that was more about a contractual conflict rather than Conteh not wanting to fight Cuello, who he'd likely have beaten.

However, while some thought Conteh had been unlucky to leave Belgrade without the title following a disputed split decision defeat to Mate Parlov in June 1978, he had failed to impress in his two outings before Atlantic City. Plenty thought he'd reached the end of the line after a draw with Jesse Burnett in London.

English promoter Mickey Duff called it, 'his worst performance ever'. Conteh was down in rounds one and eight, got away with not losing and then was floored, two months later, toiling to an uninspiring win over Ivy Brown.

Added to that, many in the sport saw him as a one-handed fighter after he had suffered two bad breaks in his right hand that hadn't been pain-free since a win over Willie Taylor in Scranton back in 1975.

'It's shit or bust,' Conteh admitted, when asked if the hand would hold up.

The challenger was relentlessly referred to as 'handsome', a 'jet-setter' or a 'playboy' by the press. He drove a Rolls-Royce, liked the nightlife and modelled underwear. It seemed he would not be short of options in his transition away from the sport, which seasoned observers thought might come if he couldn't upset Matthew. The British press pack travelled in force, ready to pen their man's obituary, but their US counterparts took a liking to Conteh. He was sharp-witted and made for good copy. One said he looked like Ken Norton but sounded like Paul McCartney and another called him 'a wisecracking glamour boy'.

Conteh didn't mind. He was a smooth fighter with a wand of a left hand but the sparing use of his right hand was a concern, and those who believed in Conteh were in short supply.

The *Boxing News* headline read, 'Sorry John! It's too late now' and editor Harry Mullan thought the new champ's heavy artillery would be too much for the experienced Englishman. Mullan, one of the great boxing scribe, wrote, 'Whether it's a matter of loss of interest, too much social life, recurrent hand injuries, or simply the inevitable passage of time, Conteh now seems a shadow of the golden fighter he was six years ago.'

Mullan added, 'Muhammad looks an extraordinarily gifted young champion with resilience, courage, strength, and lots of ability, too.'

In Matthew's camp, Belfiore predicted his charge would get Conteh out by the seventh or eighth round.

Matthew's old NABF title, which he had vacated, was going to be contested between Jerry Martin and Dale Grant on the Atlantic City undercard.

Matthew and Conteh attended a press luncheon on the Boardwalk a week before the fight and Matthew was asked more questions about religion and his name change than the bout.

There was another new face in the champ's camp, too. New Jersey photographer Paul Trace was hired by Bilal Muhammad to capture the new champion's reign. The assignment fell in his lap when a colleague was asked whether he could photograph a Teddy Pendergrass concert or the light-heavyweight championship fight. Paul chose to cover Saad Muhammad–Conteh, was taken to Matthew's hotel room and started taking pictures. Before he knew it, he was in the dressing room capturing the final preparations.

Trace had been a fight fan since listening to Joe Louis bouts on the radio with his father in the 1940s, but he'd never been to a boxing match before.

'I didn't know anybody,' Trace recalled. 'I'm the only white guy there and we then go to the ring. I'm in front, Matthew's walking down and I'm going backwards. They were playing *Rocky* music and now I'm in the centre of the ring, photographing the champion getting in, and I almost couldn't take pictures! It was incredible. The hair on the back of my neck was standing up. I could hardly think straight.'

* * *

Conteh started off behind his precise, brisk jab, looking compact and economical. Matthew, meanwhile, missed with some hearty swings and was made to look clumsy, unable to locate range or timing.

Referee Carlos Padilla, who'd overseen the third and final fight in the Ali–Frazier rivalry, didn't have a lot to do in the early going.

Conteh was slipping or blocking almost everything that came his way.

The challenger boxed with finesse. Matthew had more success in the third as he started to close the gap, thudding home a right to Conteh's torso in the fourth, but shortly after walked on to a firm right that caught him between the eyes.

Conteh was growing in confidence and at the end of the fifth, a clash of heads left Matthew cut along his left eyebrow. Cutman Adolph Ritacco and Belfiore went to work in the corner, but blood trickled from Matthew's left eye. At the start of the sixth, Conteh was having more success with his jabs and hooks. Matthew was easy to find and absorbed a heavy-looking left hook that forced him on to his back foot. Conteh was winning rounds, and he claimed the sixth handily.

In commentary, Howard Cosell said Conteh's jab was a 'work of art'. Matthew's left eye was now haemorrhaging blood. Conteh didn't give ground in the clinches, and he was throwing his supposedly bad right hand more often, too.

The fight was not just bloody, it was increasingly gruelling.

Cosell noticed Conteh blinking in the seventh and the eighth but the challenger's right hand kept connecting with the damaged area on Matthew's face.

Matthew's double jab snapped Conteh's rhythm, but the deep cut turned the champion's white Pony shorts pink. However, there was growing consternation in Conteh's corner, with George Francis claiming Matthew's corner was using illegal substances to stem the blood flow.

As the rounds progressed, Matthew's familiar mask of blood re-emerged. He was also cut down the inside of his left eye along the nose and on the cheek.

Conteh thought the fight was going to be stopped and felt it should have been.

Matthew had been bleeding so profusely that Dr Stanley P. Rogers checked the eye after the sixth, seventh and eighth rounds.

Ferdie Pacheco, commentating with Bob Halloran on a taped feed for promoters Top Rank, was in no doubt what was being used. 'They're putting in a solution which is monsel solution, it's an ointment and it's illegal, it's ferric chloride and it burns the tissue and stops [the bleeding],' snapped Pacheco.

A round later, Pacheco added, 'Right now, they're putting in that solution which is almost like cement; it burns the tissue shut and he's not bleeding as much as he had been.'

Matthew came out for the ninth with a thick dollop of what might have been Vaseline over his left eye and he pumped out his jab regularly. But towards the end of the session, Conteh landed a right over the top. Matthew smiled in acknowledgement that it hurt.

As the ninth closed, a now-incensed Francis flew into the ring and lambasted everyone from Padilla to the opposition team about what was being used in the wound over Matthew's left eye, alleging the same substance had caused Conteh to blink earlier in the fight.

Matthew looked like he'd been through a meat-grinder, while Conteh could have put on a suit and strolled down the catwalk.

Although you could see the dark crimson holes in Matthew's face, as the fight progressed, the blood stopped flowing as freely.

Writing for *Boxing News* from ringside, Mullan called the tenth 'fiercely exciting' and said the 12th was 'one of the great rounds'. Yet the most intense drama was still to come.

Matthew had never gone 15 rounds. Conteh had done it seven times, but the challenger lost a punishing 13th and knew he was tiring. His face was starting to swell and that's when things really began to unravel. He came out for the next round, telling his legs to buck up, but he knew they were no longer listening to his commands and when the Saad Muhammad avalanche came his way, Conteh could do nothing to stem the leather.

With around a minute remaining in the 14th round, Matthew broke decisively through. There were several crunching rights then a left hook-right hand and a straight left. Conteh folded, dropping to his knees with his back arching over the middle rope. Matthew hoisted his gloves in victory, but Conteh scrambled on to all fours and returned to his feet. Matthew flew in to conclude matters, with Conteh trying to hang on but he was caught by an arcing left hook that sent him lurching backwards into the ropes and then back to the canvas.

With three seconds left in the round, Conteh stood once more, and the bell sounded before Matthew could apply any kind of finishing attempt.

Going into the last round, Mullan had the fight level, Cosell had Matthew one round down. 'Matthew, Matthew, Matthew!' screamed the crowd, supporting his desperate rally, which ended with Conteh bleeding by his right eye and the fighters trading up to the final bell.

Both celebrated at the end, Conteh from surviving the final frantic nine minutes and Matthew from clawing back a deficit to be in contention for retaining his title.

When the decision was announced, Matthew had done enough on all three cards. Padilla scored 146-142, English referee Harry Gibbs marked it 144-143 and New Jersey's Charlie Spina had it 146-141.

Conteh and Matthew held each other's hand aloft. Cosell didn't agree with the decision but was in a minority. Many felt Matthew's late rally and the two knockdowns had turned the fight in his favour, even if only just.

At the press conference, the boxers again embraced, sat next to one another and answered questions.

'I picked the lock and I lowered the boom,' said the relieved champion, wearing an enormous white bandage above his left eye.

The challenger was proud of his efforts. 'He pulled it out like great champions do,' admitted Conteh, strips of plaster over his left cheek and on his right eyebrow.

Conteh later joked, 'Saad's cornermen had been bunging up enough illegal substances into those cuts to fill up three holes in a road .... By the end of the ninth round the cuts had sealed and the substance was set as solid as cement. Chunks of it were jutting out of his eyebrow.'

Mullan felt Conteh should fight on, calling the contest 'one of the most exciting championships I've ever watched', which was standard fare for Matthew's bouts by now. 'It was magnificent, unforgettable,' wrote Mullan.

Post-fight, gamblers returned to their tables and Conteh's wife Veronica stood tearfully in the arena, her voice cracking when she said, 'But if only he could have won.' Conteh's stock rocketed in defeat, however. He'd given the high-flying champion hell, could have won and proved the doubters wrong.

Talk of a rematch swirled before either of them could hit the showers.

A day later, Matthew said, 'I shall never lose my title ... I showed again I can come back from the grave and win.'

He had turned things around again, as he had against Douglas, Kates, Lopez and twice against Johnson. The *New York Times* could see a pattern in Matthew's fights. 'Matthew Saad Muhammad has forged a trademark for himself. Whenever it looks like he might be in trouble, or behind on points, that means just one thing. Look out!'

But the furore over what had happened to Matthew's cuts in the fight was just beginning. Within hours of the final bell, Francis had lodged an official protest, claiming Matthew's corner had 'used all sorts of stuff' to close the cuts. Francis contended that he'd seen 'red stuff, black stuff and clear stuff'.

'I think it was glue,' he said, only half-joking. 'He had a clever cutman. He may have won this fight for him.'

Mullan wrote of the eye damage, 'The cut was beyond treatment by normal means, and no British referee would have allowed a boxer to continue with such a wound.'

Ritacco went under the microscope. Seconds could only use Vaseline or 1/1000 of adrenaline in the corner, but he'd used something else, and he admitted it, too.

Ritacco said they would find only 'a tannic acid, which is made out of tea leaves' that he'd been using for 25 years.

'And I don't give a damn whether they like it or not,' he snapped.

Incriminating himself further, Ritacco added, 'What it comes down to is whether we're going to have boxing or not. With those two cuts today, I could have stuck Matthew's head in a pail of adrenaline and it wouldn't have done any good. If they ain't gonna stop a guy from butting open cuts like that, then they can't expect me to stop a two-inch gash with adrenaline.'

Ritacco doubled-down and half-implicated commissioner Joe Walcott, saying he'd seen him use the same mix many times before.

Speaking to Tom Cushman of the *Philadelphia Daily News* in the aftermath, Ritacco fumed, 'Matthew got one cut below the eye that was minor. The one alongside the eye took two butterflies to close afterwards and the one over the eye took five. He was sliced up pretty good by a guy who knows how to do it, but they were things we could manage. The only thing I was afraid of was that they were gonna say what I was doing was illegal and throw me out of the ring.'

Whatever was used, New Jersey commissioner Percy Richardson took samples to have them analysed and Bob Lee, also on the New Jersey commission, confiscated two packets of beige powder, one of white as well as some powder in a gauze pad, sealing them and sending them to New Jersey State Police in Hammonton.

Conteh took his boxing gloves to the British Boxing Board of Control headquarters in Oxford Street, hoping to prove an illegal substance had been used and that it could be traced on the red leather.

Francis, who'd kept the gloves wrapped in plastic since fight night, was fuming. 'If the WBC don't act, it will set boxing back 20 years,' he said.

The Board sent the gloves to the forensic laboratory at Scotland Yard, home of the UK police, to be examined and a week after the contest, New Jersey suspended both Adolph Ritacco and Nick Belfiore pending a 12 September hearing.

When Conteh got back to England, he said, 'No, I didn't think I'd got it [the decision]. You don't lie to yourself, do you? I am just an honest worker and pleased with myself that I trained as dedicated as I could and gave 200 per cent on the night.'

He was satisfied with his efforts, particularly as he'd worried about letting people down in the build-up. He'd done the UK proud, as seen on the cover of *Boxing News* that read, 'Down – But A Long Way From Out'.

Covering the fight from ringside, Steve Farhood wrote, 'There would only be one winner, but no losers. And in a gambling town, such an ending defies all the odds.'

Farhood's report in the *Big Book of Boxing* magazine saw the Philly orphan take on another name and another identity. Farhood colourfully referred to him as 'Miracle Matthew', a moniker that would stay with him.

* * *

Speculation of a rematch was everywhere, and Ritacco was on the back foot but remained indignant. He was even considering suing the commission, 'for accusing me of using monsel'.

The under-fire cutman shouted that he had never seen such sore losers and snapped, 'You won't find any of that in there. You can suspend me for life.'

At the commission hearing, Walcott suspended Ritacco for two months and Belfiore for three but the WBC took it more seriously. At their convention in Casablanca, Morocco, they considered two options, an immediate rematch and life ban for the cornermen or stripping Matthew and allowing Conteh to fight for the vacant title.

WBC president Jose Sulaiman had called it a 'serious rules violation by the champion'.

Whatever, Conteh would get another chance and the rematch had to take place in March with a 55-45 purse split in the champion's favour.

Matthew was irate, saying Belfiore and Ritacco had been 'unprompted' in their actions and that the damage had been caused by a Conteh headbutt. There wasn't much sympathy for him, and the WBC initially handed out lifetime bans to Belfiore and Ritacco, later changing them to 12 months. They fined Bilal Muhammad and Belfiore $7,500 each.

Decades on, Conteh had all but forgotten the corner shenanigans.

'It didn't bother me,' Conteh admitted. 'I let them do what they wanted to do and George would take care of that, or the people around the ring, the officials … I was just focused on what I was trying to do and what he was doing. And what he was doing, whether he should or shouldn't have been doing it, can do it or can't do it, it was down to the authorities or George in my corner sorting it.'

The challenger also knew he had emerged with real credit. 'It was great because he was a real tough fighter and I was trying to draw back the years, even though I was only 28, and I felt it was harder than when I was younger but I gave it everything. It was a great night. It went 15 rounds. I did the best I could.'

Top Rank still wanted to pair Matthew with Rossman and Matthew was open to it, even though Rossman hadn't fought him when he held the WBA title. In fact, Matthew went to the Giants Stadium with Arum to watch Rossman in a shock defeat to Ramon Ranquello.

A few weeks later, Matthew's adoptive mother Bertha Santos died and he started thinking about life away from the sport, and his future after boxing. He spoke about retiring soon, believing another three or five years of brawls would make him the greatest light-heavyweight champion of all time.

'The way I fight, I won't have ten years left,' he admitted.

'That's when I'll be in investments and be ready to settle down,' Matthew continued. 'I got a girl in mind but everybody, mostly Bilal, says I'm too young to get married.'

'Everybody's too young to get married,' Bilal chimed in.

Matthew found that funny.

'That's why I have Bilal with me. He's so smart.'

* * *

Arum outbid Don King to stage the fight by a slender margin. King offered $812,500, Arum bid $815,000. Peltz was saying to forget Matthew and Rossman because Jerry 'The Bull' Martin might be Philly's best 175-pounder and veteran Mike Quarry was back and hoping for a shot at Matthew.

Meanwhile, James Scott's prison boxing career was gaining momentum. Through 1979, Scott had four fights and worked his way up the WBA rankings as he defeated Richie Kates, Bunny Johnson, Ennio Cometti and Jerry Celestine.

'I'm gonna get that title,' Scott promised. 'I'm in the worst place in the world and I'm only this far from it.'

Incidentally, Conteh had signed to fight Kates until the rematch with Matthew was formalised.

In November, Victor Galindez lost his WBA title to Marvin Johnson at the Superdome in New Orleans. Matthew was ringside to challenge the Galindez–Johnson winner, and he was hoping it would be Johnson. The night before the fight, Matthew went into his old rival's hotel room to wish him well and give him some tips.

'He'll back up and be defensive,' Matthew said, predicting Galindez's tactics. 'He doesn't have any legs, man, and you can put pressure on him.'

Johnson seemed to find it all surreal. He was used to fighting the man in front of him, not taking intel from him.

'I appreciate your advice,' Johnson grinned. 'But I thought about all those things and I just want you to think about us going again.'

Johnson stopped Galindez in the 11th, flooring the Argentine on his way to a huge victory and in December James Scott hammered out a decision over Yaqui Lopez in Rahway to solidify his position as a top contender.

He called out Matthew and Johnson for title fights at the first opportunity.

A week later, Matthew's old rivals Mate Parlov and Marvin Camel contested the first world title fight at cruiserweight, a new weight division that had opened to bridge the gap between light-heavyweight and heavyweight. They shared a 15-round draw in Croatia.

Of course, Matthew's out-of-the-ring problems had not gone away, and he was becoming more outspoken about Gelb's role in his career. He contended that his path to the top had been too rough, and he had a point. 'He put me in with King Kong,' Matthew explained. 'Put me in with guys who could knock my head off. I got tired of that.'

Regardless of the acrimony, Gelb remained manager on paper for 10 per cent of Matthew's future purses for the next year or so, but Belfiore's fears had been realised and he was gone.

'Nick didn't really get to reap the benefits of his early work,' recalled Nigel Collins. 'More than anything else, the parting with Belfiore seemed to sever Muhammad's last link with his old persona – that of Matthew Franklin.'

Belfiore was so upset that he threw Matthew out of the Juniper, claiming he had not been getting his 10 per cent management fee and he'd been underpaid for the Conteh fight.

They'd been together for just about every fight Matthew had had, amateur and pro, and Belfiore wasn't the only departure. Rubin, the lawyer, who'd been unable to snap the Gelb contract but who was reportedly on 15 per cent if he had, was also gone. So was Jimmy Hayes, the long-standing cornerman.

Hayes asked for their agreement to be formalised, but Matthew baulked.

'Let's see how he does with a whole new corner,' Jimmy snapped.

'I'm the owner of my corporation,' said Matthew, sounding like a changed man. 'Now I have a totally new staff.'

The old guard, who'd been with him through the leanest years, would have been a part of the new money. Matthew was due to make $448,250 for the second Conteh fight.

It was all chaotic and unsavoury. As one writer put it, 'Poke around in the scenes surrounding Matthew Saad Muhammad and you'll hear more lies than Saturday night in a singles bar.'

The jilted Belfiore spat, 'Matthew lies like a rug. He is the most ungrateful, lousy ****er I have ever run across and I am going to be 70 years old on Saturday.'

People weren't unaware of what was going on. Rossman even quipped to a reporter, 'I'm watching what is happening to Matthew … he thinks his face is cut up [after Conteh]. Wait until he takes a look at his contract someday.'

* * *

For the first time in his career, Matthew needed a new trainer and trialled Philadelphia veteran Sam Solomon. Solomon, 61, had coached Philly middleweight puncher Cyclone Hart, had taken Ernie

Terrell to the WBA heavyweight title and had worked with former heavyweight champion Leon Spinks, training the young contender to victory and defeat in two fights with Muhammad Ali. Solomon also worked with another big Philadelphia boxing name, Sonny Liston.

'Sam is here for a purpose,' Matthew explained. 'Helping me fulfil things I need to be an even better champion. I am not ignoring my defensive problems. I know I get hit too often.'

In an interesting sidebar, Solomon had already gone up against Conteh. He'd trained Philadelphian Eddie Duncan to defeat him in 1972 in Conteh's hometown of Liverpool.

'He was not a taskmaster,' said Mustafa Ameen of Solomon. 'He was smooth, cool and he would go whichever way the wind would blow. He had a very dark complexion, about 5ft 9ish – he'd begun to go grey, real solid build and he was a real affable guy. It was hard not to like Sam. He was passive. He wasn't interested in what happened at night, where a lot of trainers are interested in what you're doing, if there were any girls around. He was politically astute so Sam wasn't going to do anything to upset the applecart. As long as the training went well and the cheques were coming, he was just there in the gym.'

After some thought, Collins said, 'I don't think he was a good trainer. He was a good conditioner. Georgie Benton was a good trainer. Trainer is maybe the wrong word but the best of them are teachers. Sam used to have this notebook where he'd make note of how many rounds he did, how many rounds you hit the bag, who he sparred, callisthenics, he seemed to be focused on writing all that stuff.'

But Matthew was the one who seemed to be writing a lot. He was signing a lot of cheques.

* * *

Matthew's plans sounded just fine to the writers, who were uniformed in wondering how much longer he could fight as his mileage climbed. By this point, *Boxing News* editor Harry Mullan felt Matthew 'has at least a couple more battles in him'.

Bilal Muhammad explained that the last three fights of Matthew's Top Rank deal were tiered to earn the fighter $125,000, $150,000 and then $200,000. But the Conteh rematch alone was worth more than $400,000, so there were moves to renegotiate.

In the meantime, Matthew bought a new house in Jenkintown, a five-bedroom place that Bilal didn't want him to purchase.

'Matthew is his own man,' explained Bilal. 'This is not an old-line fighter–manager relationship. I can only suggest things. In a way I'm happy he bought the big house. Now he has to fight more. He will make a million this year if he keeps winning. That's if we have a unification title fight.'

For the second Conteh bout, set for 29 March and back in Atlantic City, Matthew prepared at Steve Traitz's Montgomery County Boys Club in Eagleville.

'He was the best,' said Saad's chief sparring partner Tony Green, of Traitz.

Green was also a key confidant who'd been with Matthew since the second Marvin Johnson fight and who was becoming an integral part of the camp.

'He [Traitz] was the head of the roofers' union and had a bunch of amateur fighters and he used to use a space for their meetings but Steve turned it into a gym and he invited Matthew to use the facility.'

Matthew wasn't sure if he'd ever return to Deer Lake, and although he'd denied he wanted to be the new Muhammad Ali, Gary Smith from the *Philadelphia Daily News* thought he could see that Matthew was trying to be Ali version 2.0.

'He even tried being Muhammad Ali for a while,' wrote Smith. 'He took on Ali's religion and name and his training camp in Deer Lake, and he ringed himself with an Ali-sized legion of lackeys.'

Matthew was okay with the comparisons and admired Ali like no other, but he wanted to be his own man.

'I don't want to be a Muhammad Ali,' he shot back. 'I'm just a new Muhammad on the mountain. It was hell there at Ali's camp. Ali can live on turmoil. I can't live on that. I'm Matthew Saad Muhammad and I'm just looking for my own identity.'

That wasn't lost on those who closely covered his story. One was boxing journalist Steve Farhood.

'With the aid of caring Catholic nuns and devilish fists, three crucial elements were somehow formed; a legitimate identity, a mission to be the best, and an oversized heart,' Farhood wrote.

From the outside looking in, Matthew was the orphan made good, making big money, winning exciting fights, realising dreams. Inwardly, though, there were signs he was troubled.

He bumped into Rossman at the Spectrum and Rossman asked him how things were.

'Problems, lots of problems,' Matthew sighed. Rossman could relate. Politics had played a bitter part in his own career.

'Hey, you know,' Rossman replied. 'It's tougher to be champion than it is to be the president.'

Then, in the countdown to the Conteh rematch, Matthew told British journalist Reg Gutteridge, 'This boxing is too politicking for me. Too corrupt, too many snakes, all the swindles and conniving.'

But Matthew was enjoying the finer things in life, too. With the money rolling in, he set about working on his image. He liked the idea of being seen as cultured and erudite. He was still trying to conquer his stammer, but he returned from a trip to New York $22,995 lighter having bought a Louis XV Steinway piano.

'Let me tell you about this piano,' laughed Tony Green, many years later. 'This PR broad hooked Matthew up with some famous pianist and he went and got a Steinway piano in New York and they wanted Matthew to do some PR with this famous piano guy. Long story short, after he did the PR with this famous pianist, they talked Matthew into buying a piano. That Steinway was about $20,000. Twenty grand for this goddamn Steinway piano. He couldn't play the piano, man. We were coming back to Philly and I said, "With $20,000 you can pay me for taking all these ass-whippings you've been giving me!" He thought it was funny.'

In the gym, Matthew and Solomon prioritised defence. During fight week, WBC president Jose Sulaiman arrived in town. He was going to see for himself if there was any controversy. That only served to get Matthew's back up even more. He felt the sanctioning body had it in for him and that the Mexican was there to see Conteh have his hand raised.

Sulaiman believed he'd been fair in the aftermath of 'cutgate' but Matthew's team had issues with the purse split right until the morning of the fight, hiring Newark lawyer Norman Fischbein to get things changed at the 11th hour. Sulaiman didn't see what the problem was. They hadn't stripped Matthew and he was about to make another handsome payday, even if Matthew felt he should get an additional $165,000 of Conteh's purse, providing him with 75 per cent of the $815,000 bounty rather than the 55 ordered by the WBC.

Matthew was big business by now, Sulaiman admitted. 'In all history, no [light-heavyweight] fighter has ever earned such a payday. Why complain?'

Matthew didn't want to fight Conteh again. He was mad at the WBC. He'd had to get a new trainer. His entourage was growing rapidly, and there was a new emerging threat, as well.

Michael Spinks, the 1976 Olympic gold medallist was calling out the champions, Matthew and Johnson. The weight class was a shark tank, brimming with menace, danger and skill.

Matthew also felt pressure with the burden of responsibility that came with wearing the crown.

'I had a championship to defend and more was expected of me, plus I was on a lot of money and I didn't want to lose the funds, the physical funds,' he recalled.

Conteh had spent ten days preparing in the Bahamas on his way to Atlantic City courtesy of Resorts and he insisted he was ready to seize his opportunity. He stayed with his wife and children at the New Jersey seaside resort as he completed training camp. But he felt something was missing. Maybe the first fight had cleaned out the former champion's reserves.

'I was doing all the same training and I just felt the mental and physical reaction wasn't there,' Conteh lamented. 'The lifestyle must have been taking its toll outside the ring, but the hunger and response from when you're younger and when you tell your body to do anything you want it to do and more, that response wasn't there.'

Matthew was further incensed when he was made to have some last-minute medicals owing to incorrect paperwork being filed. Toiling on the heavy bag following a 45-minute media workout, he snarled, 'I've trained too hard for this fight. I'm tired of this man John Conteh and the way they [the WBC] keep putting him in my way. I've got to put him away once and for all.'

Matthew was having daily salt baths to try to toughen the skin around his eyes, but he got the weight wrong again at the 9am weigh-in and had to lose quarter of a pound on fight day.

Ritacco was in town, too, attending the rules meeting and threatening the WBC with legal action if they upheld the ban. He had continued to work on cuts in New Jersey, just not in WBC-sanctioned fights. Matthew's team asked for him to be reinstated. 'This man handled 22 title fights,' argued Fischbein, in a meeting with New Jersey officials and Sulaiman. 'He is being deprived of making a living.'

George Francis was there, making sure everyone knew that only Vaseline and adrenaline could be used. He had zero sympathy for Ritacco. 'It was disgusting,' he said of Ritacco's actions in the first fight. 'He should be deprived.'

Ritacco said he'd been asked to work other non-WBC fights on the bill, but tried pleading his case, saying, 'What am I going to do, take $10 for a four-rounder when I should be making $1,000 for the championship? I'm a disabled veteran, I've got a steel rod in my leg, I can't go running up and down stairs for a four-round fighter.'

'I thought they gave him a bad deal,' Matthew would reflect. 'I thought he should have been in my corner [for the rematch].'

Instead, Matthew's team hired the respected Milt Bailey to handle cuts.

In the venue, outspoken commentator Howard Cosell thought the ring looked too small and favoured the champion, so the ropes were tightened, increasing the surface area by more than a foot.

Matthew was now at boiling point and spoke to Randy Gordon, writing for *The Ring*, in his dressing room an hour before the fight.

'All of these things that have happened only make me want to end this as soon as I can,' he snarled. 'I can't see this ending any way other than a knockout in my favour. You will see a different me out there today.'

* * *

Matthew wore black trunks with white trim, perhaps in anticipation of the usual bloodbath. There were 1,700 in attendance at the Resorts. In Matthew's corner, there was no Nick and Joe Belfiore, no Ritacco and no Hayes. Strangely, Mexican referee Octavio Meyran paraded the fighters to all four sides of the ring before the opening bell in what looked like an awkward ceremonial effort to have their pictures taken together. Once that was done, the fight was on.

The first round was quiet and not a lot happened in the second, although Conteh's legs wobbled lightly from a right hand. Solomon urged Matthew on in round three, asking him to be more aggressive in pursuit of the Englishman.

Early in the fourth, the abrupt end came from almost nowhere.

'Overhand right, over his jab, baby,' yelled Solomon from the corner. Seconds later, Conteh fell flat on his back from a glancing left hook-right hand. Neither seemed to land with devastating force but they'd connected high on the head and flattened the challenger. Conteh clambered back to his feet but was in desperate trouble. Matthew started cranking through the gears with his two leather steamrollers. Another right sent Conteh crashing to the deck once more. Up at eight, Conteh struggled on but was again down as Matthew followed up. Conteh took another eight count. No sooner was he up than he was down again. Matthew wheeled away in celebration, jumping up and down. Even though Conteh courageously made it to his feet, Matthew knew it was over. Moments later, he floored the challenger for a fifth and final time with a left hook.

Matthew embraced Solomon, then commiserated with Conteh. For once, there wasn't a mark on the champion.

'Saad Muhammad's dangerous when you let him be the aggressor,' conceded Conteh, who was stopped for the first time in 38 fights. 'That's what I allowed him to do.'

'As soon as I started hitting him cleanly, his legs went,' said Matthew, who then spoke of the siege mentality he'd instilled in camp. 'There were a lot of people here to see John Conteh win the title,' he reckoned. 'That is why I had to destroy him physically and mentally. I was going to take him out. I told you all that this week.'

He dedicated the win to his late step-mother, Bertha, and told step-father John, who was in hospital, that he was thinking about him.

Conteh had been up and down five times within a two-minute spell in the fourth round. He recalled being embarrassed as he looked out to the likes of Frank Sinatra and Faye Dunaway at ringside and the word 'yo-yo' went through his mind.

'I certainly wasn't in it,' he would recall, years on.

Little-known light-heavyweight prospect Dwight Braxton, a sawn-off brawler with six wins against a loss and a draw, appeared on the undercard. He was under the radar, even if some people had started to think he could be worth keeping an eye on, and he shelled Cornell Chavis to defeat in 72 seconds.

An hour or so after Matthew had put the Conteh rivalry to bed, sports writers met him in his hotel suite in the Resorts. Wearing a green tracksuit, he laid on his bed with a copy of *The Light Shineth From the East* in his hands. People joked about how he was usually horizontal after a fight, being stitched, being brought around, with white towels pressed against open wounds and suffering with headaches from battle.

Solomon was instantly credited with Matthew's success.

They thought the wars were over. This new version of Matthew was focused, concentrated, tactically disciplined and could still knock out the very best in his division.

Years later, Matthew was unflinching when speaking of his admiration for Conteh.

'I just couldn't see how he could beat me this time,' Matthew said. 'I was focused. I knew I'd trained hard. I just couldn't see John Conteh beating me. He was a good technical boxer but I knew that I was younger, I knew I had the strength and I knew that eventually I would get to him. That was my game plan. I knew I was going to be dominant.'

Conteh, conversely, would later write in his autobiography, 'I was beaten before I started, then, and I never did get started.'

'I didn't realise how many knockdowns it was,' admitted a dejected Conteh, who said he would sit down with friends and family to decide on his future.

Many felt that was the end of the line.

'He beat me,' Conteh conceded in 2021. 'He was a great fighter. You knew he was a great fighter, puncher, he could take a shot, good boxer, experienced, all that ... How much did that fight take out of me? It wasn't the fight, it was the partying afterwards that took it out of me!' he quipped. 'That's what it was like. I was a kid. You'd get the money and you'd have a great time.'

But Conteh was an emotional wreck afterwards. In the hotel room, he ate so much chocolate cake that he threw up. Then he went and apologised to the British press who had made the journey and he and his wife went to watch Sinatra in concert. Conteh wound up in a bar with a couple of the sports writers but outlasted them and drank himself to a virtual standstill. In the small hours in one of the bars, Sinatra sat nearby and Conteh asked a 'new companion' to introduce them, but Sinatra – a legitimate fight fan who'd dabbled in promotion and management and whose father was a boxer – didn't want to know.

Conteh then licked his wounds at a disco and with his sorrows drowned, he hit his lowest ebb. He trashed his hotel room, launched luggage from his window to the street below and 'rampaged up and down the hotel corridors naked'.

Some reports said he was in his underwear, some said he turned over maids' carts.

By this point, he didn't know what he was doing and, fortunately for him, it was something he couldn't remember.

Unfortunately, however, he would be reminded of it in the press the next day.

Conteh was asked to leave Atlantic City by a judge.

Matthew would snicker mischievously when he recollected it years later, but he didn't know how serious Conteh's drinking demons were. Conteh had a far bigger fight on his hands, and Matthew had a world title to unify.

CHAPTER 9

THE MASTERPIECE

MARVIN JOHNSON was a wonderful warrior. Following the bruising loss of his WBC title to Matthew Saad Muhammad in April of 1979, he'd taken five months out, banked ten rounds against journeyman Carlos Marks and two months later knocked out Victor Galindez in 11 for the WBA belt. On 31 March 1980, he made his first defence and was stopped by top contender Eddie Mustafa Muhammad, the former Eddie Gregory. Incidentally, on the same night, two of Matthew's other opponents, Marvin Camel and Mate Parlov, boxed a rematch for the right to be called the first cruiserweight champion in history. Camel beat Parlov on points in Las Vegas to win the WBC crown.

However, back at 175lbs, things were getting even hotter and there was an increasing clamour for the two champions, and close friends, to fight. Matthew and Eddie had known each other for years. They'd boxed in Philly in 1977 before either of them had hit the big time. And just as Matthew said he changed following the Gregory fight, no longer wanting to leave decisions in the hands of the officials, Mustafa Muhammad said he'd had his epiphany in the aftermath of his prison loss to James Scott, which made him realise he needed to take his conditioning more seriously and dedicate himself to his craft more fiercely.

'The guy who lost to James Scott was named Eddie Gregory,' he explained. 'This is a different person. Mustafa Muhammad lives clean, prays to God and is disciplined.'

Mustafa Muhammad's stoppage of Johnson in Tennessee had some believing he was the best in the division. Matthew wasn't buying that. He felt he'd improved since Mustafa Muhammad had beaten him, the last time he had lost, and he had an incredible confidence that he was indestructible and couldn't be stopped. He had become a force of nature, blessed with insane powers of recovery that allowed him to routinely win from the direst circumstances.

Mustafa Muhammad thought he was by far and away the best. He, too, had been heavily influenced by Ali and promoter Murad Muhammad, who was becoming a force on the East Coast.

Murad was getting close to Matthew and saw talent.

'I knew how to pick a fighter and Saad was one of my best,' he said later. 'I did tremendous things with James Scott and they started calling me The Prison Promoter. I didn't like that name, so I wanted to go into Atlantic City.'

Murad saw a bigger, brighter future than just having a niche market in Rahway. He wanted to get to the big time and needed fighters who weren't facing long stretches to do it.

* * *

Six weeks after the Conteh thrashing, Matthew defended his world title against Louis Pergaud, who was originally from Cameroon but had moved to Germany where he trained in Dusseldorf. Pergaud was ranked by the WBC and the WBA but not as good as many of the men Matthew had already beaten. The fight took place on 11 May. Pergaud was 17-1, and he'd beaten Willie Taylor in New Orleans on the Galindez–Rossman rematch undercard. He didn't have a standout win on his record, but he had beaten Tom Bethea and Ba Sounkalo, who'd also defeated Pergaud for the African light-heavyweight title.

Saad–Pergaud was not a big fight and took place in Halifax, Nova Scotia. When asked why he was fighting again so soon after Conteh, Matthew replied, 'Why not?'

Of Pergaud, Matthew said, 'He runs faster than a rabbit. But I'm going to catch him. I always do.'

More people would have been interested in a unification fight, of course, or with up and comer Michael Spinks, who was calling for all of the smoke.

'Give me anybody – I'm the best out there,' charged Spinks. 'Eddie [Mustafa Muhammad] is not good enough. Now I want James Scott.'

Spinks said Scott was 'nothing but a bald-headed bully. I'll go in that prison and fight him with bare fists – even in his bathroom. I've got too much class for him.'

As WBA champ, Mustafa Muhammad was in Matthew's sights.

'I don't think he wants to fight me right away,' Matthew said. 'But if he's any kind of champion, let him fight me now. I'll fight him tomorrow. Right after Pergaud. I'm working to put the title together … My job is not complete.'

Matthew meant business and didn't plan on being in Halifax long.

'He sparred like he fought,' said photographer Paul Trace, recalling one training session in Nova Scotia. 'Oh my God. He was sparring Danny Schneider and there were almost no punches pulled. It was almost like a fight, and Matthew hit Danny on the top of his head and I'm on the ring-post getting aerial shots and he hit him and knocked him down and Danny didn't move for what seemed like 20 minutes. That's how hard he hit him.'

Only around 3,500 showed up to watch the first title fight in Nova Scotia in the 10,000-seat Metro Centre. ABC televised and Bob Arum promoted but organisers thought they were going to take a severe loss. Matthew made $125,000; Pergaud, managed by Mickey Duff who was in the corner, took $20,000.

The champion predicted he would beat his southpaw challenger in four rounds, and he wasn't far off. Pergaud was bleeding from his left cheek and floored by a long-left uppercut to close the show 1:19 into the fifth.

The decisive punch was aimed at the body, but the Cameroonian ducked and it connected with his chin.

Matthew knew it was all over, although he also knew he'd sustained damage to his right hand.

The challenger's trainer, Wolfgang Muller, offered both an explanation and a damning indictment when he said, 'It wasn't the punch that hurt Louis but the way his head hit the canvas. I felt he could have gone on but I guess the fight is history now.'

Arum was delighted and eulogised how Matthew was the best light-heavyweight of the last 20 years. 'Nobody is going to beat him,' the promoter said.

The Louis Pergauds of the world certainly were not.

And while Eddie Mustafa Muhammad was always mentioned, the name James Scott was a common companion in pieces about Matthew and in the many interviews Scott gave from Rahway prison or in his many letters to the outside world.

Matthew never had any intention of fighting Scott, whether he made it to the top contender's spot or not. Scott, however, was making a racket. He felt Mustafa Muhammad's win over Marvin Johnson solidified his claim as the division's uncrowned champion of the division, given that he had already beaten him.

'It's time for me to get out and fight,' said Scott, with 18 wins, no losses and a draw. 'I want to fight [Saad Muhammad] so Gregory [Mustafa Muhammad] can enjoy his title. He just got it so there's no sense taking it away. Meanwhile, I'll beat up Franklin.'

Matthew had a standard riposte when asked about Scott. 'I'm a big believer in forgiving those who do wrong,' he said. 'But giving a guy a title shot who has done as much wrong as Scott seems like a bad example to set.'

Scott dreamt that he'd be allowed out on a furlough if he could get a status change in prison, but realising there was nowhere else for him to go but the title, the WBA, who'd ranked him as high as No. 2, removed him, saying they hadn't realised he'd been boxing in prison. *The Ring* still had Scott at No. 1.

The noise stopped, however, almost two weeks after Matthew flattened Pergaud, when Scott was beaten by Jerry Martin and Yaqui Lopez was then announced as Matthew's next challenger. Lopez had always been confident he would meet Matthew again after their war in Philadelphia.

'He knew he was in a tough fight and he told me, "Yaqui, if I win the championship, I'm going to give you the rematch,"' remembered the Stockton hero. 'I gave him the thumbs up, and he was a man of his word. I didn't doubt him. He looked me straight in the eye and I thought hopefully he doesn't forget – and it came true.'

CBS broadcast Saad–Lopez II, on 13 July, and Matthew said the rematch at the Playboy Resort and Country Club at Great Gorge in north New Jersey would be easier than their first battle.

'Why Lopez?' Matthew asked rhetorically. 'I beat everybody else around. I offered Jerry Martin a fight but I haven't heard anything back. I've fought every legitimate contender around.'

The division was getting deeper, though. Martin was now on the scene, Scott wasn't going quietly, Marvin Johnson wanted a title back, Lopez was hoping to finally win the big one at the fourth time of asking, Conteh had returned with a win, Rossman was still a name and a new guy, 9-1-1 Dwight Braxton, known as the 'Camden Buzzsaw', was building a formidable reputation in the Philly gyms having sparred Scott in Rahway while he served time for armed robbery. 'I'm the dark horse,' he boasted. 'But I'll fight anybody. A bull, a moose, a Muhammad. I didn't come to kiss nobody's butt. I'd take them all on tomorrow if it was up to me.'

In June 1980, Philadelphia held a Muhammad Ali day and a bust was unveiled at what was then known as the Afro-American Historical and Cultural Museum. Ali attended with Matthew and Sugar Ray Leonard, who was a guest at Matthew's new pad, what was called by one writer 'a mini-mansion' in Jenkintown in North Philadelphia. He named it 'Muhammad's Summit'.

Being the champion afforded Matthew other lucrative benefits, and one was a sponsorship deal with the clothing label Sassoon, which specialised in jeans and activewear. The rapidly growing designer brand was owned by entrepreneur Paul Guez. As Sassoon expanded, they used several high-profile athletes and stars to wear their clothing. Larry Holmes, Juan Laporte, Sugar Ray Leonard and Matthew were some of the boxers they focused on, and they ran TV commercials using the New York Rangers ice hockey team in one, baseball star Lou Piniella in another and one featuring Elton John.

Guez and his brother Gerard had a link to boxing through a friendship with French middleweight contender Loucif Hamani and Guez also knew Bilal. Guez was thrilled to be working with Matthew. 'He was a handsome young man, very successful, champion of the world,' recalled Guez. 'He was a wonderful guy. He was a sweetheart. He was always very nice and he was a great boxer, too. He was very exciting. He could take a punch and he could hit. We were friends. We went to restaurants, I went to see him train, I went to his fights and he was an unbelievable fighter.'

* * *

Fight week came around and Lopez was grateful for a fourth title try, having come up short against Conteh and twice against Galindez.

Matthew was making $150,000; Lopez was set for $40,000; significant increases from their Spectrum purses two years earlier. But it wasn't about the money for Lopez; he wanted the title. He had won 49 fights and lost nine times. Now there was desperation in the air. It was rare anyone got four attempts at a world title and another defeat could see him lost in the shuffle of an incredibly deep pack.

Besides, an even bigger bounty was on the horizon because a week later – also at the Playboy – Eddie Mustafa Muhammad was set to defend his WBA championship against Jerry Martin, with the winners from both 175lbs clashes finally meeting to unify. Eddie used Ali's Deer Lake camp to prepare for Martin.

Sam Solomon hoped the Lopez fight wouldn't get rough but felt that with the easy wins over Conteh and Pergaud he was working with a different boxer.

'I didn't try to change him,' said Matthew's trainer. 'But I modified him. He was already a good fighter. This was a man who was a champion when I got him. He had some rough spots that had to be ironed out. He didn't have too much defence.'

The work was always hard. Sparring partner and friend Tony Green said he and Matthew regularly met in the trenches.

Young Matthew Franklin is flanked by Lil Abner (left) and Bennie Briscoe in Paris (Peltz Boxing Promotions, Inc.)

In an early promotional picture, the future Hall of Famer poses for the camera (John DiSanto/ PhillyBoxingHistory)

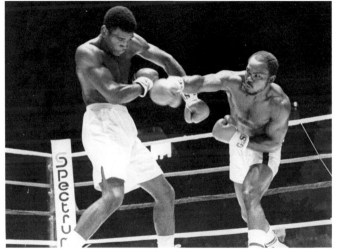

Matthew twice struggled against Wayne McGee, losing their first fight and scraping a draw in the return (John DiSanto/ PhillyBoxingHistory)

Everything changed after Matthew Franklin and Marvin Johnson went to war at the Philadelphia Spectrum (Peltz Boxing Promotions, Inc.)

Billy 'Dynamite' Douglas rocks Matthew with a huge right hand (John DiSanto/ PhillyBoxingHistory)

Matthew sizes up Richie Kates ahead of their spectacular Fight of the Year contender (John DiSanto/ PhillyBoxingHistory)

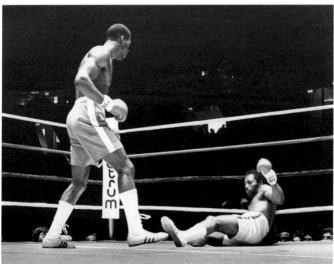

Kates crumbles, but he had been just seconds from victory earlier in the fight (John DiSanto/ PhillyBoxingHistory)

Franklin and Marvin Johnson go back into the trenches in one of 1979's most violent fights (Boxing News)

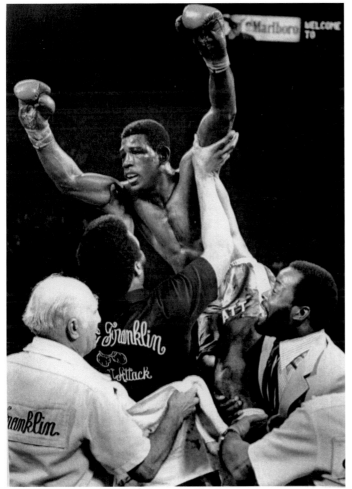

A victorious but exhausted Franklin is held aloft having captured the WBC light-heavyweight championship of the world (John DiSanto/ PhillyBoxingHistory)

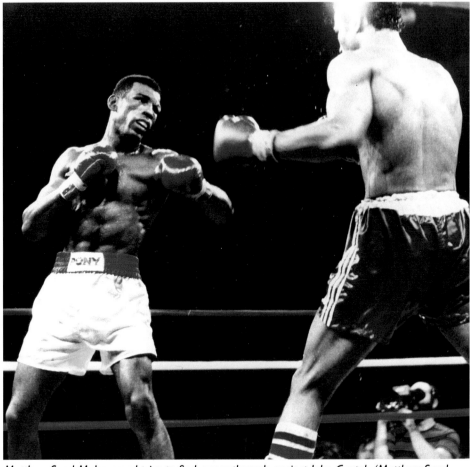

Matthew Saad Muhammad tries to find a way through against John Conteh (Matthew Saad Muhammad)

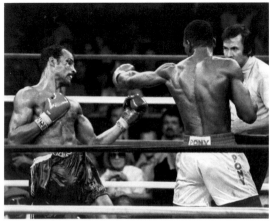

A left hook sends Conteh reeling in their first meeting in Atlantic City (Boxing News)

The warriors are all smiles afterwards, but both knew they had been in a fight (Boxing News)

Conteh is vanquished in style in the rematch (Boxing News)

Matthew shows off his championship belt in the gym, with trainer Sam Solomon sitting nearest him (Paul Trace)

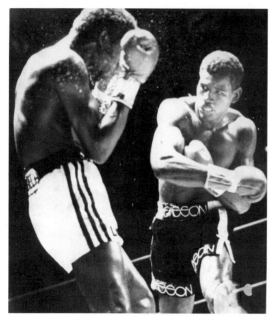

Saad Muhammad surges forward and is about to crush contender Lottie Mwale in dramatic fashion (Boxing News)

Matthew's team hold him high as his remarkable streak of stunning victories continues (Paul Trace)

Yaqui Lopez has Matthew in serious trouble, firing off around 40 shots, but Saad Muhammad smiles back

Matthew traps Yaqui Lopez on the ropes in the best fight of 1980

The money men,
Bilal Muhammad
(left) and Harold
Smith, prepare
to shake hands
as Muhammad
Ali (rear left) and
Matthew look on
(Paul Trace)

Matthew flirted with
careers in films, music
and modelling as he
explored post-boxing
avenues (Paul Trace)

Matthew and Michelle celebrate their engagement in Alaska (Paul Trace)

The couple pose for some portraits, near Michelle's hometown of Anchorage (Paul Trace)

Daddy's boy – Irish setter Topper would only listen to one person, Matthew (Paul Trace)

Matthew with his friend and rival Eddie Mustafa Muhammad and trainer Sam Solomon (Paul Trace)

'It was hell,' Green said. 'The boxing business is a rough business but sparring with Matthew was hell. Every day we were going to war but after that we were friends. If you trained hard, the fights weren't nothing.'

As Matthew's preparations for Lopez tapered, Muhammad Ali announced he was coming back, having retired after reclaiming his title against Leon Spinks almost two years earlier. He clowned around at Deer Lake, pretending to be knocked down by a topless Tom Jones a couple of days before Matthew appeared dressed as a cowboy at the press conference with Lopez. Matthew wore a white suit, red boots, a red cowboy hat, and carried a whip – which he cracked for effect. 'I am very good at my game now,' he said. 'I don't know what kind of strategy his camp has, but it won't work. Nobody is taking my title. You got to knock me out to take my title, but nobody is going to knock Matthew Saad Muhammad out.'

As far as smack talk goes, Matthew and Lopez didn't have much to offer. Matthew obviously now knew that Lopez wasn't Native American but Lopez, who always spoke ferociously in the ring, simply said, 'When I take his title, I will replace it with a $500 sombrero.'

'I guess I won't get it, then,' replied Matthew. But Matthew and Lopez would wind up swapping sombreros and cowboy hats from their publicity stunts and the red cowboy hat would remain one of Lopez's prized possessions, on display in his house for the rest of his life.

Again, the question of the damage Matthew had already sustained resurfaced. The wars made him a beloved idol, but the regular exposure to trauma was a concern.

'I don't want to end up a little whacky, like some guys,' Matthew said. 'Sam's told me it is not necessary to take those hard licks. He hasn't changed my style but he's trying to make me a boxer-puncher. Truthfully, we're working on defence to prolong my career, but don't get me wrong. I don't want to know too much defence. I've had some good, rough fights and I think I've always been a crowd-pleaser.'

Solomon insisted defence was a must. 'He's so strong he feels he can just punch a guy and overcome him, not realising that taking too many shots will curtail his career,' offered the veteran coach.

* * *

Matthew had an international audience, was one of the best boxers in the world and word had spread about his early days. Now, as he prepared to make the fourth defence of his title, he used his platform to dig into his past and offered a $10,000 reward to anyone who could give him the answers to the dark questions he had.

He might have been known as Matthew Saad Muhammad, the biggest hitter in the light-heavyweight division, a gladiator and the WBC champion, but there was one identity that still escaped him. It bothered him that he didn't know his own origin story, where he was from and what had happened to his real family.

'Saad' might have meant bright future, but he wanted to know more about his past. He couldn't block it out with success, relationships, winning titles, changing his team, moving house or upgrading his cars. He wanted to know what had happened.

On the eve of the Lopez rematch, reporters asked him to recall the day he had been abandoned.

'I think I was five years old,' he started. 'I remember racing my brother, I think he was two years older, to my grandmother's house. The only thing I can remember is the police found me on the Ben Franklin Parkway. When the policewoman asked me my name, I said I don't know.'

Journalists wondered why a five-year-old didn't know his name and Matthew couldn't explain with any authority. He knew he'd had a speech impediment that he'd worked hard to overcome, and he knew about the orphanage and being given the name Matthew Franklin. It was the part before he couldn't understand, yet he somehow remembered his brother's face, all these years on.

'I could tell him a mile away,' Matthew went on. 'I would just like to know, and that's it. I guess it's my conscience. I just would like to meet them and then I would be happy.'

Why had he been left? What had he done wrong? What was wrong with him?

The storyline was so big that Lopez found himself with only cursory mentions in many of the build-up preview articles, with headlines like 'Boxer searching for family,' 'Saad Muhammad wants to return to his lost past', and 'Muhammad offers $10,000 to the keeper of his identity'.

Regardless of what was going on outside the ring, Lopez knew it was his last chance.

Moments before Matthew left his hotel room to face Lopez, there was a knock at the door. Former heavyweight champions Floyd Patterson and Jersey Joe Walcott came in to wish Matthew good luck.

* * *

Of all the wars Matthew had been in, this bloody, brutal, unforgiving spectacle at the Playboy Club on 13 July 1980, might have topped them all.

It was one so harsh that Michael Katz, writing for the *New York Times*, said it 'made the Roberto Duran–Sugar Ray Leonard bout look like a marbles contest by comparison' while Randy Gordon wrote in *The Ring* that none of the other most exciting fights in 1980 'were as brutal, as savage, as explosive, as moving or heart-stopping as this incomparable light-heavyweight classic'.

Before the opening bell, Hall of Fame trainer and TV analyst Gil Clancy figured Matthew had improved as much as 20 per cent since becoming the champion.

Resplendent in a jet-black robe with 'Indian Yaqui Lopez' in gold across his back, the challenger tried to show he wasn't intimidated by making a beeline for the champion's corner, invading his personal space. Matthew, wearing a white silk gown with black trim and matching shorts, shrugged him off.

They came face-to-face for the instructions of Puerto Rican referee Waldemar Schmidt, returned to their corners and at the sound of the bell, turned, faced one another and made history.

You could tell what kind of fight it was going to be from the first round. Lopez had talked about using his jab and boxing more. Matthew had spoken again about his defensive work. But with a minute left in the round they forgot all of that, planted their feet and skewered one another with punches.

Lopez drew first blood in the second, causing Matthew to bleed above the right eyebrow, and he had success thudding in punches to the head and banging them into Matthew's muscular torso.

Matthew tried to back Lopez up with jabs and feints in the third, but the Mexican wasn't buying them and bludgeoned forwards. Lopez had so much success that Matthew started to smile, knowing full well he was getting caught with shots he should have been trying to avoid.

The crowd was becoming more invested by the round. Matthew was staying on the ropes and taking unnecessary punishment. The champion was steadied by a long right, then soaked up another crunching one in the fourth as Lopez varied his attack from the body to the head.

Lopez was cut between the eyes in the fifth but finished the round well on top, with Matthew again taking his back to the ropes and getting nailed.

Round six produced fireworks, with Lopez seemingly landing at will.

'They're going toe-to-toe!' shrieked announcer Tim Ryan. He and his CBS colleagues had Lopez ahead after six.

'Get off, get off,' screamed a desperate Solomon, urging Matthew to throw shots so Lopez couldn't plant his feet and fire at him first.

Matthew scored with a solid left hook, but his own head was jerked back twice by a Lopez double jab as the champion showed signs of fatigue if not distress.

As round eight started, journalists, reporters and commentators were already calling it a superb battle but what happened next converted it from a great fight to one of the greatest.

With Lopez swelling beneath the left eye and bleeding from a gash above the right, he came out bombing. For a short period, he found himself trapped on the ropes for the first time that afternoon.

Matthew, sensing a chance to turn the tide, fired in blows with all his might. Booming left hooks were accompanied by jarring straight rights. Lopez tried to avoid them and wasn't caught by all but certainly by plenty. Then, however, as he battled for a way out, Lopez landed a crisp right hand that stopped Matthew in his tracks and gave the challenger the respite he needed to escape. Lopez followed up, crashing another full power right hand off the side of Matthew's head as red leather hailed down on the champion. His back was to the ropes; Lopez held the upper hand and he was giving it all he had.

'What a comeback, what a comeback!' screamed co-commentator Gil Clancy, as Lopez teed off on the champion. Matthew reeled into the corner and tried to slip out of trouble. All he could do was smile and flash his white mouthpiece, but Lopez was throwing everything at him and could taste the title after three previous attempts. With the crowd of 1,300 in the tennis centre on its feet roaring at the action, he banged away with reckless abandon.

Matthew held his gloves high and tried to ride the punches but bomb after bomb exploded on his head, dimming the volume of the fans screaming raucously at ringside.

In the words of one writer, trying to stay on his seat rather than leaping into the air like many of his colleagues, Matthew was experiencing 'what must have been the hardest, loneliest three minutes of his life'.

Without pause, more than 30 blows poured cruelly against his face and into his body, but with around 45 seconds left in the round, Matthew found a gap for a right hand, managed to pivot Lopez around and then he had him in trouble. Lopez was almost out of ammunition. The outcome hung dramatically in the balance as the bell sounded to end the eighth. It permitted them both one quick minute to get their breath back, and the fans excitedly nattered amongst themselves at the bedlam.

The Ring voted it Round of the Year, immortalising the names of Saad Muhammad and Lopez alongside those of Tony Zale and Rocky Graziano (1946), Sugar Ray Robinson and Carmen Basilio

(1957 and 1958), Muhammad Ali and Joe Frazier (1971 and 1975) and Ali and George Foreman (1974). Another ringsider said the round was 'Hollywood-style – all-out, all-give, all-take, bombs away, with every punch landing.'

Another stunned observer wrote, 'For three incredible minutes, the irresistible force strained against the immovable object. But this force could be depleted and this object could feel the pain. That's why every eye in the Playboy Club Arena that night was fixed on the ring. For three sweeps of the second hand, nothing else existed. No joy, no personal problems. Nothing but the sight and sound of two men fighting each other for a prize that only one could have.'

It was that intense. Fans were in and out of their seats with irregular regularity.

'Draw back and box,' implored Benny Casing, working miracles in Lopez's corner as cutman.

The Mexican started the ninth on the back foot and Matthew was in no hurry to pursue. They both needed a break after that torrid eighth round with seven hard sessions left.

The fighters propped one another up with hearty blows, testing their desire and will with every weighted breath. Every time they blinked, sweat and blood filled their eyes, and each time they took a step forward or back on scorched, fatigued legs it was an enormous effort. Aided by insurmountable hearts, they stood in front of one another and punched and punched.

Matthew had stopped Lopez in the 11th at the Spectrum but this time in the same round Yaqui rallied, defended well and turned the screw with pressure. Matthew laboriously forced his work and lost his timing and rhythm.

As the 12th opened, observers thought Matthew was in grave danger of losing his title and even of being stopped as his well was running dry.

By now, Matthew's white shorts were pink, but he attacked again, taking right uppercuts to land his own shots. The crowd was fully invested. It was gory, messy and vicious.

Lopez initiated hostilities in the 13th with a thudding left hook but Matthew didn't budge. Instead, Lopez was staggered by a return right hand that was sent with severe interest.

'This is a war!' cried Clancy. It was riveting, the crowd constantly buzzing with approval. Finally, in the 14th, Matthew landed a destructive long right. The champion followed in and then, among the cluster of shots, he spun Lopez around with a brutal right uppercut that dumped the Mexican on to his backside. Beleaguered and with little left to offer, Lopez stood gamely but vacantly to hear the mandatory eight count.

'Here comes the freight train now,' warned Clancy, as Matthew steamed in. A right over the top and a follow-up left dropped Lopez once more. He rose despairingly, but he couldn't get out of harm's way. Matthew knew he had him and knew what he had to do. He had to fire until Lopez could no longer stand. Lopez wilted for a third time on the ropes. Exhausted and spent, but desperate to finally get over the line in a world title fight, Lopez rose again, but he looked forlorn. Matthew lined Yaqui up with one long final right hand and Lopez could take no more. As he dropped for a fourth time, New Jersey commissioner Joe Walcott signalled to Schmidt to stop it. The referee had already arrived at the same conclusion. The war was over.

Matthew *knew* that was it and punched his hands skywards. Lopez didn't stay down for long but got up shaking his head, wearing blood for a moustache. Matthew ran around the ring with his hands high, leaping up and down.

The sunken challenger was distraught, consoled by his team, his head cloaked under a white towel that promptly turned red.

'He wanted to try,' Matthew said. 'He wouldn't give up.'

It had been a masterpiece of a brawl.

* * *

A disconsolate Yaqui Lopez admitted immediately afterwards that he'd not fallen apart as much as he was shattered from having thrown so many punches in round eight.

Matthew, who reinforced his desire to unify the titles, said his right hand had been reinjured from the Pergaud fight, and it was little surprise that he was less coherent than he would have liked to have sounded when asked about the search for his family.

'Is that paramount of everything?' asked ringside interviewer Dick Stockton.

'It is a search being ... a watch out for my parents. $10,000 so I'm quite sure that hopefully someone will come up with something.'

Lopez had been in the Last Chance Saloon and had just sipped the dregs of his last drink but he was able to address the media first. His nose still bled 30 minutes after the bout and there were cuts all over his face; three over his eyes, one under his left eye and his lip was sliced open.

He lamented allowing Matthew to escape the eighth-round maelstrom and sighed, 'One more good one and he would have gone down.'

'Matt was hurting and I'm sure Yaqui was, but Yaqui had hit him with so many body punches,' recalled Tony Green. 'After that fight, we were taking Matthew to the dressing room and Matthew fell and we had to help him into a chair. That fight took a lot out of him.'

'He didn't have an ounce of energy to do anything,' said Paul Trace, who'd followed them up the corridors. 'He could barely talk.'

Seventy-five minutes after he left the ring, Matthew slowly walked down the hotel halls and finally emerged to the media room where he wobbled gingerly into a seat, occasionally holding his lumpy head and speaking in little more than a whisper.

He was so drained and weak, one member of the press pack wondered whether a ventriloquist was holding him up.

'His speech was slow,' wrote Gerry Monigan, and hardly audible. Quite out of character for him. His face was badly swollen and he could hardly raise his head.'

'I'm kind of exhausted,' the champion admitted. 'But I was in the best shape of my life. That's why I knew I would remain victorious. I knew he had me in trouble – I'm not denying that – but I knew

I'd come back. Everybody knows Matthew Saad Muhammad can handle wars.'

'I want another shot,' said Lopez. 'I'm not that old yet. I had him in trouble a few times. I've got to try again.'

He was rightly proud, although he also knew how close he had come.

But even in victory, what Matthew had left was being openly debated. Graham Houston wrote in *Boxing News*, 'The question arises again just how much longer Muhammad can keep drawing on his deepest resources and coming back from the brink. His savage wars are becoming almost legendary.'

Ray Parrillo, closer to home at *The Bulletin*, thought the same thing, writing, 'There must be a limit to the amount of physical abuse Matthew Saad Muhammad can absorb in the ring, although it may take a wrecking ball to show us what it is.'

Lopez had fallen agonisingly short but years later admitted the second fight, the war of light-heavyweight wars, had topped their Spectrum special for thrills.

'Somehow it was better,' Lopez said. 'I lost but we made history. He knocked me down four times and I got up and the referee, of course, saw me and he knows and he thinks that I was hurt. But I'm not. I just think to myself that it's the 14th round, I have to get up.'

Lopez knew it was close on the cards and believed there might have been skulduggery in the opposite corner.

'I know they used smelling salts and that was illegal, but we know they used it because at the end of the fight Hank Pericole [a Lopez camp member] went and checked and there were smelling salts,' Lopez claimed. 'I'd say he took at least 30 punches [in that eighth round]. Some of them were big shots. He [Matthew] was smiling because he was hurt.'

'I knew Yaqui was a great, great fighter,' Matthew said later in his life. 'I knew that he was experienced and I knew he was a warrior. Whoever he fought, they would have a fight. They knew what they had gotten themselves into. But he had never won the title and he wanted it so badly. He deserved one, and everybody – including Yaqui – believed that this was his last chance.'

After the routine rematch win over Conteh and the one-sided drubbing of Pergaud, reporters were now back searching for superlatives for a Matthew Saad Muhammad epic. 'It was as electrifying as any fight can be,' wrote one, and Arum said it was 'one of the greatest fights I have ever promoted'.

Matthew had a deep respect for Lopez for the rest of his life and appreciated the magnitude of what they had shared.

'He hit me with some devastating punches,' Matthew said. 'He threw over 40 punches [in round eight] but that's when I took his heart. I started blocking his punches, then I started laughing at him. I started laughing at him. The crowd roared and applauded and roared some more and I was getting hit but I was laughing.'

CHAPTER 10

I CANNOT KEEP THIS
TYPE OF THING UP

MATTHEW WAS ordered to fight his No. 1 contender Lottie Mwale in October. One writer quipped that after what Matthew had had to endure against Yaqui Lopez in July, October 1990 was a more realistic target than October 1980.

Bob Arum said there had been a big offer from Zambia, where Mwale was from, and that Bilal Muhammad would explore possibilities for the fight to take place there, but Matthew was reluctant to travel.

Eddie Mustafa Muhammad had been ringside for Saad–Lopez II, but while he was ambitious and confident, he had no intention of fighting a fellow Muslim, making the unification clash unlikely.

'Muslims don't fight each other,' said Eddie. 'I love him. He's my brother.'

Then, pressed for specifics, Eddie added, 'I didn't say I don't want to fight Matthew Saad Muhammad. The only way I would fight him is if we changed our names back, each got $3m for the fight and each donated $1m to the mosque. Muslims don't fight each other. I would renounce my religion for $3m ... If it's millions we are talking about, several million, we could be fighting.'

Saad Muhammad versus Mustafa Muhammad, WBC champion versus the WBA titlist, was on the lips of fight fans around the world. One night in the Garden, as Eddie sat with *Ring* editor Randy Gordon, an inquisitive fan asked him, 'If Allah is always supposedly in a Muslim's corner, whose corner will he be in when you fight Saad Muhammad?'

'That's up to Allah,' he replied with a smile. 'I might win; I might lose. I don't know how Allah has it written. But whatever happens that night, I'll know in my heart it happened because that was the will of the Almighty Allah.'

Both champions had found Islam and had inspirational back stories and both had designs on winning the world heavyweight title.

Mustafa Muhammad had even had a run-in with champion Larry Holmes, and they'd lobbed verbal grenades at one another in the boxing press. Holmes called Mustafa Muhammad a 'faggot' and Mustafa Muhammad said Holmes was, 'one of the most stupid, ugly, gross, non-speaking really dumb champions boxing has ever had'.

The feud stemmed from an altercation at Deer Lake, when Eddie was training and Larry visited. It resulted in Mustafa Muhammad offering Holmes a fight outside.

* * *

A week after Matthew turned back Lopez's game challenge, he was ringside rooting for his friend to beat Jerry Martin. Matthew was introduced to fans before the first bell to start Mustafa Muhammad–Martin, taking his seat next to Muhammad Ali.

In an interview with *The Ring*, Eddie said he would knock Matthew out if they fought again. 'I read somewhere that Saad said he's going to knock me out within five rounds,' he argued. 'That's ridiculous. That's wishful thinking on his part. He won't even hit me in five rounds. I can stand right in front of a person and make him miss. I'll give him waist and head movement like he's never seen. I'm not going to have any problem with him.'

On 6 August, Matthew boxed an exhibition in Philly to raise money for a youth boxing programme and despite Eddie negotiating another hurdle by beating the tough Martin, Arum maintained he wanted fans to salivate over the dream unification rematch rather than see it. 'There are still too many other guys for them to fight before they meet each other,' he insisted. 'This is a talented division.

Why let them knock off each other? I want the public to be screaming for the two champs to fight before they get in the ring together.'

Eddie was happy to keep his options open, even if talk always came back to Matthew. There was the beef with Holmes, he wanted to fight Scott again and right the wrong of his loss to the Rahway inmate, Rossman was in the midst of a comeback and Michael Spinks was starting to get serious attention.

* * *

In late August 1980, Matthew, Eddie and Muhammad Ali were all in camp in Deer Lake. The two light-heavyweight champions were helping Ali, who was approaching his 39th birthday, sharpen his tools ahead of his return to the ring against Holmes. Also in camp were Tim Witherspoon and Maine Miller.

In one open sparring session, Ali did six rounds with two amateur middleweights and then finished with two against Matthew.

'You're in with the heavyweight champion now,' Ali announced. The crowd laughed, and they cheered for Ali when he backed Matthew up with some sharp jabs.

Matthew was impressed and told the press, 'Anytime you take Saad's punches, you're ready.'

Photographer Paul Trace captured the session.

'Matthew was in really good shape, but after doing some rounds with Ali he felt like he'd just finished 15 rounds, and that was the difference between fighting at light-heavyweight and heavyweight,' said Trace.

In September, Eddie and Matthew attended a bill topped by Bennie Briscoe at the Martin Luther King Arena in Philly. The speculation was that there was going to be some sort of double-header, with Matthew fighting Mwale and Eddie facing Dutch contender Rudy Koopmans. Mwale and Koopmans were decent, but neither fight whetted the appetite or satisfied cravings for the big one.

Spending time with Ali in Deer Lake was a thrill for Matthew. The man he'd followed as a child and was inspired by from behind the walls of Camp Hill was now a friend.

'I was training with Muhammad Ali, I was boxing with Muhammad Ali, we had it on tape and that was the most exciting thing for me; being close with him, sparring with him, having read all about this guy and now I'm here?' Matthew said excitedly. 'We sparred but mostly we talked. He had his own cabin, but we'd talk a lot. He always talked about having beautiful women, having beautiful cars, having a beautiful house and having beautiful children.'

'Watch your money,' Ali instructed Matthew. 'Watch it. You make money, you watch it and get good people around you and handle your money right.'

Like Ali, Matthew was image-conscious. He was known in the sport for his smart dress sense.

'As time went on, I didn't want to be badly dressed. I had to keep a certain image,' he explained.

He and Eddie, who also liked the finer things in life, thought Ali might turn back the clock against Holmes.

'I can't tell you what it is, but Muhammad Ali is going to do things, he's going to come up with something to be victorious over Larry Holmes,' Matthew predicted.

Perhaps he was struggling to back his friend, but he thought Ali's mind games could be the difference. 'Mentally, I think that Larry will get beat. Ali has the strong mind – he will outsmart him. It's definitely going to be the Last Hurrah. How can I be sure? Because Muhammad Ali always comes with his bag of tricks.'

Eddie agreed. 'He's going to take Larry late,' predicted the WBA champion.

* * *

Ali–Holmes was originally set to be a co-promotion between Don King and Murad Muhammad and was headed to Rio de Janeiro, but Murad made some contractual errors – he'd originally tried to get Mike Weaver for Ali – so King wound up promoting on his own and Murad would be forever grateful not to have been involved.

Murad lived in the Beverly Wilshire hotel in Los Angeles for two years at a thousand dollars a day when Ali called him.

'Bring me out of retirement,' said Ali.

'Okay,' agreed Murad.

The promoter gave Ali $800,000 and WBA champion Mike Weaver $300,000 but the day before they were due to announce the fight, Arum got Weaver out of the country and Murad couldn't find him.

'I'm stuck,' Murad admitted.

He called Holmes as a backup and was told his fee would be $4m, and then he called Holmes's promoter, Don King.

King's manoeuvrings kept him a step ahead of Murad who wound up breaching his contract with Holmes, freezing him out of the picture.

'He checkmated me,' admitted Murad.

The morning of Holmes–Ali in Las Vegas, Mustafa Muhammad spoke to reporters while poolside.

He and Matthew were in town to support Ali and Eddie told the media he thought the fight with Matthew could happen in March or April of 1981 in Argentina. He said he'd signed a contract with a new promotional group called Muhammad Ali Professional Sports that would stage it. The fighters were set to make an unprecedented light-heavyweight purse of $1.5m each, plus 20 per cent of the gate.

Later that day, however, there was little talk of the unification fight. Boxing was in mourning.

Ringside at Holmes–Ali, on 2 October 1980, were Tom Jones, Frank Sinatra, John Travolta, Larry Hagman and OJ Simpson. Then there was boxing royalty, like Sugar Ray Leonard, Roberto Duran and Ken Norton and they saw Ali battered into a one-sided stoppage loss by Larry Holmes.

But Holmes wasn't celebrated as the champion of a new era. He was the man who'd stamped on the fingers of a legend trying to cling on to a youth that had deserted him years ago. The shellacking Holmes doled out, which brought even Holmes himself to tears, turned vast sections of the sporting world against him before he even had a chance to create his own legacy.

The only person remotely happy was Murad Muhammad. He was an Ali supporter and wound up pleased that he'd not been a part of The Greatest taking such a drubbing.

'It was the worst fight in Ali's career,' sighed Murad. 'It wasn't meant for me. It was like the angels said, "Don't do this fight. This is the wrong fight for Ali." But now you know it was Weaver all the time.'

Even with the resounding loss to Holmes, Ali considered fighting on and he had two prodigies to test himself against if he decided to try again.

'I may return,' Ali declared. 'Wait about a month, go back in the gym, see how I feel. Put me through some real tests with those two light-heavyweight champions, Mustafa and Matthew Saad Muhammad. If I can slug it out with them, then maybe I'd make a comeback.'

* * *

The story of Matthew's Dickensian start had spread internationally. He was profiled in *Jet* magazine in late 1980, pictured walking around the pool of his Jenkintown mansion with Mustafa Ameen and photographed on a hammock in the garden with his dog, an Irish setter named Topper.

The focus of the moving feature was about the reward for help to reunite him with his family. He pondered if it might lead to false hope, whether chancers who didn't really know the truth might come forward, but it was worth trying.

'As a kid, growing up in an orphanage, I often wondered who my mother was, and why she never bothered to find me … After a while, I gave up thinking about it,' he told *Jet*.

The piece said he longed for a mother–son relationship. He added, 'I would just like to know who my real parents are. I have a few details that will clue me in on the real ones when and if they show up, but I can't peep all my hole cards just yet. They have nothing to fear from me. I have almost everything else in the world I want already.'

Matthew was also the big interview in *KO* magazine at around the same time. Interviewer Steve Farhood probed at Matthew's mileage and his expanded back catalogue of gruelling wars. Matthew felt his conditioning was exceptional but confessed, 'I know time can take its toll … If I got hurt, the indication would be that my legs go first. But in all those fights you can see that my legs never did. I think that maybe when I do fall, everything will go. But I keep myself well-conditioned, and that's been saving me.'

Farhood's wide-ranging interview encompassed religion, Mustafa Muhammad, Matthew's thoughts on the other top light-heavyweights, the Lopez war, unification and the search to find his parents. But Farhood later asked an important question. 'How many more fights like that can you have and still remain strong?'

Matthew was measured in his response. 'I have tremendous recuperative powers and I have a lot of strength. I think that if I keep taking care of myself properly, and if I keep eating the right foods and going to bed early, I think I can still go on, maybe five more years. But my goal is to fight about three more years and then get out of boxing. I know I cannot keep this type of thing up. This is why I hope I can unify the title and then call boxing a night.'

Farhood also asked Matthew about Michael Spinks.

'Good young boy,' he replied. 'He's coming up. That's another money fight. His name pushes him, but as long as he keeps winning, he'll get there.'

Asked if there was anyone else to look out for, he said he'd heard of a stumpy prospect called Dwight Braxton. 'The guy they call Braxton,' Matthew said. 'A good, strong fighter.'

Matthew said the three big money fights for him were Mwale, Mustafa Muhammad and Rossman but Farhood was not just wondering what challenges lay ahead, but what the challenges in the past had taken from him.

Spinks, just 24, had been earning headlines. On 18 October, just three months after Yaqui Lopez had gone to war with Matthew, the Stockton warrior was back in action. Spinks stopped him in seven rounds.

Lopez had some early success, even building up a lead, but ultimately came up short. Spinks had made a statement in his biggest test to date. With today's knowledge of brain trauma and recovery, Lopez probably needed more time off after the savage fight with Matthew, but it was a different time then and he left Atlantic City a beaten man once more.

Spinks was a fresh and impressive 15-0 and riding high. 'I want it all,' he charged. 'I think I can do it now … I won't say which champion I want first – whether it's Saad Muhammad or Mustafa. If I name one, the other might become upset because I'm not giving him his beating first.'

Spinks wasn't the only one who wanted a shot at Matthew or Eddie. Braxton, though inexperienced, was fighting out of Philly and the 'Camden Buzzsaw' was drawing admirers. Matthew's old promoter Russell Peltz had seen Braxton's potential and witnessed his menace in the gym.

'Guys coming out of Philly with a 5-0 record might be the equivalent of someone else who is 25-0,' Russell said. 'I don't know what it is, maybe we have the worst ghettoes, more unemployment, but the calibre of young fighters in Philly is the best in the country.'

He reckoned Braxton could already hold his own with Matthew, having seen Braxton spar Jerry Martin.

Peltz continued, 'He was sparring with Michael Spinks before the Spinks–Yaqui Lopez fight, but they had to pull Braxton out of the workouts because he was making it too rough.'

Whatever happened behind closed doors, Braxton was confident.

'Matthew Saad, when he gets with a guy who's not afraid of him, who also has a big punch, he's gonna get knocked out,' Braxton charged. 'Mustafa Muhammad, he likes to stand back and pose, like somebody's taking his picture. A man pressures Mustafa, he'll beat him. Martin, Spinks, I know their flaws from working with them.'

* * *

Meanwhile, Muhammad Ali Professional Sports (MAPS) was getting rave reviews from the fighters.

Its founder Harold Smith had somehow gotten Ali to lend him his name to build a business, starting with an amateur team, signing a host of top professionals, dreaming of mega-shows and he opened the Muhammad Ali Professional Sports Gym in Santa Monica.

Smith was big news, partly because of the names he was signing and partly because of the amount he was paying. Fighters and their teams were being flown first class or on private jets for meetings, there were briefcases of cash, plush hotel rooms, exorbitant signing bonuses and excess everywhere.

Don King and Bob Arum couldn't compete. Boxing had never seen anything like it.

Smith worked with Tommy Hearns, Wilfredo Gomez, Leon Spinks, Aaron Pryor and Gerry Cooney. He also wanted to match Matthew and Eddie in the biggest light-heavyweight title fight in history.

No one knew where Smith's money was coming from or where he had appeared from. But with Ali's name behind him, he was making a difference and the fighters loved him.

Asked whether he was content with MAPS promoting him, Eddie couldn't contain himself.

'Content?' Eddie asked quizzically. 'I'm thrilled. They can promote all of my fights from now on as far as I'm concerned.'

Farhood would recall his long sit-down with Matthew at his plush home decades later. The writer was charmed by the Philly slugger and left his home thinking the orphan had turned it all around. He was winning at life.

'He was just a charming, wonderful, easy-going guy,' Farhood said. 'I had a wonderful day with him and I remember leaving, and maybe it's because I was then a pretty young journalist, but I remember leaving thinking, "This guy has everything. There's nothing missing".'

CHAPTER 11

THAT WAS THAT

'FOR THE last several years, it has been so – if you wanted to fight for the title you had to see The Man,' wrote Lewis Freedman in the *Inquirer*. 'In reality, the man was two men, rival promoters Don King and Bob Arum. The fact that there were two of them was the only thing that meant boxing wasn't an outright monopoly. But quietly, without the bombast of King or the hard-nosed-to-the-point-of-alienating negotiation of Arum, a new force has emerged at the power vortex of boxing – Muhammad Ali Professional Sports, which is called MAPS.'

The outfit was being run by Harold Smith, who was billed out of Santa Monica in California, and was said to be in his thirties, a former jeweller who rarely returned phone calls and would go to big fights around the country before hurrying home.

There were suspicions about him and where his apparent fortune had come from. People wondered how Gerry Cooney was paid $125,000 to beat Ron Lyle, who was paid $90,000, even though Lyle was through as a fighter and an attraction. The likes of Randall Cobb, Ken Norton, Tommy Hearns, Hilmer Kenty, Eddie Mustafa Muhammad, Matthew and others were beginning to benefit as Smith tried to build the stable of stables and the show of shows.

As Freedman put it, 'All of these fighters are getting bigger paydays from MAPS than they could get from King or Arum, which raises the question of how MAPS can afford to throw money around like this. The purses are so high they can't profit on many of the promotions. There is no official documentation on the source of the money, but there are unconfirmed suggestions it comes from Japanese and Argentine businessmen.'

Another speculated the money was coming from 'Arab oilmen or investors of questionable character from the Orient and South America.'

Everyone was guessing. Bahar Muhammad, who was now working for MAPS, joked of Smith, 'He's the adopted son of Howard Hughes.'

Then, with a straighter face, Bahar said, 'The man can deliver the best situation for the athlete.'

Russell Peltz, who was handling Jeff Chandler, the brilliant bantamweight and friend of Matthew's from South Philly, had no idea what the source of the money was, or how long it would last.

'You can't compete with them throwing money around,' Peltz said. 'They've got both light-heavyweight champs [Matthew and Eddie], Hearns, Kenty, [bantamweight Julian] Solis. Those are some pretty heavy champions. And they've got a lot of top-flight amateurs. They can just outbid anybody right now.'

'The world wondered,' said Mustafa Ameen, who was now looking after Matthew's finances. 'Harold's competitors had different views. Don King said he was a drug dealer and it had to be related to drugs, Arum said it was a bunch of malarky and Harold's schtick was he had a wealthy wife whose father had died and left her a mad inheritance.'

Smith, trying to get in front of the intensifying speculation, claimed $12m had come from friends who set the group up. 'My wife and I put up $4m, another friend $4m and two others $2m apiece,' Smith lied.

Eddie Mustafa Muhammad was certainly living large. He had a high-rise apartment that looked over the Hudson from Guttenberg, New Jersey, with a Datsun, Rolls-Royce and Triumph cars outside.

Matthew was driving a two-door BMW and his split-level home on Woodpecker Road was a good-sized house. The champ had spared no expense inside. There were 11 rooms, four bathrooms and an outdoor barbecue area by the pool.

In fact, Eddie had been one of 300 guests at Matthew's housewarming.

'You don't see too many ivory pianos around, do you?' smiled Matthew to Eddie, nodding proudly at the unused Steinway in the reception room.

'To be quite frank with you, as time goes on, you realise it's not quite the mansion people thought it was,' offered Ameen. 'Don't get me wrong, it's a very wonderful house on about one and a half acres with an in-ground swimming pool but in retrospect, the house wasn't particularly large. I guess you'd be talking 3,000 square feet, which is not mansion-size. But coming from where Saad came from, a house with a pool and a garage, a one-car garage, it was a very nice house.'

Matthew wowed people with the facilities but, again, Ameen played it down. 'What we called a disco, in retrospect, was painting the basement, putting some strobe lights in there, having a nice sound system, speakers, music and saying "I have a disco at my house" and having the lights and playing the music. It was just a basement with some lights.'

But some of the furnishings were lavish, or at least Matthew's expenditure was. He was featured in the 'People' section of the *Philadelphia Inquirer* in the home, perched in one picture on his 'curved sectional sofa in the living room'. According to one *Inquirer* picture caption, 'Contrasting inserts in the living room carpet were created to conform to the [silk] sofa's curves.'

Matthew liked being caught up in high society given his meagre start. He paid local designer Marilyn Cutler to plan the interior. Cutler brought in the linens, dishes and stemware and it took six months to complete five rooms. They converted a closet into a trophy room by adjusting the size of one of the bathrooms. The pretentious *Inquirer* article continued, 'The bedroom pleases the owner with a colour combination of turquoise, wine, black and white. A built-in platform bed is placed next to one mirrored wall: the other walls are covered in silvery mylar ...'

Cutler had colour-coded the front room around the piano, using burgundy, camel and cream, and there was recessed lighting with dimmer switches. Matthew wanted a couple of chandeliers, which Cutler graciously allowed him, with one in the dining room and one in the foyer. There was a TV room/library with purple lacquered walls and custom rugs by an apparently well-renowned Nigerian artist.

'I had access to Matthew's chequebook,' remembered Ameen. 'I wrote his cheques. I paid his bills and I remember to this day – and I was surprised because I knew he was having some walls painted and the couch replaced and some things – he told me to pay her and I wrote a cheque that day for $65,000 for some decorating advice and a couple of pieces of furniture. So yeah, did the colour scheme match and all that kind of stuff? Yes. But there was nothing structurally done. There were no additions, it was just some furniture ...'

Sparring partner and friend Tony Green added, shaking his head, 'He paid about $85,000 just to get the insides renovated, just to have extras.'

The house was great, but Matthew was running up wasteful expenditures, with a piano he couldn't play and a pool he couldn't use because he couldn't swim.

'He had that piano shipped from New York and never took a piano lesson and it just sat there,' sighed Ameen. 'It looked beautiful in the living room – that wasn't frequented too often – and no one ever played that piano. It was a great accessory and I guess it made the house look refined and cultured, but it wasn't a practical piece.'

On one occasion, Ameen and Matthew sat by the pool. Ameen was reading the newspaper and Matthew jumped in to cool off, not realising he was jumping into the deep end. Mustafa leapt in and rescued him.

Matthew had been a guest of Eddie's on a visit to Brooklyn as their friendship grew. 'He slept in my bed and went out with my girls,' Eddie remembered. 'We had an agreement that if either of us were to win the title, he would give a shot to the other. But when he won the title, I didn't hear from him.'

Now, it was just about all they could manage not to hear from one another. They were going to fight again, they were travelling together, spending a lot of time together, sharing the covers of boxing magazines and getting ready to headline possibly the largest boxing card the world had seen.

Knowing the business, they talked up their proposed clash.

'Mustafa's fights are so boring you go to sleep,' argued Matthew.

'When I'm 40 years old, I don't want to take ten minutes to answer somebody who asks my name,' Eddie countered.

They had many similarities, but in the ring they were different. Eddie was a defensive whizz with great power and Matthew was a slugger with an unquenchable will. Neither of them had enjoyed an easy road to this point.

'This could be my last fight,' Matthew teased. 'My fights reflect my life, the way I had to come back.'

Harold Smith was building to a crescendo, a huge show at Madison Square Garden that he was calling 'This Is It'.

Gerry Cooney would fight Ken Norton in a heavyweight attraction on February 23 and amid headlines of '2 Muslims to box for one world title', Matthew would fight Eddie in the long-awaited unification clash. Also on the show, WBA welter champion Tommy Hearns and No. 2 contender Wilfred Benitez would unify the welterweight title, junior-featherweight WBC champion Wilfredo Gomez would defend against No. 4 Mike Ayala and WBA lightweight ruler Hilmer Kenty would fight No. 3 contender Alexis Arguello.

It was an unprecedented night. Tickets would be priced as high as $5,000 to produce a record-breaking gate. The total of the combined purses was more than $8m.

MAPS teamed up with Tiffany Promotions, which handled Cooney, and it was the first big boxing show at the Garden in more than a year.

'All the contracts are signed and we're all set,' boasted Smith, ready to pull off boxing's heist of the century.

It was so big, the *Boxing News* headline simply read, 'What a bill!' Most news items covering the announcement of the card used the words 'extravaganza' and 'spectacular'.

But nothing was more spectacular than the amount of money Smith was spending ... and losing.

The close-knit team of Bilal, Matthew and Mustafa went everywhere together, making frequent trips from coast to coast, from Philly to Santa Monica. That team often included Tony Green, Paul Trace and Salim El-Amin.

Mustafa Ameen recalled: 'After we signed the deal [with MAPS], we took the [Lottie] Mwale fight and the girl calls up and says, "What kind of car do we like?" At that time, Matthew's driving a [Mercedes] 380SL drop-top convertible as his personal car, and a BMW in Philadelphia, so we said we'd like a 450SL. We fly to California – and this is the first day I met Harold Smith personally – there was me, Milt Bailey, Salim [El-Amin], Sam Solomon, there's a van to pick us up at the airport and we go to the office in Santa Monica and she says, "Here's the keys. Look out the window and you'll see a white Mercedes." It was a brand-new drop-top convertible. And it didn't stop then ...'

* * *

Former WBA champion Victor Galindez had been forced to retire after suffering two detached retinas in a loss to Jesse Burnett in June 1980. With his boxing career over, at 55-9-4, he followed another passion and became a stock car racing driver.

On October 25, he entered his first Turismo Carretera, a road racing series in his native Argentina, making his debut as a co-driver to Antonio Lizeviche. Not long after the race began, their car suffered a mechanical failure. The dejected duo trudged towards the pits alongside the road when another competitor lost control of his vehicle, and spun off the track. The car struck both the former world light-heavyweight champion and Lizeviche, killing them on the spot.

Meanwhile, despite Mickey Duff's efforts to work with the Zambian government to stage Mwale's title attempt in Africa,

Smith's money dictated the fight took place in San Diego. Mwale's coach, George Francis, had his fighter running more than 100 miles a week and sparring ten rounds a day. Francis was more than familiar with Matthew after twice training John Conteh to face him. Some, particularly in the UK, were high on Mwale's prospects. 'Saad Muhammad can't continue to take the poundings he's taken and Mwale can be as good as he wants to be,' asserted Duff, who was also no stranger to Matthew, having worked with Conteh and Pergaud.

Sam Solomon was frustrated because he couldn't find any tape of the little-known African to study but he was confident in his charge.

Only around 3,000 fans attended the 10,000-capacity Sports Arena in San Diego on 28 November to watch Matthew defend his title for a fifth time in 19 months. Some reports had the sparse crowd at fewer than 1,000.

MAPS took a financial hammering. The undefeated Mwale, who had been a sparring partner for Conteh, earned $250,000 and Matthew made a record light-heavyweight payday of $750,000. You can only imagine the financial disaster it was given the meagre size of the crowd. There was no income from TV and the gate receipts came in at $41,785.

Incidentally, California State Athletic Commission files showed that Matthew was paid a $150,000 purse for the fight, but he'd somehow cleared $600,000 in extras from Smith. Arum knew it all because Saad had sought his advice. 'He has reported every penny to the IRS,' insisted Arum.

Explaining how Matthew had been wrested from Arum's Top Rank, Mustafa Ameen remembered an example of Smith's extravagance. 'Bilal went to a meeting in California through our good friend Bahar Muhammad and [it was] just at meeting to discuss business, but he came back with a gift from Harold Smith,' recalled Ameen. '[He] opened the briefcase and said, "Harold sends this." It was $25,000 in cash just for having the meeting.'

Mwale had won 21 fights. He had climbed off the floor to outpoint Jesse Burnett, had beaten a couple of Matthew's early foes in Dave Lee Royster and Vandell Woods, had stopped England's tough Tony Sibson in a round and in 1978 defeated Marvin Johnson via decision over eight rounds in Belgrade.

His team wouldn't fight Matthew in Pennsylvania or neighbouring New Jersey, making it the first world title fight in San Diego's history. Muhammad Ali was in attendance to cheer Matthew on.

Mwale entered to the sound of drums beating, the Zambian flag waving.

Matthew's step-father John Santos was ringside to support his boy.

Ritacco was back in the corner for Matthew, too, along with Solomon and veteran Philadelphian Milt Bailey.

Matthew lost two early rounds against Mwale but only ever looked calm and composed. In the third, he smashed in a left hook that had Mwale out on his feet. Referee Tony Perez could and perhaps should have intervened, but Mwale staggered, covered and wobbled in a corner until the bell sounded.

As the fourth progressed, Solomon shouted from the corner, 'Open up, Matt! Open up!'

Matthew fired over a crushing right hand and, before Mwale could register the impact, a follow-up left uppercut pierced his guard once more.

Matthew knew that was it. It was the hardest punch he ever threw.

Mwale's head snapped back, his mouthpiece went into orbit, he catapulted backwards, his right leg folded beneath him and his head clattered against the ring canvas. He lay motionless on his back.

Commentating for UK television, veteran Reg Gutteridge shouted, 'Oh … It's as perfect a knockout punch as you'll ever see.'

The ring physician leapt between the ropes and Mwale was out cold 15 seconds after the referee's count had stopped. When Lottie reacquainted himself with his senses, Matthew checked on him.

Muhammad Ali, in a black suit but showing the signs of a hard career as he slowly searched for words, was asked if he'd ever thrown a better shot.

'I threw a lot, maybe harder but the men didn't look so bad,' said The Greatest. 'Everything flew out of his mouth, his mouthpiece, blood, I never saw such a hard punch.'

Then, asked for his opinion on Matthew, he said, 'He's young, man, and we may look to hear about him for at least another ten years.'

Duff, again in a losing corner against Matthew, said Mwale had deviated from his gameplan to outbox Matthew because he'd had some early success, adding: 'Saad Muhammad is the strongest fighter at the weight that I've ever seen … The punch he hit Lottie with would have knocked out any fighter in the world.'

'He's a very strong man,' conceded Mwale. 'Stronger than anyone I've met before.'

Matthew, who won for the 15th time in a row since the disputed loss to the fighter then known as Eddie Gregory, said he'd been hurt a couple of times in round two, but that seemed like charitable praise.

Eddie fought Rudy Koopmans the following night in Los Angeles, retaining his title with a stoppage, arising from a cut, in the third round.

Saad Muhammad–Mwale and Mustafa Muhammad–Koopmans were financial disasters, but they didn't kill the momentum for the super-fight, so Smith forged ahead with the New York bill that he believed would change the course of boxing.

Matthew cranked up the pre-fight smack talk saying, 'I still call him Eddie Gregory. He's not a real Muslim like I am. I'll knock him back to Africa.'

'I was amazed at what he said,' Eddie shot back. 'I'm going to make it short and quick. Saad is a robot. We're not going 15 rounds … he is a very ignorant champion.'

Matthew and Eddie didn't really want to fight one another, but the purses were extraordinary.

'Eddie and Matt were tight, man,' said Tony Green. 'Even though they had fought, they were tight. They were Muslim brothers and they were close.'

'We were friends with Eddie, it was the money,' said Ameen. 'We were getting $2.5 [million] and that was a lot of damn money, so each guy wanted to win, but it wasn't anything deep-rooted. It never reached that level at all.'

Eddie admitted it was just about them both getting paid. 'I said, "Harold, I will fight Saad again but this is what I want, I want a million and a half and the majority of it up front for training expenses." I got it and the fight was on.'

Ameen's suspicions about Smith were heightened further when he was given a cheque for $100,000 for 'training expenses'. The team travelled in a stretched limousine to the Wells Fargo bank branch in Beverly Hills and Matthew and the crew were directed beyond the counter and into the vice president's office where they met Sammie Marshall.

'My senses were lit,' Ameen later admitted.

Even more so when Ameen was asked how he'd like the $100,000. Ameen only wanted to take $10,000 out. Payday for the team was Friday and he needed payroll to distribute but without asking for ID, information or having to fill out forms, Ameen could have cashed the $100,000, no questions asked.

* * *

The media rumoured that Sam Solomon was going to be replaced by Detroit's Emanuel Steward, who had Kenty and Hearns in action on the big Madison Square Garden bill. Meanwhile, the story about Matthew's childhood and search for his identity was still big news. When asked by one reporter how old he was, Matthew guessed he was somewhere between 26 and 30. 'Yeah, he could be 400, too,' Mustafa Muhammad, then 28, quipped.

Matthew's backstory was getting so much coverage it was on the verge of making him a crossover star. One *New York Daily News* columnist wrote of Saad and the wide appeal of his sad story, 'Will this man unseat Sugar Ray Leonard as media darling of the boxing world?'

Matthew was also a guest on *60 Minutes with Morley Safer*, talking about his childhood, the search and the reward, but the media was becoming increasingly fixated on Harold Smith and MAPS, and about where the money was coming from.

The outfit had lost around a million on the San Diego show and about $800,000 on the Eddie Mustafa–Koopmans bill. Sources reckoned they'd haemorrhaged anywhere from $3m to $7m since they started in 1979.

Reporters were doing simple maths and trying to work out how the blockbuster bill at MSG was going to do anything but disastrous numbers, with far more money going out in fighter purses than coming in from ticket sales, priced from $1,000 down to $50, with only 700 available at the top end. There were around 500 closed circuit deals.

Eddie and Matthew were the top earners, set for $1.5m apiece, although some sources had Matthew's purse at $2.1m or $2.5m. Cooney was getting $1.25m for Norton, who was making $1.1m. Tommy Hearns was on $1.2m, Benitez was at $1m with Gomez, Arguello and Kenty earning $300,000 each and Ayala at $150,000. MAPS was paying Ali $150,000 just to show up.

It just didn't add up. It's not as if journalists weren't asking the questions, but no one knew the answers.

John Conden was the director of boxing at the Garden, and he said they were renting MAPS the building for $250,000 and profits from concessions. He admitted he had never seen anything like the amount of money that was being tossed about.

'The flow of money is unbelievable,' he said. 'I have no idea where their money is coming from. But they pay their bills. No fighter, no arena, no one has been stiffed.'

That was rare in the sport, too, so there were few complaints.

Not only were MAPS paying well, but they were doing so almost all the time in good faith, without small print clauses or options on future fights. The boxers were not tied down, but none of them wanted to go anywhere else. Those behind MAPS wanted to be known as 'The New Team in Town'.

Of their astronomical losses, Arum said, 'That would be more than Don King and I and all the other promoters together cleared for the same period. I am totally bewildered why anybody would go into boxing ventures for the purpose of losing substantial sums of money ... They are paying double and triple what other promoters could afford to pay and remain solvent. How they do it and why is a mystery. Where does the money come from? How deep is the well?'

Greg Logan at the *Record* in Hackensack, New Jersey, was circumspect.

'In the best of all possible worlds, this is the way the boxing business would be run,' he wrote. 'But the sport's cynical fans have come to expect the worst. The climate in the boxing business is permanently shady. One assumes that someone is being ripped off somewhere along the line, whether it is the fighters, the public or both.'

But fighters and their teams were on the ride of their lives, living larger than any of them could have possibly imagined just months before they had met Harold Smith.

'He wasn't brash,' said Ameen of Smith. 'He had a certain electricity about him. You knew he was "The Man" when he walked into a room and among his staff – but he wasn't brash or rude. He was affable. He was just a cool guy. And he really did like Saad as a fighter.'

* * *

Harold Smith was thick-set, thirty-something, stood 6ft 2ins tall, had a high-pitched voice, a beard, dark glasses and a white cowboy hat. He didn't stint on the jewellery, either. He had a luxurious top-floor apartment on Sunset Strip in Los Angeles and condos in Marina del Rey. He'd used interior decorators to fill them with extravagances; there was a sunken hot tub and a pool. He couldn't turn down a party invite, and plenty thought he was a drug dealer doing great business. But how would one explain the private jet, the racehorses, the yacht, the first-class travel and all the rest of it? His boat came in at more than $80,000, he drove a $40,000 custom El Dorado and his wife Barbara – one of many aliases – had a Mercedes.

Smith was a mystery. People had heard who he was, but nobody knew him.

In 1976, Smith listened to the story of Florida sprinter Houston McTear, a decorated high school athlete who was struggling to make ends meet away from the track. Smith either wanted to make things right for the potential star, or saw an opportunity, and rang McTear to see how he could help. A few calls later, Smith had managed to get hold of Muhammad Ali. (One of Smith's qualities was chutzpah.)

He told Ali he'd found the next Jesse Owens. Ali said he'd buy McTear a house and pay his training expenses and Smith, emboldened by his success, asked Ali if he wouldn't mind lending his name to Smith to form an amateur athletics team. Ali, who didn't say 'no' often, agreed and MAAS (Muhammad Ali Amateur Sports) was born.

'My impression was that he was a clean young man, striving to do business,' said Ali. 'Honest, I thought, and I liked him enough to let him use my name.'

Smith promoted some track meets in 1976 and 1977 but couldn't land TV deals, often leaving a trail of red ink on his invoices.

He met 48-year-old Beverly Hills banker Ben Lewis, who had worked at Wells Fargo for more than a decade. Lewis was a dapper black man who was enthused by what Smith was trying to do, helping poor kids, giving them an opportunity and platform to a better life. Lewis soon realised Smith's cheques often bounced, but Smith pleaded with the bank for clemency and argued, 'I'm doing it for the kids.'

Sometimes operations manager Lewis would delay collecting debts until Smith could finally pay; he wanted to help his community, too.

At first, it was a one-off, but it became a regular thing. Then, despite his better judgement, he started helping Smith.

Smith, after all, had introduced Lewis to his idol, Ali. This gave Lewis the taste of wealth and celebrity that would otherwise have been a fantasy for someone making $1,750 a month.

Smith's debts to the bank climbed to around $14,000 so Lewis called his colleague, loan officer Sammie Marshall, at the Miracle Mile Wells Fargo and implored him to help Smith clear his debts and start making big money.

Marshall, too, was reluctantly in. Smith told them, 'Brothers, do you know how much money can be made in sports? We could make millions.' That's not often the case in athletics, so Smith – with the Ali name behind him – switched his attention to boxing. He kept an eye out for promising amateurs and even took Marshall and Lewis to Ali–Spinks II in New Orleans, all expenses paid. It turned out the trip cost $19,000. Lewis and Marshall knew because when Smith gave them the cheque to pay for it, it bounced.

But Marshall and Lewis had sampled a new life and despite the panic and stress of knowing what they were doing was illegal and could not just cost them their careers but their freedom, they followed Smith as though he were the Pied Piper.

With Ali's permission, Smith launched Muhammad Ali Professional Sports. He signed erratic heavyweight Tony Tubbs – even buying Tubbs's parents a $50,000 home as a signing bonus – as well as middleweight Jeff McCracken and light-heavyweight JB Williamson. They had an amateur team and opened a gym in Santa Monica.

But the money going out overwhelmed the money coming in. They took Ali to Australia to fight Joe Bugner in an exhibition no one wanted, with barely 4,000 attending in a 45,000-seater stadium. After each titanic loss, Smith told Marshall and Lewis, 'We'll get it all back. I guarantee you.'

Smith signed Leo Randolph for crazy money. Randolph was a 1976 Olympic gold medal winner, but he weighed 112lbs and there was no money in flyweights. Smith matched Randolph with Oscar Muniz in 1979, paid the boxers a combined $41,250 and the show made $9,656.

When he put Henry Lumpkin in with Marty Monroe, the boxers split $41,250 but only brought in $5,281.

Later in 1980, on a show in Sacramento, Wilfred Benitez was handed $250,000 to fight little-known Pete Ranzani, who took home around $75,000. Again, it went on without TV, and 4,507 fans put just $89,992.50 back into Smith's seemingly bottomless pot.

MAPS lost another $200,000 when Marty Monroe stopped Eddie Lopez and Smith had sunk about a million into Ali's pockets for the use of his name and to attend shows.

Smith tried to signed Larry Holmes, but had an angry altercation with Don King – Holmes's promoter – in Las Vegas, which had King reaching for a gun. Whatever money was offered, Holmes was tempted.

Smith also tried to sweet-talk Sugar Ray Leonard, but Leonard's astute lawyer Mike Trainer saw through whatever Smith was selling and moved on.

Constantly, Smith tried to tell the bankers he was close to the big bucks. Even with a TV deal, the MAPS show that featured Ken Norton–Randy 'Tex' Cobb lost a further $200,000.

There was another problem as well as the losses, though. Smith didn't know a whole lot about boxing. He launched money at a washed-up Earnie Shavers, passing him $100,000 in a briefcase in a Vegas hotel suite and in a meeting with English promoter Mickey Duff, Duff returned to the UK with $300,000, with $250,000 for Scotland's Jim Watt to defend his WBC lightweight title and $50,000 for John L. Gardner to box on a show, likely an Ali exhibition. 'I thought I was dreaming,' said Duff, who'd been in the sport for decades and who had just about seen it all. 'I just couldn't believe it.'

Smith told Duff he'd just won $5m gambling in Las Vegas.

'I thought he was a crook or crazy,' Duff later said.

Smith flew Detroit trainer and manager Emanuel Steward and his star Tommy Hearns to his plush Santa Monica office – Suite 208, 3231 Ocean Park Boulevard – for a meeting in mid-1980. 'The Hitman' had never made more than $85,000 for a fight, but Smith opened the bidding on Hearns's services, handing over a bag with $500,000 inside.

Before Hearns could reach for a pen, Smith turned the screw. 'I'll give you another $100,000 if you sign.'

The condition was that Hearns fight WBA welterweight ruler Jose 'Pipino' Cuevas, so Smith boarded his leased private jet, with $1m in a duffel bag, and signed the Mexican.

Smith made history on 2 August 1980, when he had two boxing shows on television at the same time. In Detroit, Hearns iced Cuevas in two rounds, with one of the sport's most ferocious knockouts. Hilmer Kenty defended his WBA lightweight title against South Korean Young Ho Oh on the undercard and Cobb knocked off a tired Shavers. Meanwhile, in Cincinnati, Ohio, the brilliant fighting windmill Aaron Pryor stopped veteran champion Antonio Cervantes to win the WBA super-lightweight crown in front of Pryor's own fans on a bill that also featured Tony Tubbs and Jeff McCracken.

Smith would fly ring-card girls around to travel with him, putting them up in penthouses in luxury hotels and apartments, even buying some of them cars and presents, but he still lost money faster than his jet could travel.

At one point, Smith flew Matthew, Bilal and Ameen to San Juan for the Hilmer Kenty–Ernesto Espana lightweight title fight. 'That was the first engagement when I thought, "This is over the top,"' recalled Ameen. 'When we got there, there were 50 other people [guests], the card girls, his staff and we walked through the casino with Harold and I saw him lose $15–20,000 in 20 minutes. He just shrugged his shoulders and said, "I'll come back later." Everyone was at the Hilton, everyone had their own suite. This was something new here. You talk about extravagance.'

Matthew told someone in the camp, 'Something ain't right.'

Smith wanted to buy boxing. He would outbid everyone until he had control of the major titles and all but eliminated the competition. Then he would reduce and regulate pay scales.

But with Smith becoming paranoid and running out of road, he made what some saw as his last big move. The Madison Square Garden show could break records. It could break MAPS even. It could set everything straight. It could rewrite two years of red ink with one fat line of black. As the New York event neared, limousines filled with sacks and cases of cash were showing up at the gyms and houses of fighters to make sure they were paid. As the late Jim Brady wrote, 'With Smith's "money men" frantically juggling debit chits, and with sacks of cash leaving Wells Fargo like garbage on New Year's Day, the plotters nervously counted the hours till the show took place.'

* * *

Smith had roped Lewis in around October 1978. A year later, and around $200,000 could not be accounted for. As 1980 was ending, and Smith's foot was to the floor promoting the card, more than $15m had gone.

Smith was flying Matthew and his team, which was expanding into a serious entourage, everywhere with no expense spared.

'I can't say nothing bad about him,' Matthew said years on.

'Harold Smith paid you good money?'

'Always.'

Those who found themselves in Saad's inner circle were Bilal, Mustafa, Tony Green, Salim El-Amin and photographer Paul Trace.

'Let me tell you something, I've got nothing bad to say about Harold,' said Green. 'The guy treated us like kings. I guess when you're using other people's money, you can do that. I fought for Don King, Bob Arum … [but] Harold Smith was the best.'

'One thing about Harold, I never questioned where he got the money from,' Eddie Mustafa Muhammad said, decades on. 'I didn't care where the money came from.

'As long as he kept paying and giving me what I wanted, we was cool.'

As 1980 closed the top six in a packed light-heavyweight division saw Matthew recognised as the champion. The contenders were Eddie at No. 1, Spinks at 2, James Scott at 3, Jerry Martin at No. 4, with Marvin Johnson at No.5.

In December, Matthew was on a dais with his friend Teddy Pendergrass, Dionne Warwick, Patti Labelle, Joe Frazier, Julius Irving and other dignitaries at the Franklin Plaza Hotel in Philadelphia, when 1,000 gathered to pay tribute to Pendergrass for selling a million records for his fifth consecutive album.

Over Christmas, Matthew was thrown a party in Beverly Hills by Paul and Gerard Guez, his sponsors at Sassoon. Matthew was pictured with actress Farah Fawcett at a glittering celebrity-filled Hollywood bash that Ryan O'Neal, Lou Ferrigno and Cathy Bach, from *The Dukes of Hazzard*, also attended.

Ali was there, of course, and so was Paul Trace, who was now known in Saad's camp as the 'White Shadow' because he went everywhere the champion went. Trace had been reluctant to meet Muhammad Ali through Matthew for fear of looking unprofessional. Trace also realised he was just about the only non-Muslim in the camp so, out of respect for the others, he learned the Muslim greeting, 'As-salamu alaykum,' and the response, 'Wa alaykumu s-salam.'

At a governor's banquet for Tim Florio in Newark, New Jersey, filled with senators and officials, Matthew told Trace he was going to introduce him to Ali.

'My job is to photograph you and Ali,' Trace protested.

Matthew wasn't having it. He shook Ali's hand and looked towards Trace.

'I want you to meet my photographer,' Saad said to Ali.

Trace extended his hand. 'As-salamu alaykum,' he said.

'Wa alaykumu s-salam,' Ali replied.

'And I went to move away and he called me back and said, "You boy,"' Trace recalled.

'Come here.'

Ali bit his lip and said, 'What did you just say to me?'

'As-salamu alaykum,' Trace repeated.

Ali smiled and shook his head. 'My God, they done make a nigger out of you already.'

* * *

On a team trip to New York, Sassoon outfitted the whole crew with new clothes and tracksuits, and while Matthew was in town, LeRoy Neiman invited him to his studio to be painted.

Matthew and Eddie were also flirting with futures in Hollywood. Eddie had been cast in the role of Billy Fox, going against Robert DeNiro on screen who was playing Jake LaMotta in the Martin Scorsese epic *Raging Bull*.

Matthew had gone for the part of Clubber Lang in *Rocky III*, along with other legit fighters Earnie Shavers and Joe Frazier.

'Matt, even prior to *Rocky*, would mention his relationship with the Stallone brothers, Frankie in particular, who did the music scores for *Rocky*,' remembered Mustafa Ameen. 'Frank wasn't as well-known as Sylvester, but Matthew had a kinship with Frank more so than Sylvester. When the *Rocky* movies took off and they decided to do the sequels, Sylvester decided he wanted to try for authenticity and use a Philadelphia fighter. And who better than Joe Frazier and Saad Muhammad? We hired an acting coach and had less than two weeks to prepare and we had the full script.'

They were staying at the Beverly Hills Hilton. Having spent some time alone in his room, Matthew approached Ameen in the lobby.

'Mustafa, did you really read this script?'

'Yeah.'

'Well, did you see they have me losing to Rocky? That can't be ...'

'What do you mean?'

'I'm the champ. Nobody beats me. I'm not going to lose my title. You need to call those people and ask them to change it ...'

'Champ, I'm not calling anybody. It's a movie. It's a movie about Rocky. Rocky has to win.'

Matthew stormed off and came back 20 minutes later.

'Okay, you're right,' he said, shaking his head. 'But can you call them and see if they can at least make it a draw.'

Mr. T eventually got the role he was born to play, as Clubber Lang, and as soon as he auditioned it was a one-horse race. Stallone, the directors, the whole team knew the muscle-bound bodyguard with the mohawk was a perfect fit.

Matthew told reporter Nigel Collins another version of the audition back in 1981. 'I've got my pride, man,' said the then champion. 'I don't get beat in the ring and I'm not about to be beat on the screen. And besides, they weren't going to use my real name!'

* * *

A few weeks out from the huge New York card, Matthew and Eddie attended the press conference to formally announce the rematch.

They were pictured comparing threads alongside Tommy Hearns, Gerry Cooney and Wilfred Benitez.

The media ate up their 'feud'. It was not just about the two fighters but the one name. Matthew Saad Muhammad was managed by Bilal Muhammad. Eddie Mustafa Muhammad was managed by Ben Muhammad. Eddie had a sister, Salilah Muhammad. The whole show was being put on by Muhammad Ali Professional Sports. Muhammad Ali was going to be there.

As Will Grimsley, for the Associated Press, broke it down, 'Muhammad fights Muhammad with each having a Muhammad in the corner and another Muhammad sitting among the relatives, not to mention the Muhammad which is paying the freight.'

Matthew tried to stoke the promotional fires, even though there was no bad blood. 'It will be a war, a rumble,' he insisted. 'It won't be "I touch you, you touch me." There will be bloodshed.'

Then, clarifying his intent, he said, 'But we'll take it as a sport, in a good way. Our intention is not to go out there and kill each other, but you can bet that we won't be holding our punches, that's for sure.'

Michael Spinks, who'd moved from St Louis to Philadelphia to further his career, was the first out of the top half of the division to see action in 1981. He beat Brooklyn's Willie Taylor inside eight rounds in Philly on 24 January to move to 16-0. He was asked who would win on 23 February and made his answer wholly about him.

'I can't predict which Muhammad will win,' said Spinks. 'All I'll say is they both have a deep respect for me.'

'I think Spinks is a good young prospect, but he still has a lot to learn,' said Matthew, while Eddie's trainer Slim Jim Robinson said, 'This guy [Spinks] should be an easy fight for Eddie.'

But in mid-January, Harold Smith went missing. He was wanted by the FBI, who were making an inquiry into the embezzlement of funds. An internal Wells Fargo investigation revealed that millions of dollars was missing. The MAPS accounts were instantly frozen and by 31 January – with Smith AWOL and thought to be in Puerto Rico, but also rumoured to be in Australia or Mexico – the Madison Square Garden show was in trouble.

Despite the venue making a vague effort to salvage at least a portion of the card, 'This Is It' went down the drain on 6 February.

'Matt and I were rooming together in a hotel in New York and we got a telephone call. Bilal was on the line and Matthew's jaw dropped. He went silent and that's when we learned that Harold Smith had absconded with $22m dollars,' Paul Trace recollected. 'That was the shocker to end all shockers.'

As a last-ditch measure, organisers tried to get Eddie and Matthew to split $1m for the fight to go ahead, but they were not interested.

The fallout was severe.

As prosecutors quickly built their case against Smith, they uncovered the system that had been used. Wells Fargo was one of the largest American banks with thousands of transactions taking place daily. The bank used a computerised process, called a branch settlement system, that allowed customers to withdraw from any of their locations. With each transaction, two halves of a ticket were created, and they were put together for debits and credits. The numbers of each operation needed to match, and the case was settled. However, if two bankers in two different branches knew the transaction code, they could keep the matter unresolved, and therefore undetected.

Ben Lewis, in Beverly Drive, and Sammie Marshall, at Miracle Mile, had been pedalling as fast as they could to keep Smith's unlikely dream alive. They had been vital to the operation. Without them frantically trying to cover the paper trail, and each other, the game would have been up long before. They were in so deep they couldn't take holidays because they needed to stay on top of the embezzlement.

They had also become MAPS employees. Lewis was on the original board of directors while Marshall had become the company's president.

But when a member of staff, Julie McLardie, at the Miracle Mile Wells Fargo branch called Lewis and told him she couldn't find half of one of the outstanding chits, they had a major issue.

Agitated about being rumbled, Lewis played it down. 'It's nothing, it'll show up,' he said.

McLardie escalated the problem, and Lewis was summoned to the office of his boss, Brian Feeley.

'I advanced Harold Smith some money,' Lewis confessed.

It all unravelled from there.

Lewis called Smith and told him it was all over. The game was up. That was that.

The FBI was soon involved, as was the Los Angeles District Attorney's Office. Cops descended upon the Santa Monica branch, and all 12 Smith and MAPS accounts were stopped.

On 31 January, when Matthew's friend Jeff Chandler defeated Panama's Jorge Lujan in Philadelphia to defend his WBA bantamweight title, CBS refused to allow MAPS to be involved in the co-promotion with Russell Peltz, insisting Peltz went it alone as the network moved to distance itself from what federal agents were calling 'the biggest bank fraud in American history'.

On 7 February, the missing Smith called into a radio station and made a bizarre plea. 'I appeal to the media to go to the Wells Fargo Miracle Mile branch,' he stated. 'It is there you will find the beginning of what I guarantee is the biggest case of fraud, embezzlement and illegal loan kickbacks, including numerous branches and personnel in the Wells Fargo system. I am not afraid, and I am not alone because I know God is with me.'

But Muhammad Ali no longer was. He held a hastily arranged press conference to disown the man who'd been using his name as auditors sunk their fangs into one of the deepest paper trails in banking crime.

'I saw him with all those beautiful girls, planes, boats,' Ali explained. 'I used to say, "You sure everything's okay, Harold?" He always said everything was fine.'

A staggering $21,305,705.18 had been plundered.

'It's all gone, all spent,' said federal prosecutor Dean Allison.

The investigation was so intensely thorough all but seven cents was accounted for.

Smith made all kinds of false accusations to get off the hook. He claimed a Wells Fargo insider had pushed him into it, alleged that the bank's security force was trying to murder him and shouted about links to the Japanese Yakuza. Smith even launched a near-$300m lawsuit against Wells Fargo claiming defamation because 'my good name has been tarnished'. But no one could take him seriously, and all of his assertions were false.

As everything came out in the wash, it was revealed that Harold Smith was named Ross Eugene Fields.

That didn't mean much to anyone, but it did to Bob Arum, who suddenly realised why he'd recognised Smith.

In 1972, Ross Fields – who had been born in Birmingham, Alabama in 1943 – had run off with the North Carolina takings from the Arum-promoted Ali–Jerry Quarry fight, and was wanted around the country for any number of bad cheques. The man who had been looking for the new Jesse Owens when he tried to help Houston McTear was actually a latter-day Jesse James.

'I never put it together when he was Harold Smith and spending all this money on all these wild schemes paying these light-heavyweights $750,000 when I was paying them $250,000,' sighed Arum, who'd recalled Smith as a slender, clean-shaven man years earlier.

Smith had wanted to be a somebody. He had grown up poor, five boys to a bed, bologna for breakfast daily. One day, he found a can of dog food beneath his mother's bed she had been making last so that at least the kids could eat their cheap tinned meat.

In July 1981, following a six-month investigation, a grand jury returned a 32-felony indictment against Smith for conspiring to defraud Wells Fargo. The jury took eight days to convict him. They ignored his final plea when he asked for a short sentence saying, 'I've got a beautiful wife and a beautiful son. Please don't take them away from me. I'm a good person.'

But even before the trial was over, those in boxing knew the game was up. Harold Smith and his looted millions were gone, and they were not coming back. That golden, halcyon period of endless money, cars and cases full of cash and limousines was over.

'It's time we get back to basics,' said Gil Clancy, matchmaker for the Garden. 'Managers are going to come in and be shocked at what we offer and at what Bob Arum and Don King offer, but the offers will be just exactly what the fighter is worth. A $300,000 fighter is going to get $300,000. If he wants $1m, let him go and find Smith.'

Just days away from his biggest heist, Smith was denied his greatest score, and perhaps his only real profitable venture. The $80m he thought he was going to make, that would settle everything, that would balance the books and make everyone rich, had gone up in smoke.

'MAPS goes boom ... and the "Card of the Century" goes bye-bye ...' read a *Boxing Illustrated* headline.

'It was great while it lasted,' said Cooney's manager, Mike Jones. 'Now we'll have to go back to reality.'

'I can't say anything bad about MAPS,' said 'KO' Becky, Chandler's manager. 'They treated us royal.'

For Team Saad, they had enjoyed every minute. There had been no downs, only ups. 'Everything was over the top,' grinned Ameen. 'There was no rollercoaster for us. We fell in love with Harold.'

* * *

Before Sammie Marshall was dragged into the prosecutor's crosshairs and implicated, he tried to salvage Smith's doomed New York card, but no one could pay the $8.1m in fighter purses and still have a company left afterwards.

On 2 February 1981, Ben Lewis walked into FBI headquarters to come clean, but by 24 February, a day after the proposed show date, Smith still couldn't be found. His five lawyers, however, arrived in a federal courthouse to meet with prosecutors in an attempt to cut him some slack. The authorities were hot on Smith's heels, however, and on Saturday, 4 April 1981, he was captured in a police sting at Elysian Park near Dodger Stadium after 71 days of hiding. The FBI made an official announcement later in the day. Smith couldn't make the $400,000 bail.

When Smith was sentenced, he tried to flatter district judge Consuelo B. Marshall but it didn't work and she gave him ten years. Lewis made a plea with the government and was sentenced to five years. Marshall was given three.

Professionally, Eddie and Matthew went their separate ways. Both had been paid $300,000 up front, with Matthew due to get his balance on 8 February. 'We're not holding our breath,' said a camp insider.

'I was looking forward to it,' Matthew said. 'I was looking forward to unifying the title. I'm very, very disappointed. I don't even like to talk about it. I get a headache.'

Eddie was worse off. He had paid his $300,000 into Wells Fargo Bank, where it had been seized.

'It was a big payday. I was disappointed but it wasn't the end of the world,' he recalled.

There had actually been turmoil in his team before the super-fight, with Archie Moore replacing Slim Robinson as trainer just days out. Eddie was closer to the story than he would have liked.

'I went to the bank to make a withdrawal,' Eddie remembered. 'I was living in Santa Monica, California, and as I go to the front door, one of the guys who was my banker ran out. I thought he was saying hello. "Don't come in here. Don't come in. I'll call you later." I got to my apartment and there was a newsflash that came over the TV about Wells Fargo and Harold Smith, whose real name was Ross Fields. I was like, "I ain't got nothing to do with that. This is how I make my money; I fight. I didn't rob no bank." It was crazy, man. The FBI came to my house and told me what had happened.'

CHAPTER 12

I HAVE TO LOOK FOR OTHER GOALS

'I HOPE his mental state is down,' fight manager and trainer Angelo Dundee said. 'Way down from not getting the fight.'

Dundee managed Vonzell Johnson, who was drafted to face Matthew at short notice.

They couldn't make the 23 February date, the bill collapsed and 'This Is It' was cancelled, but promoter Murad Muhammad gave Matthew the option of fighting Johnson, Jerry Martin, Dwight Braxton or Murray Sutherland.

Martin turned it down, saying there wasn't enough time to get ready, but Johnson had been training to face James Scott in Rahway. That bout had also been scrapped, and Scott's fighting future hung in the balance as he'd been found guilty of the murder that went along with his previous robbery charges.

Matthew was making around $300,000 while Johnson, earning considerably less at around $50,000, said he would have fought for free; he just wanted the opportunity.

They met inside Atlantic City's Bally's Park Plaza on 28 February, so at least Matthew's camp for Eddie Mustafa Muhammad had not been wasted.

The fight put Tony Green in an awkward situation. He was in Matthew's inner circle, but he was also trained and managed by Dundee, and Johnson was his stablemate. With Matthew's blessing, Green left for Miami to help the challenger prepare to take his employer's title.

Green and Johnson went way back. Johnson had stopped Green in three rounds early in their pro careers as part of Don King's aborted televised tournament.

'I remember I was getting my hands wrapped and Angelo came in the room and watched my trainer and told him to take the wraps off,' Johnson recalled. 'He was trying to intimidate my trainer, so I told my trainer, "Do whatever he wants, take them off." I looked at Angelo Dundee and I told him, "You just got your guy knocked out." And in the third round, I knocked out Tony Green. I looked over to Angelo and said, "You did that. I told you."'

Vonzell and Tony had become friends, however, a mutual respect born from fierce competition. But the impressive win hadn't done Johnson many favours. He was nearly 6ft 5ins tall and a nightmare to box. He was rangy, had an expert left jab and had learned his craft in the fight city of Detroit. In around 90 amateur fights, he had won 80. He'd captured National AAU and Golden Gloves titles, and no one wanted to fight him. It resulted in him having just one professional fight in 1978 and one in 1979 as the phone stopped ringing.

'I guess the word was out that I had three heads and eight arms and nobody wanted any part of me,' Johnson remembered.

That was when he reached out to Dundee, who subsequently guided him to five comparatively speedy wins and a shot at the WBC title. Johnson had beaten Matthew's early conqueror Wayne McGee, and Johnson's lone loss was to another fringe contender, Jerry Celestine, who wound up fighting Marvin Johnson, Eddie Mustafa Muhammad, Jerry Martin, James Scott, Richie Kates and Michael Spinks.

The WBC rated Vonzell, 23-1 as a pro, at No. 8, but the bookmakers didn't give him a shot at Matthew. His odds ranged from 6/1 to 25/1.

'Angelo mentioned about the three weeks [notice] and I said I was going to try and get Matthew out of there,' Johnson remembered, thinking he'd be the one to end Matthew's reign. 'Back then you couldn't turn down a world championship fight. I couldn't turn it down.'

Getting prepared for the changes in opponent, date, venue and stakes wasn't easy for Matthew. He laboured in sparring sessions against Jody Ballard and Pete McIntyre in front of around 50 members of the media who were distinctly unimpressed. Losing the opportunity to become a millionaire, to unify the titles and then having to face a tall, hungry and ambitious challenger like Johnson in a no-win bout hadn't got Matthew's competitive juices flowing.

He'd been in a different place psychologically before the cancelled fight. 'I'm still ready but life goes on,' Matthew said during fight week media engagements, adding that he only wanted to fight two more years at the most. 'I have to look for other goals. It [not unifying the titles] prolongs my boxing career. It was just at the tip of my fingers.'

'You've got to forget about it,' said trainer Sam Solomon. 'You're fighting another man now.'

But Matthew kept getting asked about what might have been.

'My remaining goal is to bring the two titles together,' he continued. 'After I beat Eddie, there would be no reason for me to continue. Maybe one more fight, then retire. Sit back and let my money go to work.'

Boxing was becoming boring to him, and Frank Gelb had also filed a $65,000 lawsuit against him wanting his 10 per cent from the Mwale fight. Gelb's contract had expired on 20 October, the fight was at the end of November, but the bout had originally been set for September so Gelb felt he should have had his slice.

'Next to Sugar Ray Leonard, I see myself as the biggest star attraction,' Matthew told the media. 'I don't know whether I'll ever be able to get a fight with Eddie, or whoever is the other champion. I want to come out of this job looking good, talking good and walking straight. Money, I just want to know I've got enough not to have to worry. Then I'll get into something else.'

He thought there could be fights with Braxton and Spinks and still attached value to a Rossman clash that was well past its sell-by date.

'Spinks stinks,' Matthew said, lightly chuckling. 'He's a legitimate contender but he should wait until I retire. He's in over his head with Matthew Saad Muhammad.'

Then, he added, 'I don't really want to fight anymore. I have to get my mind back together. I had a thought that I was about to write the end to Matthew Saad Muhammad, boxer. Instead, the way things have gone, I guess it will have to be just another one of those stories that says at the bottom, "To be continued."'

* * *

Away from the ring, the search for Matthew's family was turning up empty. There had been one lead, but it went quiet.

'I think there's too much guilt after all these years,' Matthew said. 'I'd know my brother, but he hasn't come forward. Maybe he just ran off that day and left me.

'I think people who do well in life have a tendency to reminisce,' he went on. 'But when I tried, I really couldn't. There were blanks in my life. When you get in my position, being a champion, you start thinking, "Where did this greatness come from? Could my father be Sugar Ray Robinson?"

'I had always promised myself that when I became financially equipped, I'd find out. The investigator has worked for a long time. I talked to people who claimed to be relatives and weren't. I knew, because there were a lot of things I remembered that I never discussed with anyone.'

Journalist Nigel Collins felt that Matthew's search was what drove him to his superhuman performances and motivated him to battle back from the brink. 'Being abandoned as a child and bouncing around foster homes and reform schools, that was a double-edged sword,' Collins reasoned. 'It drove him to endure those fights, but it was going to ruin him physically.'

Matthew was also trying to help other people. Money from endorsements from the likes of athletic-wear brand Pony and Sassoon went towards a foundation that assisted underprivileged children. He also helped on a programme called FOCUS (Fresh Opportunities

Create Useful Students), which worked with the education system to give jobs to troubled youths.

'I see kids struggling,' Matthew said. 'Looking lost, reaching out. Hey, I know the feeling.'

Now, with his wealth and celebrity, people wanted to know Matthew, and they wanted his help. He'd get regular requests to share his fortune, and he was overly generous.

'It's not easy living when somebody hears you're making millions,' he said. 'Someone's always ringing the doorbell, saying "Matthew, please help me, my baby needs milk." I know there are a lot of people who make a lot of money without getting their picture in the papers, and I want to be one of them.'

But with the Johnson fight days away, Matthew managed to find a bit more enthusiam for the contest. In all, he'd sparred almost 140 rounds and run almost as many miles. Dundee, who more famously worked with Muhammad Ali and Sugar Ray Leonard, talked up his charge's chances and felt he had a knack for coaching boxers to beat Philly battlers by offsetting their aggression.

Johnson was asked about Matthew's recuperative powers, to which he answered half-jokingly, 'I think he's a masochist. He likes to take punishment. I'm taller. I have the reach advantage. I can keep him at bay, away, keep him outside with the jab.'

He felt Matthew's opponents had lost heart against him and was determined to not only take the lead, but finish Matthew off.

'They seen this guy on the other side, they beatin' him to death and he's standin' there like he loves it and they think, "What am I in here with?" Then they give it up and lose their heart ... I'm going to be there in the later rounds and I'm giving it my all. I'm never, never giving it up.'

* * *

In the first round Johnson, quick and lanky, moved equally well from left to right and right to left. He easily avoided Matthew's jab and made the champion miss with cumbersome hooks and overhand rights.

Matthew knew almost instantly it wasn't going to be straightforward.

With seconds remaining in the opener, Johnson caught Matthew with a short check hook that caused Matthew's legs to dip. Johnson's reach and movement were making him hard to hit and he racked up points by pumping out a pole-like jab with long right hands shooting in behind them.

Matthew bled from the nose in the third. He was ponderous and disorganised.

'Calm down, steady yourself,' instructed Solomon from the corner.

But the champion was looking for one big shot. Johnson was reading his every charge.

'Forget about the right hand, feint it and throw the left hook,' urged Solomon.

Johnson led and Matthew followed. The challenger boxed with increasing confidence in the fifth, dropping his hands, moving and then planting his feet to fight when he needed to.

Towards the end of the sixth, Matthew swiped erratically with a left hook and a back-pedalling Johnson crossed his feet and stumbled back and to the floor. Referee Tony Perez picked up the count. It had only been a slip, and Johnson tried to tell the official as much.

By the eighth, Matthew started to get his jab working with improved timing and accuracy. He was also investing more energy in working the challenger's body to try and hinder his movement.

Johnson's corner – Del Williams and Dundee – urged him to back the champion up, but Johnson was slowing. His swift movement from the earlier rounds was deserting him and his feet were heavy.

The crowd was engrossed. Johnson had run up a significant lead, but this is what they'd paid to see, Matthew claw his way back to life as he always did.

Johnson's decision to stand and trade was suicidal at worst, regretful at best, but he was too tired to move any more. He looked almost out of gas by the end of the tenth. Dundee again instructed him to back Matthew up but the challenger was exhausted and the game was nearly up.

A right hand-left hook had Johnson locked in reverse as round 11 opened and Matthew ploughed in with a flurry of shots before one final right dropped Johnson. The challenger made it back to his feet but Matthew hacked away with both hands. As Johnson tried to hang grimly on, Matthew couldn't be stopped. His last shot, a stiff left, caused Johnson to crumple beneath the bottom rope. When the man from Columbus, Ohio, stood, referee Perez waved it off. Johnson protested, but Perez was only looking after the fallen challenger's well-being.

Matthew hadn't unified but he had made his sixth championship defence and he'd done what he'd made a habit of doing. 'As always, Saad Muhammad comes back,' he smiled.

He thanked Steve Traitz again for letting him use the Montgomery County Boys Club to train in and admitted he'd taken time to loosen up.

'I kept the pressure on,' he said. 'I knew that he'd get tired. A man can't keep boxing. He's no Muhammad Ali.'

He dedicated the win to the 19 children who were missing or who had been killed in Atlanta – with a serial killer on the loose – and wore a green ribbon on his trunks in tribute to them.

Then he picked up with his pre-fight talk.

'I want to announce to the world and to the public that I think I'm ready to retire,' he continued. 'There's no money there [for the unification fight]. If they can hurry up and unify the title within one year then I'll stay there, but I'm getting ready to retire. That's the main reason I'm in boxing, to unify the titles. That's it.'

Years later, Matthew gave Johnson props for his spirited challenge. 'Vonzell Johnson was very tall and it was hard to throw punches up at him but Joe Frazier used to tell me that if you kill the body, the head will fall,' Matthew recollected. 'I kept trying to kill the body but I was always just inches away from being in danger, so I kept throwing one punch, just one punch. Then Sam Solomon told me to put my punches together and that's what finally caught him, combinations. If I just kept throwing right hands it would never have happened. He would have gotten hurt but it wasn't enough.'

'I knew that I could outbox him,' said Johnson, some three decades on. 'I'd studied him. I knew he was durable and if I'd had six to eight weeks to train, I'd have beaten him. It was a 15-round fight back then, and you just can't get in shape for 15 rounds in three weeks. I was hoping to get lucky and get him out of there in nine or ten rounds, but Matthew was just so durable it was kinda hard to do. He had good power in both hands. It was a matter of outmanoeuvring him and outsmarting him because he had power. He was the strongest and most durable I fought. He got stronger as the fight went on, that was his forte.'

Despite Matthew again battling back with another display of brinkmanship, not all of the media was favourable and Bill Lyon pointed out in the *Philadelphia Inquirer* that Matthew's corner was brimming with unnecessary team members who were doing little for their money. Lyon looked at them as Johnson had the upper hand and wrote that the corner was 'stuffed with a retinue that is beginning to rival Muhammad Ali's entourage, all those hangers-on in their red warm-up suits began to squirm anxiously. They had the same uneasy feeling the blackjack players down below [in the casino] get when the dealer gives him an ace face up.'

Matthew's vulnerability also illustrated that 'Miracle' Matthew could be running out of miracles, with rivals lining up to fight him next.

'He was lucky it wasn't me in there,' Eddie told one ringside writer, and although Dwight Braxton was only 12-1-1, he thought he was ready and believed Eddie was a stiffer test. Matthew would just be target practice.

'I would love to fight Mustafa,' Braxton reasoned. 'I don't get no pleasure out of beating a man senseless. Saad's got the perfect style for me. He will get his head knocked off. I will beat him unmercifully. If he stands in front of me, I'll break his jaw. I'll break him up. He's a slow starter.'

Matthew didn't care. He said about $20m would get his attention, knowing that was a pipedream. He was losing interest. He couldn't find his family. He couldn't get unification fights. Smith was gone, and so were the millions.

'I'm thinking about retiring because I fight too hard,' he said.

And if he needed a reminder about how serious his day job was, it came on the Saad–Johnson undercard when Youngstown lightweight Fred Bowman was stopped by Isidro Perez and fell into a coma. Bowman died a year later, having never woken up.

But Matthew was not just thinking about the short-term risks. He knew about the long-term jeopardy of carrying on too long and the old punch-drunk stereotypes conjured by boxing.

'Look at me. I can walk okay, I can talk okay, I can think okay,' he said. 'I don't want to be one of those guys who go "uhhh" when you talk to them.'

CHAPTER 13

I KNEW I WAS GOING TO FIND THEM

IT WAS love at first sight. A couple of weeks before the win over Lottie Mwale, Matthew Saad Muhammad and Mustafa Ameen were outside the MAPS gym when two girls pulled up to use the facilities.

One was Jeanita, Muhammad Ali's *au pair*, and she was with a friend, Michelle LeViege, who was from Anchorage, Alaska. They lived about 20 minutes from the gym.

'Matthew had the world at his feet and he was immediately smitten,' said Mustafa Ameen, of the day his friend set eyes on his future wife, Michelle. 'When Cupid hit him with Michelle, it was one of those once-in-a-lifetime things – like you see in the movies – where a guy is just smitten. Michelle was young, beautiful, very good looking, really something. [She was] twenty-something, Miss Black World, she has a wonderful personality, I can't deny.'

'His smile. That was what made me go out with him,' Michelle remembered some 40 years on about their first meeting. 'The person that introduced me to him said, "I want you to meet this guy" and I said, "I don't want to meet no boxer; he's going to be ugly and stinky!"'

Michelle didn't follow boxing. She supported the Lakers and preferred watching figure skating and gymnastics. But she went to the gym, and then she saw Matthew.

'He's handsome,' she thought. 'And he was just so sweet, and he said, "I'd like to take you to dinner and get to know you ..." And then the smile. And you know they say one nibble and you're hooked?

That was it. I kind of knew he liked me but I was smitten, too, and I was mad because I didn't want to be.'

After only a day or two, she came round to see Matthew at his place.

'He said nothing happened,' Ameen added. 'I chewed him out; he could depend on me to be honest with him. We were maybe eight or nine days from the fight and we came from an era where the fighters strongly believed in no sex before the fight, so it was the camp's job to keep the fighter from temptation. Matthew was single at the time. He had a bunch of children and everywhere we went there was opportunity, but this was the first time he was just smitten.'

It wasn't long before Matthew was confiding in friends saying he wanted to get engaged to and marry Michelle.

'Pump the brakes,' said one voice in the camp.

'Not so fast. She's a gold-digger like the rest of them,' said another.

But Matthew was in love, and so was Michelle.

The team went up to Alaska and stayed at the home of her parents, Sam and Catherine.

'I liked Michelle,' said Tony Green. 'Michelle had good intentions – but Matthew had a lot of girlfriends, man.'

Matthew took Paul Trace with him on one visit to Anchorage. There was a parade for Matthew and Trace did some portraits of the couple. But, on the flight, the showman in Matthew surfaced.

'Can you talk to the pilot and see if you can get some pictures of me in the cockpit?' Matthew asked.

'No problem.'

Trace took shots of Matthew. Then, with Matthew back in his seat, Matthew leaned over and said, 'Get the stewardess to announce I'm on the plane, that the light-heavyweight champ is on board.'

'No problem.'

'He was playful in certain ways like Ali,' smiled Trace. 'The only difference was Ali would have done it all himself!'

Matthew and Michelle got engaged in December of 1980. She was due to go to Europe on a seven-week singing tour but Matthew didn't want her to leave.

'It was goofy,' Michelle smiled at the memory.

'We were in the car and he was like, "Are you going to marry me?" And he gave me the ring and I said "Yeah, okay."'

* * *

Michael Spinks knocked out Marvin Johnson with a picture-perfect fourth-round left uppercut in late March. Johnson had an overnight stay in hospital where he was treated for concussion.

Straight afterwards, Spinks and Matthew quarrelled alongside ABC's Howard Cosell. Spinks challenged Matthew, who accepted. Matthew told Michael his name was 'Stinks'; Michael told Matthew he was 'Sad Muhammad'.

The professional animosity was clearly there with Spinks, who told reporters he'd beaten Matthew up in a 1977 sparring session.

'I jumped on Saad Muhammad,' he claimed. 'Had him bleeding so bad they almost had to stop the workout.'

Spinks wanted either Muhammad, but it seemed like a fight with Matthew was easier to make because the WBC rated Spinks as their No. 1 contender and wanted the contest to happen before November.

A day after Spinks stopped Johnson, it was announced that Matthew would fight Murray Sutherland, the WBC's No. 4-ranked contender, in late April.

Sutherland was a Scotsman who had emigrated to Canada. He'd been a kickboxer, learned his trade on Toughman circuits and was a handful, always in shape and with a passion for fighting. Boxing out of Bay City, Michigan, Sutherland had given Spinks a hard fight in May the previous year before dropping a ten-round decision.

Joking about the light-heavyweight landscape, Murray said he might change his name to McMuhammad.

Matthew said his incessant schedule was what he needed and he wanted to keep busy as he closed on Bob Foster's light-heavyweight record of 14 championship defences. Without a fight lined up, there was a tendency to get bored, distracted and lazy.

As Saad finalised his preparations for Sutherland at Resorts in Atlantic City, he was roped into a publicity shot with the location's resident 600lbs tiger, Bombay.

Matthew had Topper at home, but Bombay was a different proposition entirely.

'Matthew and Topper were close,' Michelle said. 'That dog was all about Matthew. He walked Topper and I hated that dog because he didn't like me. Topper was very much about his daddy and he had little interest in anyone else.'

Matthew just hoped Bombay wasn't as interested in him.

Matthew didn't want to do the picture but Bilal Muhammad and Mustafa Ameen coaxed him into it and the champion perched nervously on the animal's back, gingerly raising a fist, barely cracking a smile for a picture that appeared in the next day's papers.

'He was scared shitless,' laughed Paul Trace, who snapped away. 'You could see him sweating.'

Sutherland was a good fighter, but more were discussing Matthew fighting Spinks. The talk of retirement had set a clock ticking in the media and they wanted the Saad Muhammad–Spinks super-fight.

'The people handling Michael Spinks are not going about it the right way,' said Murad Muhammad. 'We are waiting to fight Michael Spinks. We'll sign it today.'

'I get the impression Saad doesn't want to fight Michael,' countered Butch Lewis, Spinks's charismatic and outspoken promoter.

Bilal was getting agitated and publicly lashed out at Lewis. 'One thing we want to do is establish Matthew as one of the greatest light-heavyweights in boxing history,' said Bilal. 'Trying to duck a guy like Spinks wouldn't show everyone what a true champion is. We welcome the fight but not on his conditions. Butch Lewis is a nice guy, trying to do his best for his fighter. But tell him to stay in his own league.'

Matthew simply stated that if the money was right, he was in.

But things were getting busy for Matthew away from boxing. He talked about going back to school. He'd never graduated, and he didn't want his kids to have a dad who didn't have a diploma.

Matthew had a lawyer, Tim Crawford, and his wife Dorsena was going to teach him to read well and even get a General Educational Diploma GED. 'Of course, there were people in the camp who said, "You don't need that now. You're making money,"' Michelle remembered. 'But the sense of accomplishment he would have had from that, I can't imagine.'

Still, the *Rocky* trial had given Matthew a taste for Hollywood, and a story came out that he had a record to release, called *Climbing to the Top*.

'Matthew was a great dancer, he liked to fashion himself as a singer but he was not a great singer,' said Michelle.

Meanwhile, he was about to get started on a book with biographer Richard Durham, who had ghosted *The Greatest* for Muhammad Ali. Everyone seemed certain that it would wind up as a motion picture, with Matthew's story hitting the big screen.

'The best scripts are those that come from real life,' Matthew said.

* * *

In early April 1981, almost out of nowhere, Matthew got a call informing him that his family had been found. Both happy and nervous, he raced home to tell Michelle that his lawyer, Crawford, had completed background checks. The search was over.

On 19 April, he released a statement, convinced that he had found them.

Of course, there were sceptics. Who wouldn't want to be related to the guy making hundreds of thousands of dollars, with the celebrity friends, the big house with the disco and the other trappings of fame, not forgetting the $10,000 bounty on offer?

But a friend from his former family named Ann Young had seen the article in *Jet* and called Matthew's attorney to say she could put Matthew in touch with his family.

Matthew felt that hiring a private investigator, who had cost a lot of money, had paid off.

'I would just like to know and that's it,' he said, believing he was on the cusp of having the answers he had waited a lifetime for. 'I would just like to see them and then I would be happy.'

More information concerning his family would be detailed in the upcoming book, but Matthew was certain he had his family and with that, finally, he knew his identity. Headlines read 'Muhammad's long-lost father found' and 'Saad Muhammad's search for his family completed'.

His mother Helen, however, had died in 1966, and no one knew where his father was. But he was getting answers. He might have been Matthew Saad Muhammad, no longer Matthew Franklin, but his real name was Maxwell Antonio Loach.

Years later, he thought he might have got the name 'Matthew' as he'd tried to tell the nuns his name and couldn't manage any more than just, 'Ma ... Ma ....' because of the speech impediment.

He had been born on 5 August 1954, according to his birth certificate, which Crawford had been able to locate – not too far away from the nuns' guess of 16 June.

'When I met the ones I'm convinced are my step-brothers and step-sisters, I knew right away because everything they said I remembered quite well,' Matthew told the media. 'I interviewed them individually, and it all fits together.'

His family had told him that they'd reached a point where they could no longer care for everyone, so his mother told his brother Rodney to take him out and turn him loose.

'If you don't obey,' the boy was told, 'it will be you.'

Matthew could always remember being left, chasing Rodney, running as hard as he could for as long as he could.

'It's deep, man,' he said. 'The story made me cry. It shocked me. I'm still stunned.'

Rodney Loach was older, and he'd met Matthew several weeks before Team Saad had gone public with the story.

'If he was an actor, he's a great one,' Matthew said. 'He looked really scared. But he had the heart to admit to doing this thing to me. And when I'm asked how the hell I can accept these people after all the years, I have to say that my religion has taught me how to forgive.'

Matthew also thought about the positive side of his upbringing, and how he'd been blessed to have the nuns who cared for him, the Santos family to look after him and the people he subsequently met who had imprinted upon him.

'Now, at last, I don't have to search anymore,' Matthew said.

Nigel Collins always felt Matthew had genuinely wanted answers. 'He had this backstory everyone was talking about, the kid that nobody knew who he really was,' said Nigel. 'I don't think he would do anything to get publicity. Not many fighters did that shit back then, really.'

'It was about a year before someone came forward,' remembered Ameen. 'We finally got a hit through our attorney and we had him vet and investigate and they were able to verify and authenticate that they found Matthew's family. We had a show called *Good Morning America* and they televised it [the reunion] live because we'd not met them. The attorney was the buffer, so once it became authentic *Good Morning America* televised the first reunion of the brothers and sisters. They all had different fathers, but they had the same mother and the way the story was always told was his older brother abandoned him, he was older and faster and he ran and Matthew couldn't keep up. Well, we met that brother, Rodney.'

With so much going on, and the constant chatter about a Spinks fight, the champion could have been excused for paying scant attention to the Resorts bill he was headlining on 25 April against Sutherland. Asked whether Matthew's attention was elsewhere, Sutherland said, 'I hope so.'

Sutherland's trainer Bob Every doubled down on that. 'Saad doesn't want to fight anymore. He's been a great champion but you can't be champion forever. He's only fighting because his people want him to fight. He has too many other things he wants to do.'

They studied Matthew intricately, watching fight after fight on tape. Matthew, on the other hand, said he'd hardly seen Sutherland at all.

Matthew was making $275,000, not unification money but still extraordinary 175lbs money, and a full crowd of 1,500 was ready to witness another roller coaster.

Sutherland, wearing tartan shorts, wasn't overawed in the opening round. He was patient, waited for openings and threw punches with precision. With around 30 seconds left in the round, Sutherland pierced Matthew's guard with a right uppercut. Blood dripped from Matthew's bottom lip.

'I'll be truthful with you, the first round I threw a couple of jabs and a right hand; I hit him with all three punches,' Sutherland would later recall. 'Flush. Right in the face. And I said to myself, "I can't believe this guy is so easy to hit." I threw an uppercut and I hit him with it. Blood was spurting out of his lip. The whole lip was split wide open and I thought, "Holy shit. How the hell did I do that?"'

Sutherland was enjoying himself in the second round. He pinned Matthew on the ropes and poured on the pressure, taking only a few counters in return.

In commentary, Gil Clancy was concerned referee Paul Venti might stop it because of the injury.

Ritacco did his best with the cut but it needed stitches. It was split in half and both left and right parts dangled instead of meeting in the middle.

Sutherland was punching and moving smoothly but in the fifth Matthew began to close the distance. It became a contest of big swings.

Matthew finally found his stride in the sixth and Sutherland had to retreat or face being run over.

Murray's right glove had to be changed after round six because of a split, thought to be caused by Matthew's bottom row of teeth in the first round.

Saad bled from a cut above his right eye in the seventh but his size, strength and power was taking a toll. A wicked left hook-right hand and then a spiteful right hand-left hook landed in quick succession and caused Sutherland to crash to the mat for a mandatory count. Blood seeped from a wound above the Scotsman's left eye.

Sutherland absorbed another huge right hand that had him groggy as the bell sounded to give the challenger a brief reprieve.

'I was hoping they'd stop it [for the cut] because he was beating the shit out of me,' Sutherland would later say. He tried to hang with Matthew in the eighth and, early in the ninth, he added to Matthew's woes, slicing him open above his left eye. But Matthew pressed and caught Sutherland with a booming right. Sutherland's legs locked and he dropped, being pushed down by a straight left as he fell.

'It was an overhand right,' the challenger recalled. 'I can remember it vividly. He backed me up into my corner with a couple of jabs and then all I saw was his shoulder rotating and the next thing I knew, I was on my ass thinking, "How the hell did I get here?"'

Sutherland fell in an ungainly heap, somehow stood up, but referee Venti didn't allow him to continue. The challenger and his camp seethed, complaining vociferously that he could have gone on but commentators Clancy and Angelo Dundee thought the intervention was timely.

Matthew, holding an ice pack on his lip, was joined by Sutherland and Venti for post-fight interviews in the ring for CBS. Sutherland complained he could have gone on and he'd beaten the count. Venti claimed he had counted to ten and Sutherland was out.

Matthew thought Venti had done a good job. 'I think he [Sutherland] was hurt several times, I was definitely going to get him,' Matthew reckoned. 'I had him pretty hurt that second time he went down.'

'He was a warrior,' Sutherland, who made $35,000 for his efforts, conceded, decades removed from the fight. 'He was like one of those Viking guys. It didn't matter what you hit him with, he kept coming. You could hit him with a baseball bat and he'd keep coming. I hit him with some right hands that I've hit people with before and they've gone to sleep. But he'd just look right back at you and walk at you with that mummy walk he used to do.

'He was pretty busted up. He had to have stitches all over his face. In fact, when they interviewed both of us in the ring after the fight, we were standing side by side and his face looked like a butcher's shop. He had a big split on his bottom lip, he was cut over both eyes, but boy could he hit. Him and Michael Spinks were the two biggest punchers I faced.'

Paul Trace took no pleasure in seeing his friend so beaten up. 'That was hard to see,' admitted the photographer. 'I got close photographs of that during the fight, in the corner, and it was painful for me to look at. You know if you get a papercut on your lip from licking an envelope how painful it was.'

The gap in Matthew's bottom lip took five stitches to close and needed plastic surgery. He had to give the press conference a miss to get it fixed up.

'Matthew's a warrior,' said Spinks, who'd been monitoring the fight closely from a ringside seat. 'That's what I like about him. He'll go down fighting. You can hit him all you want, but to beat him you'll have to knock him out.'

Matthew simply said that what happened was what always happened. He fell behind, took on plenty of damage and then roared back.

Both fighters went to the Atlantic City Medical Center to get stitched up. They weren't the only ones there from the bill. Matthew's sparring partner Tony Green, who fought an eight-round draw on the undercard, was also in for observation.

'They put us in the same emergency room, bed to bed,' Green said, smiling at the recollection. 'Him with his lip and me with bruised ribs and a damaged ear.'

* * *

As Matthew's entourage grew, friends and relatives would come to the fights.

Photographer Paul Trace brought his young son, Doug, to the Sutherland battle when he was about 11 or 12.

'My dad got that shot, a series of three shots where Matthew's winding up and he then hits Murray, Murray goes flying and you see the blood flying like a burst tomato about seven rows back,' Doug could later recall.

It hadn't been a fight for the faint-hearted. Mustafa Ameen took his mother, her first and last ringside experience. Ameen always felt the punches Matthew took and described a Saad Muhammad fight experience as 'horrible' as a friend.

'It's almost as if I was getting hit,' Ameen explained. 'You just cringe, and my beloved mother ... I ended up bringing her to her very first fight and my mother talked about it to the end of her life, having blood on all her clothes and when she got the blood on her light-coloured dress that day, she wanted nothing to do with it.'

But Matthew had done it again. He was behind on the scorecards, had his lip ripped open, was cut above his eyes and still won.

'At the end, you just breathe a sigh of relief and thanks,' Ameen said of those post-fight emotions.

'How much longer these spectacular resurrections can continue is anybody's guess,' wrote Nigel Collins at the time. 'Certainly not indefinitely.'

But Matthew was being told other things by loud voices within his team. Bilal and Sam Solomon insisted that Matthew was not taking much damage, certainly not like he had in his old NABF title years.

'He's not as strong physically,' said Bilal. 'But he is stronger mentally. I think his defence is improving a whole lot.'

Solomon even snapped at one writer, 'He's not taking punches. He's blocking them with his hands, with his arms. People who refuse to acknowledge that are being fooled. They're seeing something that isn't there. He's catching jabs in the palms of his hands, in the shoulder. He's rolling with punches or slipping them. He's not being given credit for those things.'

The hospital visits, the stitches, the cuts and his depleted energy levels after the wars said otherwise, and there were concerns Matthew was in decline as a fighter. The theories were that the wars were starting to catch up with him. He constantly talked about retirement.

Five days after the Sutherland fight, Matthew and attorney Melvin Bell appeared on *Good Morning America*. More details emerged about his family as interviewer David Hartman asked Matthew questions.

Matthew's sister, Andrea, recognised him instantly when watching one of his fights on TV. She called another sister, Desiree, who agreed. The women, along with two further sisters Tondylea and Frances and, of course, Rodney were on the show.

The siblings all told Matthew that they'd missed him, that they loved him and that they knew they would all be reunited one day.

'I knew I was going to find them,' Mathew said. 'I knew if I set my mind to it, I could do it.'

'It feels unreal,' Tondylea said. 'We're overjoyed with the idea of finding him. He definitely looks like us – his smile, his eyes.'

Michelle was by Matthew's side as he gathered his family around him for a photograph.

'Different people have told different stories, but I was there and it wasn't an aunt [who had asked Rodney to lose him],' Michelle recalled. 'Matthew even changed the story, [but] it wasn't an aunt that gave him away. It was his mother. That's a hard pill to swallow, because when you look at nature, a momma dog looks after her puppies until they can take care of themselves. You look at other animals in nature, they don't just abandon their young, but clearly there was something going on emotionally and mentally that would make someone do that. The father was always unknown. No one seemed to know who his father was or had contact with him and his mother had died so we are left to wonder. Was there alcoholism? Was there abuse? All we can really do is speculate because no one really knew.'

Instead of wondering whether his father was Sugar Ray Robinson, he now wondered whether his dad had abused his mother, or worse, if she couldn't bring herself to face him. Maybe it was just down to simple economics, and not being able to afford another mouth to feed.

'There had to be something deeper than something on the surface,' Michelle explained. 'I'm a mother. I can't imagine leaving my child on a parkway. Cars are flying by, so you don't know if the child is dead or alive. Something snapped. Something wasn't right. It's not like you put him in a basket, put him on the Nile River and the Princess of Egypt happened to see him and adopted him.'

It had caused suffering for both boys, Matthew for being abandoned and Rodney for having to do it.

'How does he live with that?' Michelle wondered. 'That had to be traumatic for him. Am I next?'

* * *

Murad Muhammad was planning for Matthew to have two more fights before meeting Spinks and he hadn't given up on Eddie Mustafa Muhammad.

Eddie was tired of waiting for the unification unicorn, however, and signed to fight heavyweight contender Renaldo Snipes on 17 May in Atlantic City. Eddie realised the big money, with Harold Smith out of the picture, meant going up in weight. He also found worthy challengers hard to come by because they all fancied their chances against Matthew.

'Everyone thinks they can beat him [Matthew],' Eddie explained. 'He looks like he can be beaten.'

Eddie lost a wide decision to Snipes in a turgid bout, and faced ridicule from Spinks who taunted him saying, 'The Champ is a chump.'

Then, on 31 May, the career of Mike Rossman was all but ended by Dwight Braxton. 'The Camden Buzzsaw' swarmed Rossman, making 'The Jewish Bomber's' height redundant and nailing him in the seventh round. They had met to decide who would challenge Matthew later in the year.

Of the size discrepancy between the 5ft 5in Braxton and the bigger fighters in the division, one reporter said Dwight 'turned big light-heavyweights into small light-heavyweights and tore them to pieces'.

The Rossman thrashing meant one of Matthew's most lucrative options was gone, and Rossman had actually deputised for Matthew. It was supposed to have been Matthew in there with Braxton on 4 June, but the lip had taken time to heal so Rossman stepped in.

The break suited Matthew. He'd made seven defences of his title in two years.

'My doctor says I need three months off,' said the weary champion. 'My body – after two title defences in 56 days – is crying out for a rest.'

Bilal echoed those sentiments. Matthew needed to organise his personal affairs and to reassess the last 18 months. Bilal also hired the New York firm Rogers and Cowan to package Matthew's story and image so he could join the likes of Leonard and Duran as a closed-circuit draw rather than just being a must-see TV attraction.

Braxton didn't care about that stuff. He was on his own mission and just wanted to beat people up.

'They wanted me to wait around until September, but I have to make a living,' he said, explaining his choice to annihilate Rossman. 'Everyone else has been beaten up. I'm the only fresh kid out there.'

There was truth to that. Everyone knew about Matthew's wars, Yaqui Lopez had been in them for years, Eddie had been boxing at a high level for almost a decade, Scott had been in some hard brawls, as had Marvin Johnson. Rossman was done, Galindez was gone, Conteh had retired. Qawi was 15-1-1 and Spinks was 17-0. Many of the others had boxed 30, 40, even 50 times, and it was not just the volume of fights, but the incessant schedule and how brutal many of them were.

Matthew's time off included a wedding and a honeymoon. Michelle had been meant to be going to college in Los Angeles when they'd met, but she was living with Matthew in Philadelphia. One day her father, Sam, called and asked them where their relationship was going.

'Alright you two, what are you doing?' Sam started.

'Let me speak to Matthew.'

Matthew took the phone and could barely get a greeting out when Sam interupted.

'You're not going to shack up with my daughter. Either she's going back to California or going back to school. I just want to know; you're engaged but when are you going to get married?'

Matthew came off the phone and the couple discussed their future.

'What's today?' he asked.

'July 2nd,' Michelle replied.

'We're getting married August 2nd.'

But the boxing world didn't stop turning. Eddie Mustafa Muhammad had dropped back down to light-heavyweight in an ill-advised clash with Michael Spinks, who the WBA made him fight within 60 days of facing Snipes.

Mustafa Muhammad had to trim off more than 25lbs from the heavyweight experiment against Snipes to defend his title against Spinks just eight weeks later. Eddie came in overweight and had to shed a pound hours before the first bell.

Matthew provided moral support as Eddie put on a sweatsuit and jumped rope until the weight came off.

Spinks ended up battering an eye shut and knocking Eddie down and almost out during their 18 July fight in Las Vegas. Matthew had been yelling support for Eddie, and even afterwards interrupted the Spinks press conference to say the wrong guy had won.

'I was talking,' Spinks shot back. And then Spinks and Matthew erupted into another argument.

Asked if he was going to unify against Matthew, Spinks smirked, 'If he'll sign.' Eddie said Spinks was only borrowing the title and he'd get it back.

On 31 July, Murad announced Matthew would face Jerry Martin later in the year. On Sunday, 2 August, at Abington Country Club in Jenkintown, Matthew married Michelle.

At short notice, Michelle had found a sample dress off the rack and Matthew called his friend, Philadelphia Eagles quarterback Ron Jaworski, to ask if they could use his venue.

Boxing guests included Jeff Chandler, middleweight contender Frank 'The Animal' Fletcher and 'KO' Becky O'Neil.

The service included three verses of the Koran and a gala reception.

'We were so goofy,' Michelle laughed, looking back. 'We were giggling at our wedding ceremony. We were supposed to be all serious but the air conditioning had gone off in the country club and I've got this stupid veil on because my mother wanted me to wear it. We had a lot of laughs.'

Eddie Mustafa was also there. He lined up for the throwing of the bride's garter but was beaten to the punch. 'I guess you could say I'm on a losing streak,' he sighed.

Ring magazine said, 'The marriage of England's Prince Charles to Lady Diana was not the only royal nuptial of the summer' and the couple went on honeymoon to Carmel in California and a cruise to Hawaii.

Nigel Collins was at the wedding and remembered Michelle as, 'a beautiful woman. She was very nice and I was miffed when I got there and found out it was a Muslim wedding and there was no alcohol! It's funny how I remember that. It was top drawer at some country club with a lot of money spent.'

* * *

While much was written about Matthew's proposed fights with Eddie Mustafa and Michael Spinks, and also about finding his family, plenty of journalists opted to cover the size of his entourage. Collins had known Matthew since his early professional days with Nick Belfiore and Frank Gelb and he had visited Matthew in his three-bedroom suite on the top floor of Resorts overlooking the Atlantic Ocean as he tapered training for Martin.

Of the people Collins namechecked, there was Mustafa Ameen, 'his personal secretary and buffer' and Yuseh Shah, 'a large shaven-skulled man, whose task it is to push a cart loaded with boxing equipment to the gym and back once a day. The rest of his time is spent watching television.'

Bilal was 'away on business' when Nigel visited, but also present were sparring partners Tony Green and Kenny Ringo, photographer Paul Trace, trainer Sam Solomon and assistants Salim El-Amin and Milt Bailey.

Then there was his personal chef, Lana Shabazz, who'd had the same role for Muhammad Ali. But Resorts wouldn't let her use the kitchen so her job was to select Matthew's meals from the room service menus.

'I am just enjoying the comforts a champion is supposed to have,' Matthew told Collins. 'That's all. I had to sacrifice a lot of things to get where I am and now I'm not going to let myself go.'

There was a problem, though. He had a heavyweight entourage on light-heavyweight's wages, and not Harold Smith wages, either.

'Matthew had two teams. One was his permanent team of which there were only seven or eight guys. I was one of them,' Trace explained. 'Then, during a fight, that team grew to like 22 people.'

Lawyers, friends, a masseuse, more sparring partners, security and others joined the circus.

Then there was bombastic promoter Murad Muhammad, who saw the group expanding, which was something he'd seen before.

'Muhammad Ali had a reason for what he did,' Murad said, discussing entourages. 'When Bundini Brown used to say, "Fight for the little people," Ali was doing it for the little people. That's what he does. And the reason Ray Robinson started all this, with his entourage … those people [in his entourage] would have never been out of this country if it wasn't for him. These people from the inner city would not be able to travel if it wasn't for their expenses that they could write off against their taxes. That's what the entourage were … we don't call them hangers-on. A friend in need is a friend indeed. Most athletes in the boxing world didn't go to school to learn to invest their money, and so you don't have people who know how to invest their money, they lose it.'

But Collins had concerns. He'd seen Matthew before anyone else was around. Now he witnessed a swollen camp with too few making any real contribution.

'Who are these fucking guys?' he thought, on one visit to the Traitz gym at the Montgomery County Boys Club.

At the back of the gym was a dormitory and a rec room. Collins went in there and introduced himself to one of the team. 'There was this guy sitting on the couch and I said, "I'm Nigel Collins, what do you do?" And he said, "I'm independently wealthy" and I thought, "This guy's an asshole." He didn't want to tell me who he was.'

It was one of the few times Collins ever quizzed Matthew about his spending habits.

'I asked him why he needed all these people,' Collins recalled. 'Everybody was on the payroll, 13 or more people. I said, "It's crazy"

and he [Matthew] said, "Well, I'm the champ now. I deserve it."
What are you going to say after that?'

Matthew and his team were headed back to Ali's old camp in
Deer Lake but the entourage, although huge, was changing, and there
was a new face in camp. Rodney, the brother who had abandoned
Matthew all those years ago on the streets of Philadelphia, was now
part of the team.

CHAPTER 14

BURDEN AND GUILT

BEFORE MATTHEW married Michelle, another union was dissolved when Sam Solomon left the camp following a dispute. While Solomon claimed it was about money, Bilal denied that.

Coach and fighter had been together for two years and for six of Matthew's seven title defences. 'He didn't do too bad with me,' Solomon contended. Bilal had begun to think that Matthew had been taking too much punishment, after all, and Angelo Dundee was in the frame to take over.

'Bilal seemed to think I was not worth ten per cent off the top of the money,' Solomon argued. 'I thought I was.'

Solomon was being asked to take five per cent, and targeted Bilal with his ire. Even though that showdown meeting between Solomon and Bilal was on 31 July, Sam was still a guest at the wedding and there were no ill-feelings between the fighter and the trainer.

Mustafa Ameen spoke with Sam about his problems.

'Sam reminded me that he had a verbal agreement that was standard and that are semi-standard to this day between trainers and fighters, so, at the end of the [Mwale] fight, Sam reminds me that he had been cut in for ten per cent,' Ameen recalled. 'But as fighters develop, once you leave a couple of hundred-thousand-dollar range, you're not going to give a trainer ten per cent out of an $8m purse That's $800,000 for training you for a few weeks. That's not common reality, but Sam said, "My cheque should be for $65,000," and he and Saad got into a dispute.' Sam prevailed.

In the long term, it didn't help Solomon's cause, so he was gone. Some in the team were also under fire, from the likes of columnist Stan Hochman in the *Philadelphia Daily News* who alleged that, 'Matthew Saad Muhammad has accomplished boxing's hat-trick. He is the most mismanaged, mis-promoted and now mis-trained championship fighter in America.'

The assertion in the press was that the champion was all-but training himself, and he didn't vehemently deny that when he said he knew his body and he only had to be reminded of certain things.

The focus for his upcoming opponent, Jerry 'The Bull' Martin, Matthew said, was 'slide and glide', two words that had never been used to describe his fighting style, ever. With camp back up in Deer Lake, Lana Shabazz returned to her old kitchen, where she had worked for Ali. Even she complained how swollen the camp had become, having to cook fresh food for 15 or 16 people at a time, so she was shopping almost daily. Matthew figured she could use help, so he assigned Rodney to go and help her with the groceries.

Matthew also formally announced his work with FOCUS at the Martin Luther King Arena in Philadelphia. There were two surprise guests. One was Jerry Martin, the other was Dwight Braxton, but they were more interested in the championship than the champ's programme to help disadvantaged youths.

FOCUS had been created with the help and stewardship of Matthew's brother, Joe Johnson, who was one of the Santos family's adopted boys and who had remained close to Matthew. Matthew had always been passionate about getting kids off the street, both out of harm's way and into employment.

Braxton, tired of waiting to fight Matthew, didn't care about waiting in any kind of holding pattern for a title opportunity. He wanted to force the fight and agreed to fight James Scott in Rahway. Scott had been greenlit to continue his career, but Matthew still refused to take his title to jail.

'There is no way I will go inside of those walls and fight him,' Matthew told reporters for the umpteenth time. 'Suppose he beats me? How can little kids look at him as a champ?'

Braxton didn't mind. Not only had he served hard time in Rahway, but he had been part of the prison boxing programme Scott ran. The two had sparred and Braxton even claimed Scott owed him $400 for sparring. The bad blood was real and Braxton was unfazed going back to Rahway. In fact, the pocket lunatic relished it.

Organisers gifted tickets to Saad Muhammad-Martin to high-rolling gamblers, and they were a substantial gift given Matthew, with 30 wins against three losses and two draws, unbeaten in 17 since that defeat to Eddie Mustafa four years earlier, was making $425,000 and Martin, who had 22 wins against just two losses, was due $60,000.

Only 812 seats were set up inside the venue's Opera House.

Martin's biggest win had come in Rahway, where he'd beaten up James Scott in an upset. He'd suffered an early career defeat in a ten-rounder and then Eddie stopped him in ten rounds in July 1980. Martin then scored three stoppage wins and was ranked No. 2 by the WBC.

Matthew remained impervious to critics who contended he was using up every conceivable miracle and that the well was running dry.

'It will never happen,' he said. 'Just when you think Matthew Saad Muhammad is gone, he's just begun. I will fight and die in the ring. Will another man do that? I am like fighters who came before. Fight hard, no matter what.'

Martin, originally from Antigua but fighting out of Philly, countered, 'I guarantee you, if I hit Saad like these other guys hit him, he's going out. If he doesn't go down, he's a miracle man. I've got power those other guys don't have.'

Martin was also going to target the body and figured Matthew would fold if he kept the pressure on. 'The Bull' did that from the first bell. In red silk shorts with white trim, he tried to overpower the champion, not just with his punches but by trapping Matthew on the ropes, attempting to cut off any possible exit routes by shoving Matthew back into the strands and firing away.

It was hard, again.

After two rounds, Matthew – wearing emerald shorts with a gold waistband – hadn't started but in the third he began to find some range and refused to back up. Then, in the closing moments of the round, Matthew landed a terrific right that had Martin in real trouble.

A third-round blitzing of Martin would have been an incredible result, but early in the fourth not only was Martin back in the fight, but Matthew was cut by the corner of his right eye. Matthew was too static and taking yet more punishment, but he had flashes of success towards the end of the fifth. The pace of a hard battle slowed in the next but Martin was a handful in the seventh, pumping in a series of debilitating bodyshots after repeatedly snaring Matthew on the ropes.

It was another violent brawl, but as the eighth ended, out of nowhere Matthew boxed with a freshness he hadn't had in round one. He dangled his left hand low and launched in rangy rights. Martin had no answer. 'The Bull' recklessly pursued to open the ninth, perhaps thinking one last push would put the champion away, but the round was Matthew's biggest win so far. He peppered the challenger with several enormous left hooks and a number of stiff right hands.

Martin was feeling the effects. He was heavy-legged and his punches looked lethargic, but he then connected with a bone-crunching right. Matthew was hanging on grimly as Martin found a third wind. But Martin might have punched himself out and was open to a terrific right that froze him like a statue. Matthew launched an onslaught through the final seconds of the round. It was a seesaw fight and another thriller.

Shortly after the 11th began, Matthew swiped with the left and missed but followed up with a right that hit. He drained Martin of almost everything. The challenger's arms dropped by his side and he swung like a drunken uncle at a wedding.

Lewis Freedman, for the *Inquirer*, wrote that Martin 'teetered and weaved forward like a skyscraper in the wind, about to fall'. Referee Larry Hazzard did not hesitate waving it off. Within seconds, Martin and his furious team crowded around the official to remonstrate.

There was prolonged booing from the fans. Even those with complimentary tickets felt short-changed, but they had witnessed a savage war.

'He was in very bad trouble,' Matthew told ABC's Howard Cosell. 'The man was hurt. He completely dropped his hands. I would have hit him with a couple more combinations and that would have been it.'

But Martin and trainer Leon Tabbs were having none of it. Martin knew he'd been in a fight. He also knew he'd been hurt, but he was certain he could have fought on.

Hazzard, who had noticed Martin getting weaker by the round, believed the challenger had suffered a 'concussive episode'. Commissioner Joe Walcott stood by Hazzard.

'His eyes went up,' Hazzard told Cosell. 'He was hurt. He was a sitting duck for Saad Muhammad. I was not going to take a chance of his getting seriously hurt or killed in that ring.'

As for Matthew, the 'slide and glide' certainly wasn't there. It was the same story on repeat. Another challenger had hit Matthew with everything they had and then, exhausted, they'd succumbed.

By the end, Matthew was narrowly ahead on two cards while a third scorecard couldn't separate them. As the champ again licked his wounds, he told members of his team he had no more than two fights left.

Michelle had seen the damage of the wars and she didn't like it. One day at home a couple of days after a fight, Matthew was urinating blood.

'But you knocked him out so easily, why do you let people beat you up?' she asked.

'It's like a pride thing,' he replied. 'I like to take their heart. I like to take everything they've got and then it's like night night. I have to get a little mad, as if to say, "Okay, that's what we're doing? Boom."'

Michelle was pleased Matthew was looking at life after boxing. He wanted to work with kids who had been dealt a bad hand in life, open a facility where they could train, box and learn trades, like carpentry. He wanted them to have breaks he didn't have. He just needed one big win, a unification fight and then he could retire.

'There is one big money fight on the horizon, and that's Stinks,' said Matthew, looking clearly beyond Dwight Braxton. 'Uh, Spinks,' he said, laughing at his own gag again.

Braxton had claimed his prison debt by ending the career of James Scott, on points in a ten-rounder. That remarkable chapter of boxing when it seemed like there could possibly be a world title fight in prison was over.

Spinks, meanwhile, had made the first defence of his title by toppling Vonzell Johnson in seven in Atlantic City in November. Matthew had jumped into the ring to hype their clash. In the crowd, Mustafa Ameen was becoming concerned by the continuous 'build to the next fight' mentality that had been in the camp. He'd read all the obituaries about Matthew's career and figured there was no use taking another fight for a few hundred grand when the million-plus for Spinks was there and interest was at an all-time high.

Others just thought the good times, the comebacks and the wars would last forever.

But nothing does and Rodney was gone again. During the Martin training camp at Deer Lake, Rodney told Ameen he had a routine medical appointment.

'We had a rule, that once you enter camp, you're in camp,' Ameen explained. 'You're not going to New York, or hanging out in Philly, you're in training camp and the champ used to say, "If I gotta lock my balls up and not be around women for four or five weeks, you're all going to lock your balls up. No sneaking out of camp."'

'Can I go to Philadelphia?' Rodney asked Ameen. 'I'll leave in the morning and be back by the evening.'

Ameen didn't consult Matthew. He didn't see the harm and told Rodney to go and get himself checked out without troubling Matthew.

'Where's Rodney?' Matthew asked that day.

'He had a doctor's appointment,' Mustafa replied.

'Man, you know the rules. What kind of camp are you running?'

And Rodney never came back. They never heard from him again.

'He was always looking away in Saad's presence,' Ameen recalled. 'When Saad would speak to him, he would never engage. You could see the burden and the guilt and he would not look at Saad.'

Michelle saw the same thing when the brothers were together. 'I sensed that,' she agreed. 'He was the only one when we first met them that didn't have his hand out. I think he was just trying to feel his way. When he did meet his siblings, it overwhelmed him because I think what he was hoping for was, "Oh my brother, you finally found us." But because he was a known figure, he felt that if it had been an emotional thing, they would have reached out to him. But they wanted things. Like, "Can you buy me a car? Can you pay my rent?" And Matthew kind of just recoiled. After a few meetings, Matthew changed his phone number and thought, "I don't want to do that."'

'Matthew was very suspicious about it,' said Paul Trace. 'That never turned out very well because, for lack of a better explanation, they were more interested in what they could get out of Matthew than a family reunion.'

It didn't seem as though there were many happy stories for Matthew. As far as the search for his family was concerned, the journey was the destination and his identity was in the search rather than his findings.

'It was not only anti-climactic, I think it was very disappointing and heart-breaking,' said Michelle. 'And I remember him saying, "I wish I'd never found them."'

CHAPTER 15

PEANUTS

MATTHEW SAAD Muhammad rode back into Atlantic City a hero. He'd trained in Florida and purchased a shiny new red Rolls-Royce, so he could arrive for his ninth title defence in style.

Matthew was unbeaten and unbeatable as the champion. He was looking at two more fights – Dwight Braxton and Michael Spinks – and then a long, happy retirement.

Before the Braxton fight had been agreed, Mustafa Ameen and Bilal Muhammad met with Butch Lewis in Atlantic City to crystallise the next steps. Ameen didn't want to challenge Bilal's authority, but he started to think Spinks should be next as the money was far greater.

'There's a $5m kitty for Michael to fight Matthew,' the always flamboyant Lewis started. 'We're going to chop it up right down the middle. Now is the time. We have to pull the trigger on this one.'

Ameen listened attentively, trying to read what Bilal was thinking, knowing Bilal preferred to let things percolate.

'Everything Butch says makes a whole lot of sense,' Mustafa offered, gauging his friend.

Bilal was silent. Then, looking at Lewis, he said, 'You know, Butch … One thing I can say about you and Mustafa … neither one of you know what the fuck you're talking about.'

The meeting was over. Lewis might not have been Don King or Bob Arum, but he wasn't far off, and in Spinks he had a world champion, a former Olympic gold medal winner whose brother had beaten Muhammad Ali for the world heavyweight title and who was drawing big numbers on network TV.

'Bilal's excellent idea was, "We'll fight Braxton for $350,000,"' Ameen lamented. 'We walked away and I never told Saad at the time what had happened.'

* * *

Despite speculation that Angelo Dundee would be hired in a consultancy role, Sam Solomon returned as Matthew's coach, but the fighter had an ambivalent attitude towards his training. Matthew was distracted as they prepared in Florida, setting up a base in Jacksonville. He was helping a friend raise money for a local gym.

Before the team headed south, Matthew and Braxton attended a press luncheon where Matthew spoke almost entirely about Spinks. Murad Muhammad, who'd promoted Matthew's last three fights, told Matthew to stay focused. Braxton agreed. 'Let's keep this talk on the business at hand,' said the challenger.

But Matthew's mind was elsewhere. As Nigel Collins wrote at the time, 'A million dollars in the bank and a lovely lady at home can take the edge off any competitor.'

'I want to make some more money quick and get out,' Matthew informed Collins.

Matthew was on the home stretch, as the *Philadelphia Inquirer* wrote with the Braxton fight imminent: 'Matthew Saad Muhammad is on the verge of accomplishing what the most ambitious of all American capitalists dream about – retirement as a millionaire before age 30.'

Something wasn't right, though. Matthew's outlook was changing by the day. Michelle was pregnant and she had started to show.

'Man, I don't want to fight this guy,' Matthew told Ameen.

'Let's not fight?' came his lieutenant's reply.

'What are we going to do? How can we get out of it?' Matthew asked.

'Let me call Bilal and say you've slipped. You've hurt your back and you can't train.'

'It's bad,' Ameen told Bilal, who called promoter Murad Muhammad to let him know.

Murad called the camp and talked Matthew round.

'Hey, brother. You can't do this, man,' Murad pleaded. 'My credibility is on the line. I'm not that entrenched with the networks and a cancellation is a big thing ...'

Murad went on. And on. And he prevailed.

'Okay, I'll fight,' Matthew conceded.

But his mind was wandering and photographer Paul Trace could see it. Michelle and her mother were also in Jacksonville for a while.

'I was running more miles per day than he was and I was twice his age,' said Trace. 'He became undisciplined, and he wasn't listening to Sam and basically Sam said, "No, you can't have your wife here in training camp or her mother" and they came anyway. They spent time together, going out shopping, eating ... Not with the team, and it was a very undisciplined training camp.'

Michelle felt like she wasn't wanted in the camp. 'They made it very clear,' she said.

But she was cooking for her husband because Lana Shabazz was in the Bahamas, working as the chef for Muhammad Ali as he prepared for one last calamity against Trevor Berbick.

After lunch, Ameen would get some time with Matthew. They'd either go for a drive or a walk and talk.

'Pull over,' Matthew insisted, as they went by a Rolls-Royce dealership. Matthew looked over the lot and made small talk with a salesperson. Eddie and Ali both had Rolls-Royce Corniches but Ameen thought Matthew was just trying to kill time. They got back into their car and returned to the hotel.

A little later in the day, Matthew approached Ameen. 'Hey Mustafa, I need you to go back down and take the guy $15,000.'

'What guy? Ameen replied.

'The guy with the car.'

'You've got to be kidding me,' Ameen said.

'No. I've got to have the car.'

Matthew was serious. Before tax and any kind of modification, the Rolls-Royce was listed at $179,000. Matthew didn't negotiate and the car was shipped to Philadelphia.

'He and I drive to AC in this brand-new red Corniche that looks like something out of a movie,' smiled Ameen, before he became more serious. 'But that shouldn't have been his mindset.'

Braxton's mindset was seek and destroy. He'd become increasingly impatient.

He thought he'd get his title shot in April, but Murray Sutherland got the call. Then it should have been in June, but the cut to Matthew's lip prevented that. Finally, on 19 December, he would get his chance.

Braxton was making around $50,000 against the champion's rumoured $400,000 and coming off big wins against Rossman and Scott. The fighter had found boxing late, using the sport to turn his life around from an armed robber who did about seven years in jail to a hungry contender. He was a short Joe Frazier type, and he'd gone to Frazier's Gym on Broad Street to hone his craft. He drew, won and lost in his first three fights, was unbeaten since and was a firework of menace and belligerence, both fearsome and fearless.

At 15-1-1, the 28-year-old Braxton was battle-tested if not battle-hardened like the veteran champion. While other opponents had talked up their chances, Braxton's prophecies were laced with malice and intent. 'He'll go no more than eight rounds with me,' said the diminutive, barrel-chested, trunk-necked challenger. 'He's going to be almost half-dead ... I'll bet his face will wear out before my arms do ... It will be like two lions fighting. That's what made him champion – not skill. I think it will make a good fight.'

'All I want to do is get Spinks and retire,' Matthew countered, somewhat meekly.

Michelle could see a clear difference between the two, and she feared for her man.

'I think his management was so greedy that they threw him to the wolves,' she said. 'He had no reason to fight Dwight. This man was coming straight up out of Rahway. He has nothing to lose. I was no boxing connoisseur, but the guy looked really scary to me and how do you balance, "Babe, I'm afraid for you" with "I believe you can knock out anybody." And I'm 20-something. Of course, in retrospect, you see things a whole lot clearer, but I didn't want him to take that fight and it had been such a short time [since the Jerry Martin bout less than three months earlier], his body hadn't had a chance to heal. He didn't need that fight.'

In late November, Matthew was due in New York with other division leaders Aaron Pryor, Larry Holmes, Marvin Hagler, Alexis Arguello, Wilfredo Gomez and Jeff Chandler to be presented with their *Ring* magazine belts, worth $6,000 apiece, by Seagram's. But Holmes was in LA, testifying in the MAPS case while Matthew was in camp in Florida, so he sent Bilal.

Chandler, incidentally, was carving out a fine career for himself as the WBA bantamweight champ. He and Matthew, from South Philly, were representing the city, and one wondered where Tyrone Everett would have figured. But Chandler, even though he was doing well, knew he was not where Matthew was. 'More people know me now,' said Chandler. 'But they haven't come in droves like they do for Matthew Saad Muhammad. It still takes time.'

But things were not as they seemed for Matthew, and they got even worse when news leaked that he was planning to leave Murad to join Don King.

Once Team Saad arrived in Atlantic City, the pre-fight business threatened to blow out of hand, putting an enormous strain on the promotion. When one radio station presenter told Murad he was 'The King of Atlantic City', Murad scoffed, 'I don't know if I like that word.'

Even during fight week, Murad admitted that the Braxton fight had come close to not happening, while Bilal informed journalists there had been contractual adjustments.

King had been beaten up and hospitalised in the Bahamas while he was there for Ali–Berbick but the Saad Muhammad–Spinks fight was the key in the camp's negotiations.

Butch Lewis had said publicly the fight would be easier to make if Matthew was under King's promotional umbrella but Murad had three options left. King brought the big money.

When asked whether Team Saad had threatened to withdraw from the Braxton fight if he didn't drop his three options, Murad wouldn't be drawn on specifics but conceded, 'I can't say that, but it looks that way.'

Bilal reckoned it was simply business and said they'd leave Murad if he couldn't match King's offer.

'Saad Muhammad decided to go with Don King in the middle of that contract,' Murad, who was only 30 years old at the time, revealed many years later. 'Don King ended up stealing him from me. I got a call. I went to see King and said, "Donald, you cannot take this fight away from me. What I'll do is winner-takes-all, or I'll fight you in the courtroom for tortious interference. It's winner takes all." So who did he [Saad] fight? Braxton. I called Saad's trainer [Sam Solomon] and said, "I'm making a helluva bet, but I've got to do it. I'm going to put Saad against Braxton." He said, "You're going to win." I said "Okay." I signed a deal.'

'With Murad, he was looking at Saad as all he had to work with,' reasoned Lewis. 'He probably felt he was out of business after that fight. He was always wanting to talk about ongoing stuff, about the future.'

Matthew had been his ticket and now Murad was pitching the unification bout to Spinks and his team as 60/40 in Matthew's favour but Lewis wasn't entertaining that. Regardless, Lewis and his WBA light-heavyweight champion headed to Atlantic City to cheer on Matthew, hoping for the best, hoping for the big-money unification fight, but fearing the worst.

'Somebody, eventually, is going to catch him,' Lewis warned. 'I'm worried this could be the guy.'

But the same thing had been said many times. The miracles would run out at some point; it's just Matthew seemed to have an inexhaustible supply of them. Braxton's strategy was to control the fight with his pressure and, if he saw Matthew coming back at him, not to give up as he claimed others had.

'I've had harder street fights,' Braxton bragged. 'I've been hit with sticks harder than he could ever think of punching me.'

But Matthew had taken his eye off the ball and on the morning of the fight, he was 7lbs over the weight. Adolph Ritacco told the media Matthew had not trained on Thursday and Friday and his weight had ballooned.

'He ate peanuts and I told him not to do that,' said assistant trainer Salim El-Amin of what had happened. 'I told him the peanuts put on weight. He had to lose weight and that really killed him before he got into the ring.'

Others in the camp pointed the finger at Solomon.

'In a scenario like that, who do you think takes responsibility? The trainer,' said Ameen. 'That's Sam's job. People began to put the blame on Sam.'

Bilal told Matthew to come in overweight, relinquish the championship and smash Braxton over the weight.

'Forfeit your title,' Bilal urged his client. 'Go in at 182, beat the hell out of him and we'll get a rematch for the championship.'

'My pride won't let me do it,' Matthew replied. 'I'd rather take off the seven pounds in one day.'

Exhausted, Matthew showed up 20 minutes late for the 8am weigh-in and was still 2lbs over. He took off the remaining poundage in a sauna, by running on the beach and up and down stairs, further depleting himself.

Seven hours before the fight, six days before Christmas, Matthew finally made weight.

Some were convinced the fight was going to be violent. Russell Peltz had already seen the pair spar in Philadelphia and heralded their exchanges as some of the city's iconic gym wars while *Boxing News* predicted the contest was 'expected to be as ferocious as any in modern ring history'.

But as the fighters started to find their stride in round two at the Playboy Casino in Atlantic City, Matthew was boxing neatly, striking first with the jab and catching Braxton rushing in.

El-Amin noticed, however, that Braxton didn't have the same respect for the champion that others had shown. 'He thought Matthew was ready to be taken. He wasn't even scared of him,' El-Amin said.

Solomon was aware of the threat, too. 'Your left is too low,' he shouted from the corner, but Matthew didn't listen. Instead, he nailed Braxton with a crisp right hand.

Braxton grinned, leering at the champ after taking a couple more. He lobbed a right hand over the top and everything changed. Matthew went into a shell and tried to cover. Sensing blood, Braxton flew in to finish the job, rocking Matthew's head back with right hooks and uppercuts that would have blown away lesser fighters.

Matthew carried his hands higher in the third, trying to outbox the stocky 'Buzzsaw'. In Matthew's corner, Eddie Mustafa implored him to stay focused and keep his gloves up.

Matthew was well in the fight after three, but had not won a round. Braxton hurt Matthew to the body in round four. ABC commentator Howard Cosell told his viewers it was business as usual, that they had seen it all before with Matthew losing early rounds. 'Yes, it's a war,' he said, as Braxton hammered away, causing blood to rain from Matthew's nose.

'He's tired, Saad. He's tired,' shouted El-Amin in Matthew's corner.

Matthew was trying to pop Braxton with jabs and rights in the next. Braxton tried to forge his way in, stepping in behind jabs to the body and head. Matthew's low left again invited Braxton to bowl over a vicious right.

'Hands up! Hands up!' yelled Eddie Mustafa on repeat.

The fifth had not been bad for Matthew but the sixth was a wide Braxton round. He was winning the fight on the inside and winning the battle of the jab.

Matthew looked shell-shocked between rounds, while Braxton grinned maniacally in his corner but the Matthew die-hards had seen this before and thought their man was due to get started in the next round or two, making the challenger pay for his insolence.

Solomon wasn't so passive any longer.

After Matthew trudged back to his stool, Solomon warned him, 'You're blowing the title, man.'

Cosell saw Bilal shaking his head.

'At times, the punishment Saad was taking was almost sickening to watch,' wrote *Boxing News*.

Braxton thudded more brutal looping right hands over Matthew's low jab, then jarred the champion's head back with a shocking uppercut. He kept the pressure on, working the body. Matthew's battered nose pumped blood round after round, and he smeared it across his face as he tried to wipe his airway clear. Matthew was slowing down, trying to cover on the ropes, and Braxton pounded away with volleys of unforgiving punches.

'You're four rounds down, you've got to pull these rounds out,' Bilal told his client before the tenth.

Matthew's weight-drained legs saw him standing in front of Braxton, trying to punch with him but getting dominated bar a brief rally that only caused Braxton to fight back even harder. In doing so, the 'Buzzsaw' snapped ferocious shots into Matthew's body and pulverised him with short, clubbing right and left hooks. Matthew's legs gave out and he was rocked backwards into Braxton's corner, rolling on to his back with his legs in the air. He'd been in trouble in his title reign before, but this was the first time he'd been knocked down since he'd won the crown.

Matthew used the momentum of falling to roll forwards and on to his feet. He listened to Arthur Mercante's count, his top lip dripping in blood, but, as the rout recontinued, Ritacco stepped between the ropes. With only Matthew's heart holding him up, the threshing machine before him was stopped.

The incredible title reign of Matthew Saad Muhammad was over.

* * *

The Spinks millions were gone. Matthew's championship had been lost. Ritacco knew that despite the fables of Saad Muhammad, the miracles ran out on 19 December. Enough was enough. Matthew briefly complained but was soon comforted by members of the entourage. The warriors embraced.

Mercante hadn't even seen Ritacco, and had made his own mind up to stop it. He would have intervened moments earlier had

Matthew not managed a small salvo to buy an all-too temporary reprieve.

Spinks was ringside telling everyone he was the true champion. Cosell interviewed the winner. 'I knew it was going to be a hard fight,' the new champion said. 'I knew he'd take a lot of punishment, but the man is good. He's a great champion.'

Braxton was up on all three cards by miles; two lots of 7-2 with one 8-1.

'I'm glad they stopped it because he would have got hurt,' Braxton added.

'I won because I have no fear,' Braxton charged. 'I looked into that corner and I didn't see Superman. He's no monster. I saw just another man.'

A dejected and forlorn Matthew tried to maintain a positive outlook but could only say softly of his title, 'I've only loaned it to Braxton. I'll get it back.'

The new champ, who had initially compared Matthew to a heavy bag, was more gracious by the time the post-fight press conference began.

'It was a life-and-death situation all the way,' Braxton said, revealing he'd been shaken in round seven by a right hand. 'He hit me with some punches – I ain't going to lie to you – I saw the ceiling turning around … That man hits as hard as a mule kicks.'

When asked whether he recalled people saying Matthew had run out of miracles, he replied, 'I don't know about that. People used to say about him coming back from defeat. He did that because he was always hungry and that's how he fought, he sacrificed, but he wanted to win and there was a cost to that because it takes it out of you too,' he said.

Ritacco, moved by the beating his man had taken, said, 'By the fourth round, he was spent. When I was wiping blood off him, he told me I was rubbing too hard. It's a shame. Maybe this whole thing will teach him something. Matthew is a nice person but he's a kid. He thinks he's indestructible.'

Nigel Collins was outspoken in his fight report for *The Ring* about the level of care and sympathy in Matthew's corner.

'Before he went in to the final round, I knew he didn't have anything left,' Solomon told the reporter.

'Okay, Sam,' Collins responded. 'Then why did you permit the slaughter to continue ... Was he [Ritacco] the only man who cared more about the human being than the title?'

Matthew couldn't attend the post-fight press conference and was hospitalised overnight for observation. The ex-champion had a possible concussion and was examined for a fractured left cheekbone but staff at the Atlantic City Medical Center said his condition was stable.

Experts reckoned the defeat was down to a combination of crash weight-making and the hard fights taking their toll, but Matthew had not been alone thinking that he would always be able to fight through any kind of adversity.

Despite warning signs that one day Matthew wouldn't be able to fight back from the brink, that the well would run dry, even his staunchest supporters figured he would come good in the late rounds.

'I felt sick to my stomach,' recalled Paul Trace, who was shooting photos from ringside. 'I had seen Matthew take that horrible beating by Yaqui Lopez before knocking him out, and a couple of other fights where he was taking some heavy shots, so I was used to him pulling it off. We all thought, "Just hang in there. You'll get him." In the Braxton fight, I was so close to Matthew when he sat on his stool – it makes me so sick when I think about it – he was taking a beating. Adolph said, "I'm stopping the fight." As Adolph jumped in the ring, I grabbed his leg and said, "No." It was in a split second, and Adolph was screaming at me and he stopped the fight. That sticks in my mind.'

Trace was trying to hang on to the glory years. No one in the team was ready to let them go. Matthew just couldn't hold on to them any longer.

Murad Muhammad, hailing the fight as one of the upsets of the year, had another angle on the reason for the loss. He thought that the pre-fight promotional rows had taken Matthew's mind off the job. 'If Saad was 100 per cent, even if he had lost, I don't believe he would have took a whupping like he did,' Murad said.

'I begged him not to fight Braxton,' lamented Butch Lewis, realising the Spinks fight had gone. 'My Christmas would have been a lot merrier.'

'It broke my heart,' said Spinks. 'It's like losing my girlfriend or my wife leaving me or something. It's going to take a while to get over. You can't get it back.'

Explaining the defeat for the *Atlantic City Press*, Dave Bontempo wrote, 'Houdini ran out of solutions.'

'This time, he didn't come back," wrote Nigel Collins. 'In fact, the cavalry never left the fort ... boxing's Lazarus had struck out.'

Many years on, Braxton was asked if Matthew was already a 'shot' fighter before they fought.

'No,' came the reply. 'I shot him.'

CHAPTER 16

MERCY KILLING

'FIRST, WE take a few months off,' Bilal Muhammad said of the plan for Matthew moving forwards.

'He's not hurt at all. Then, in say March, we take an easy fight, nothing too tough. We can make a quarter of a million dollars in March, yes we can. And after that fight, we're right back in it. Matthew Saad Muhammad is still the hottest commodity in the division.'

Writing in the *Philadelphia Daily News*, Richard Hoffman argued, 'Bilal, like many of his managerial brethren, has an occasional difficulty with the interpretation of facts.'

Sam Solomon had been sacked within hours. The weight loss, 7lbs in four hours, had been the reason and Larry Holmes's trainer, Richie Giachetti, wanted to work with Matthew, having watched the Braxton battering from ringside.

As the new champion, the 'Camden Buzzsaw' wanted to follow the money. The lucrative choices were the Saad Muhammad rematch, a clash with Eddie Mustafa and, of course, Spinks.

As Braxton bathed in the glow of his new belt, reporters took time to get to know the sawn-off champion. He wanted to inspire those with hard lives in Camden. 'I know I can't change the world,' he thought. 'But if I can encourage even just five or six kids to stay in school and get an education, it will be worth it.'

Ten days after the loss, Matthew was described as 'cheerful and relaxed' for a piece in the *Philadelphia Inquirer* that was held over for the 'Design' section of the newspaper on Valentine's Day.

When asked about Braxton, Matthew said, 'What happened, I think happened for a reason. But so much for that. I'll go on to win back my championship – and then the unification. That's what I've dreamed about for a long time.'

Matthew and Michelle escaped to Hawaii for a few days to put the defeat behind him.

But the fighter was caught between admitting he hadn't prepared correctly and denying his career was all but over.

'Too many times, a fighter loses his title and everyone says he's washed up, that he took too many shots,' he said in one interview. 'Look at me, I'm not all beat up. I don't mumble, do I?'

In another, he would say, 'Sometimes a champion has a tendency to relax and get too confident. Then someone comes in like Dwight Braxton and makes him pay for it. No one takes the blame for that but me.'

But Michelle knew her husband was in pain. He wondered if the journalists were right. He wondered if he could defeat the Camden brute and he wondered whether he wanted or needed to.

'I think that fight took something from him,' Michelle explained. 'Because it was such a devastating loss. He was very disappointed and dejected and there was a certain amount of disbelief, like "I can't believe I allowed this to happen to myself." He tried to be very, "I'm going to get it back," but to me his heart wasn't as into it as it had been. I think there was a certain apprehension. There was all the talk like, "You let this jailbird come out of Rahway and take your championship?" Dwight was hungry and he had nothing to lose. Matthew was the only one with something to lose, and I think it took something out of his heart.'

Matthew didn't confide that in sparring partner Tony Green, but Green had been with Matthew from the Marvin Johnson WBC title fight through to Braxton and sensed a change. 'I could tell from fighter to fighter that Matthew had doubts about Braxton,' Green said. 'I could tell just talking to him that Matthew wasn't as confident. I knew him.'

The cover story remained that he was weight-drained but he doubted himself in quieter moments.

'I think, in the back of his mind, he thought, "This guy really beat me,"' Michelle said. '"He beat me up and now in order to get where I want to go, I've got to through him again." I'm not saying he didn't think he could, but he knew it was going to be very difficult. This guy hadn't had nearly the fights Matthew had, and all of those fights have to take a toll.'

The WBC installed Matthew as the No. 1 contender for his old title, doing their bit to get the Spinks fight back on track, but Spinks and his team seethed behind closed doors.

'Greed,' fumed Butch Lewis. 'Instead of waiting for Spinks and making $2m, they wanted to grab a quick $200,000 with Braxton, then get Spinks. It was bad management.'

Despite the public anger, it wasn't a personal issue, it was a financial one.

'Matthew and Butch were buddies, and Michael too,' said Michelle. 'None of them were enemies. Their thing was to get in here and make money.'

Matthew hired his old friend Steve Traitz as a trainer. He didn't condemn Solomon for his weight, talking about faulty scales, weighing himself on a carpet, eating too many peanuts and whatever else – but he did not hang Sam out to dry.

Matthew had often used Traitz's Montgomery County Boys Club in Eagleville and Traitz wasn't interested in money. He and Matthew liked one another and Matthew thought Steve could help him get punched less. 'Maybe I've been getting hit too much lately,' Matthew finally admitted. 'Steve's a basics guy … Maybe I need a man to keep on me constantly.'

'Matt's the best light-heavyweight around,' Traitz boasted. 'The problem is that everybody around him let him know how hard he hit. He relied on that too much. He'd get way behind in fights, then look for that one-punch knockout. With me, it'll be a different story.'

Traitz wasn't just a union guy and a boxing trainer. He was a Mob associate with close ties to Nicodemo 'Little Nicky' Scarfo, boss of the murderous Philadelphia crime family.

'If you were his friend, there was nobody more loyal or trustworthy,' said a friend of Traitz. 'The man was tough as nails, but also the most caring guy in the world.'

Team Saad prepared for Matthew to fight his old sparring partner Pete McIntyre, the No. 6 light-heavyweight contender with a spotty 16-10-1 record. The bout was the first main event inside the new Harrah's Hotel and Casino in Atlantic City, and McIntyre was trained by the brilliant Eddie Futch. The winner would get Braxton. McIntyre had won his last seven but he had been stopped twice by Yaqui Lopez, and defeated by Marvin Camel and Tony Mundine. However, there was another row over money in the build-up. Promoter Butch Lewis wanted to pay Matthew $100,000 while Bilal was holding out for $200,000.

'He's asking championship money,' Lewis said. 'He may still be in shock, but Saad's not the champion anymore.'

Matthew didn't have the title but he had a profile. He used it when he and Jeff Chandler went to Children's Hospital in Center City, Philadelphia, to help them with a fundraiser. But by fight week in April, he was not feeling as charitable, telling the press, 'Come early, or you'll miss the funeral.'

Matthew said it with a light-hearted smile but there was tragic news in Philly when – on 17 March – Matthew's friend Teddy Pendergrass was left paralysed following a car crash. One of the most promising and potentially iconic music careers was over after he sustained damage to his spinal cord.

'Teddy had a long battle, paralysis. He went through a real dark period where I don't think people saw him for years,' recalled Mustafa Ameen. 'Keep in mind, Saad's demise had started around that same time as well. Saad was on the downstroke and I'm sad to say it, but Saad and Teddy went from being the young princes and heroes of Philadelphia to, in Saad's case, doors not opening any more. You lose the title, you're down, you're living a different kind of life ... He wasn't viewed in the same light.'

* * *

Matthew and Michelle's child was due shortly after the McIntyre fight and there would be another addition to the family. Matthew collected a pit bull, Chopper, from Florida. What was supposed to become a guard dog was 'Michelle's baby'.

Not long after bringing back the new dog, it would run up to Michelle, lay on its back and insisted she rub its belly. 'You're making such a punk out of my dog,' Matthew joked. 'This is my puppy,' she smiled, because Topper had not been so welcoming.

Matthew saw McIntyre as a tune-up and was telling everyone he was desperate to go back in with Braxton. But the murmurings were that he was done as a fighter. The mileage was too high.

He knew what they were saying, too. 'Everyone wants to know if I'm through,' he admitted. 'I'm not through. All I did was lose one fight.'

There was friction in the camp, though. With Michelle pregnant, she found it increasingly difficult to contact her husband.

As Matthew trained in Eagleville, Michelle took her father to see Patti Labelle in Philadelphia. The McIntyre fight was set for 17 April and the baby was not due until mid-May but as father and daughter went to the show, Michelle began to feel unwell. When she got home, she struggled to walk so laid down. She called Matthew and Bilal picked up.

'He's in camp, he doesn't need to speak to anyone,' she was told.

'But I'm pregnant,' Michelle replied.

'Well, are you having a baby now?'

'Erm, no but I need to speak to my husband.'

She was not put through.

'Matthew didn't even know. They would try to separate us.'

The old team didn't want Michelle to take their friend or 'brother' away from them or, more cynically, to remove their meal ticket, and Michelle didn't want them to isolate her husband from her. Neither side liked the other, and the ex-champ was caught in the crossfire.

On 9 April 1982, Michelle had an emergency Caesarean at the Hahnemann Hospital – eight days before the McIntyre contest. Matthew got to the hospital as the baby was going into stress, but the couple were all smiles when pictured with a little Matthew Saad Muhammad in the papers the next day. You'd never have known about the toxic chaos behind the scenes.

Matthew quickly said of his newborn son, 'He's not going to be a fighter. There's only one fool in this family, and that's me. He can be a doctor, a lawyer, a judge, anything but a boxer.'

The focus quickly shifted to McIntyre, with Matthew wanting to see how he would bounce back. The former champion was comfortable in the first round. Michelle was still in hospital but couldn't bring herself to watch after what had happened last time.

Her husband broke through with sledgehammer rights in the second. One saw McIntyre spin into the ropes, turning his back and picking up a count for using the strands to support him, and then, when the action resumed, McIntyre went to throw his own clumsy right but Matthew's was faster. The effect was dramatic, the visual somewhat disturbing as McIntyre's punch carried on but his lights were shut off.

He swung and fell into the darkness. Matthew put his feet together and punched his arms into the air. McIntyre toppled before him. He rose groggily and didn't dispute the call of referee Tony Perez, who waved it off after 2:28 of the second round.

Matthew embraced Murad, Traitz, then Ameen and Ritacco. He was back to winning ways but content rather than happy.

'I wasn't really pleased,' he admitted. 'I won't be pleased until I fight Braxton. I want Dwight Braxton. I want him right now … This fight alone does nothing to satisfy me … And I won't stop until I unify the title.'

Sports columnists rounded on Saad Muhammad–McIntyre as a futile effort to rebuild the ex-champ that proved nothing and provided little by way of entertainment. No one knew what Matthew had left in the tank because he'd blitzed McIntyre or, according to some reports, McIntyre had conceded.

Regardless, Butch Lewis wasn't far away, gate-crashing the post-fight press conference to try to salvage Spinks–Saad Muhammad. 'We have a contract for you if you have the heart,' Lewis goaded Matthew.

But Lewis and his gang were thrown out and Matthew said, 'I want Braxton first, then I'll go after "Stinks". This is only the beginning.'

The light-heavyweight division was percolating. Richie Kates was making a comeback, Braxton was set to fight Lottie Mwale to keep busy, but Mwale had to withdraw and Jerry Martin was drafted in and stopped in six rounds as Murad tried to make a splash in Las Vegas. Spinks beat Mustafa Wasajja in February, stopped Murray Sutherland in their rematch a week before Matthew fought McIntyre and was about to defend his title for a fourth time against New Orleans dangerman Jerry Celestine.

Eddie Mustafa Muhammad had tried to find his groove, retiring and unretiring before scoring a routine return win, and he said he wanted the Spinks rematch. Marvin Johnson was also ticking over.

Matthew had little interest in the rest of the division. Only one man consumed his thoughts.

He called promoter Murad Muhammad. 'Give me Shorty,' Matthew said, referring to Braxton. 'You owe me Shorty. We've been together a long time.'

'Not now,' Murad replied. 'Take another fight and I'll give you Shorty.'

'He begged me to take the fight now … His manager and him was pushing me. The fight I wanted was Spinks.'

* * *

One can only imagine what went through the minds of Matthew and Michelle when they attended the world premiere of *Rocky III* in Philly's Sameric Theatre on 24 May.

Michelle's parents looked after baby Matthew as they saw Rocky lose his title to Clubber Lang, doubt his chin, health, desire and ambition before facing his fears and going back in with his tormentor.

Mr. T was almost Braxton-esque, a crude, menacing slugger testing Rocky's manhood while making Rocky question himself. Rocky wondered if he still had it. He'd lost the first fight, blitzed by Lang, and then trained for the rematch. The hero of the piece pulled it off. But that was Hollywood, and if all Hollywood fairy tales came true, maybe it would have been Matthew up on that silver screen instead of Mr. T.

Braxton–Saad Muhammad II was initially going to Jacksonville, then Vegas, but it was actually signed and headed for the Spectrum in Philadelphia on 7 August. The venue had been home to many of Matthew's North American title wars from a lifetime earlier, and Braxton knew the place well, having worked maintenance there.

'I don't usually go to the Spectrum,' said promoter Murad Muhammad. 'The Spectrum's like a pink elephant. Russell Peltz does a good job, but he never liked TV. He just liked wars, the North against the South. So I always say, "When you come to me, I save you from the wars. You get beat up on by the time you get to the title." But Matthew was like a freak of nature and he'd had some great, great fights.'

At the opening Braxton–Saad Muhammad II press conference some six weeks out, both talked up their chances.

'He didn't beat Saad Muhammad, he beat a shadow of Saad Muhammad,' Matthew contended. Braxton said he'd knock the 'a' out and make him 'Sad Muhammad'.

He also told Matthew that having heard about the weight issues for six months, Matthew should move his scales to the kitchen.

Matthew could do little but applaud that one.

But despite the needle, Matthew and Braxton were friends. They had both turned their lives around through boxing, they'd spent time on the wrong side of the tracks and were making each other wealthy. The only time Braxton really bristled was when Matthew joked, 'I took this short crab too lightly.'

'I'm going to bury him in Philadelphia,' snarled the champion, but the media found them to be more a double act than anything sinister, smirking at their one-liners.

Matthew, in pursuit of the Spinks bounty, was making around $400,000 while Braxton's pay was more than ten times what he'd made the first time around, in the $650,000 range.

HBO televised and fronted up most of the money. Tickets for the Liberty Brawl were priced from $15 to $200. Five weeks out, Matthew had to miss several days of training after twisting his knee sparring. He had X-rays and cortisone injections; the newspapers speculated about a postponement but he was back to full training after some rest. Chef Lana Shabazz was back, too. After Ali's loss to Trevor Berbick, she was on hand to make sure Saad had no weight issues.

The fighters couldn't stop poking fun at one another when they met again for the press inside the plush Barclay Hotel ballroom during fight week. Matthew brought Braxton a newspaper with the headline, 'Saad Muhammad destroys Braxton' but Braxton hadn't come empty-handed. He presented Matthew with a red shopping bag with kneepads and glue, in reference to Matthew's training injury.

'This is going to be the Battle of Wounded Knee,' said the Camden star. 'I like to be humorous in a situation like this. All the serious stuff will come Saturday.'

Despite plenty of publicity, ticket sales were slow with only around 2,500 sold. 'This is embarrassing,' someone connected with the promotion said. 'I thought this was supposed to be a great fight town. The way things stand now, we may end up having more fighters on the undercard than people in the seats.'

Matthew didn't go to the final press conference. Braxton said he, as the champion, was being made the underdog but he wasn't. The consensus was that the miracles were over for Matthew.

'They're saying I'm through,' Matthew said earlier in the week, predicting he would win in seven rounds. 'They're saying, "He can't take no more punches." I have more to prove for this fight than for any other fight I've ever had.'

'He's caught up on the Superman myth,' Braxton contended. 'Okay, so last time I caught him when he was Clark Kent. This time I'm giving him time to get to a phone booth. Hell, he can't scare me. He's only a man ... I want to go on record, I'm going to beat the hell out of him ... I know what he has, a big right hand. He threw it last time.'

* * *

Matthew had lost to a hungrier fighter back in December and knew things had to be different. Through much of the build-up, Michelle stayed with her family in Anchorage. Bilal said a lot had needed to be changed.

'I just think all of us didn't do our job properly,' he told HBO. 'We've been in seclusion now for five weeks. Matthew sent his wife all the way home to Alaska … it's a different day. It won't happen this time.'

The entourage was still there, though. Matthew had so many people with him jammed in the corridors in the bowels of the Spectrum on fight night there was hardly enough room for them all.

Eddie Mustafa was part of the team, having won a fight on the undercard. Braxton had a few close camp members, but brought a demonic and determined scowl with him, eating up the crowd's boos.

The fighters were in the ring more than quarter of an hour as they waited for boxing stars to be called up and introduced, including Joe Frazier, Larry Holmes, Spinks, Joey Giardello, Aaron Pryor and others. Michelle was tasked with showing off her vocal skills and singing the national anthem.

'I did it because [Matthew] told me he wanted me to,' Michelle said. 'I never personally had this great desire to be some famous singer. That was a dream my father had for me. I wanted to please my dad, but I was never comfortable singing in front of people I knew. I was always so much more comfortable singing in front of strangers. I wanted to represent Matthew well that night, but I was nervous and I just wanted the night to be over.'

She didn't stay for the fight. She couldn't. 'I would literally be physically sick,' she said. She sang, went back to the dressing room and waited.

Matthew was the romantic favourite but for those allowing their heads to rule their hearts, there was only one winner.

As legendary trainer Eddie Futch said, 'I have mixed emotions about the fight. Sentimentally, I favour Saad. I've always liked him personally, but I'm afraid he might have gone to the well too often.'

* * *

Matthew tried to establish his attack behind a busy, hard jab and an even harder right hand.

Braxton, however, asserted himself by lobbing that heavy overhand right every time he saw the slightest opening. A few cracked off Matthew's jaw in the first round and Braxton – wearing oversized blue trunks that came down almost to his shins – had that malicious grin on his face again. Knowing Matthew was in his crosshairs, Braxton smiled and stuck out his tongue at the bell to close the first round. Well, those ringside thought it was the bell. The crowd, announced as a still disappointing 6,781 (it could hold 15,000) by fight time, was so loud that referee Carlos Padilla thought he'd heard the bell and came between the fighters. The timekeeper told him the round still had nearly 30 seconds left, so Braxton climbed back off his stool, Matthew's cornermen returned to the floor and the fight was on again.

The boxers smiled at one another when the bell eventually sounded but the first round had been fought at a hard pace and it clearly wasn't going to be a contest for the faint-hearted.

Halfway through the second, Matthew was caught in the pocket by a right hand that thudded into the side of his head and caused him to lurch awkwardly backwards. Braxton raced to follow in and Matthew found it impossible to fight his way out of trouble. He did whip in a couple of left uppercut-right hand combinations, but rather than put a dent in Braxton, they caused the champion to come bombing back with heavy right hands. Braxton was finding it hard to miss the legendary Saad Muhammad. It was brutal and one-sided. Matthew's nose oozed blood again as he clung on to his career by his fingertips and covered up from another assault at the bell.

'I told you to hold him on the inside,' implored Traitz, when Matthew sat on his stool. The challenger barely had time to stand before Braxton appeared in his corner and poured on painful pressure and aggression.

At one point, Matthew started dropping his left again, trying to pop Braxton with the jab, but the champion's head movement was extraordinary. He was able to move from side to side, attack from a crouch and make Matthew miss every which way. For Matthew, it was another punishing night. He struck Braxton low in the third, was warned to keep them up by Padilla and, as Matthew extended a glove to apologise, Braxton smiled and tore in behind a right hand. Braxton crashed in hooks from both gloves and Matthew, the man of a million miracles, needed something else. He needed a resurrection. He dropped to the canvas, beaten and bloody, hauling himself back to his feet using the middle ropes, but he had a vacant stare. Matthew was looking for answers, unaware how he could turn around the mismatch.

'How do you feel?' asked Traitz, before round four.

'Okay.'

'You sure you're alright?'

'I'm alright. I'm going to fight him now.'

'You've got to fight him. You've got to fight him now. Hands high, you hear me?'

But Matthew's power gauge was running dangerously low, and he was brutalised some more, pummelled without any sign of hope or respite.

Matthew's blood-smeared face was towelled down between rounds. The white fabric was almost red. Ritacco looked painfully nervous and concerned, but Matthew squeezed his eyes shut and let Traitz do his work.

Fights had been stopped for less, but everyone knew about 'Miracle' Matthew and how he could turn a fight around.

Braxton had a laser-like focus. He didn't look as though he was out of second gear and wasn't breathing heavily.

'I'll finish him,' he grunted, coming out for the fifth.

Matthew's legs were tired. His punches were slow and not having any effect. His nostrils were filled with cascading blood. He couldn't keep Braxton off him and his head was continuously jolted backwards. 'I never like seeing a fighter take this much punishment,' said Sugar Ray Leonard, on commentary.

Referee Padilla looked closely, waiting to jump in. During the sixth, Braxton hurled some bombs that detonated with thuds, jarring

Matthew's brain this way and that, sending sweat and blood spraying into the audience. Matthew staggered backwards now, his legs doing little to support him. With Matthew's back to the ropes, Braxton burrowed in low and fired off damaging shots, initially to the body and then to the head.

Matthew tried to throw back desperately but there was no strength left.

He wilted as his shots misfired, failing to deter Braxton. Padilla had finally seen enough. It was over.

'It's a mercy killing, I assure you,' announced Barry Tompkins.

Moments after the slaughter, Braxton picked Matthew up for the applause of the shell-shocked crowd.

'Yes, I will fight Spinks,' Braxton charged. 'I want Mike. I'm the boss.'

'He was very aggressive,' said an honest and sporting Matthew. 'Once again, I was in tremendous shape. I tried to box Braxton but he proved to be a little stronger than last time. I guess he was eager to keep that championship … I can't take anything from him. It seemed that after the first round I was easy to hit … I have plans on retiring. I accomplished all my goals. I tried to come back for my title. I think I may retire after this one.'

Asked who might win the big unification clash, a crestfallen Matthew replied, 'I like Braxton now, he's a much stronger guy. [But] Spinks is very awkward and he might clip Braxton.'

* * *

Matthew was only 28 but his reflexes had slowed and his timing had deserted him.

'He was sharper last time,' Braxton admitted, somewhat damningly. 'You hate to see it happen to such a legend.'

'I don't know what I'm going to do next,' Matthew shrugged. 'I don't think I'm through. I just want to leave walking and talking and still looking good.'

Boxing News called it 'Saad's final blow', but in their preview they had considered the cost of a second defeat.

'It really will be time to bow out,' they had written. 'He [Matthew has] achieved financial security through boxing, has a beautiful wife, Michelle, and a baby son, and it would be a shame to see this brave warrior wind up as just an opponent.'

The *Inquirer* was in no doubt as to what to do next. 'He has won a world championship, he has assured himself of being a wealthy man for a long, long time, and now Saad Muhammad must ask himself if it might not be time to get into a safer line of work.'

Matthew had been caught in an even more violent maelstrom than the first time. As Bill Lyon wrote in the *Inquirer* the next day, 'To fight Dwight Braxton is to climb inside a washing machine that is set on high rinse.'

Over the years, Braxton said Matthew hit him harder than anyone else and confessed, 'I peaked during the second fight. That was the best performance of my career. I just went through him … He was sharp and he was boxing and moving but I caught him again. You get to that point where you take a lot of damage and two people are going at it, it's war. He had a lot of fights, he had a lot of hard fights, but he could still punch. I had to get him out of there. He fought that fight wrong with me.'

There was still a dream match to be made at 175lbs, but it didn't involve Matthew. Nigel Collins was at both Saad Muhammad–Braxton bouts and was saddened by what he saw, and the predictability of it.

'That was pretty much the end of the line and he sort of dropped out of sight,' said Collins. 'I knew that it was all going to fall apart for him at some point, he would burn out, and so I wasn't surprised. The second fight, there was money involved but it was unnecessary.'

Matthew had been the sport's sentimental favourite because of the wars he had given the fans.

That night, a young amateur heavyweight had a learning bout in the Bronx. Mike Tyson was only 15 years old and he'd watched Braxton destroy Matthew once more.

'I cried like a baby, watching the fight,' Tyson later recalled. 'I couldn't stop crying. I won my fight by knockout, and as soon as I got back to change, I was crying again.'

Matthew's old friends from South Philly watched sadly on the night Matthew was thrashed a second time by Dwight Braxton and shook their heads.

'I don't think Dwight would have beat a prime Matthew,' said Eddie Everett. 'I tell people all the time.'

'Agreed,' said Stephen Chandler. 'No way, he didn't beat the prime Matt, he beat what was left.'

CHAPTER 17

COMING APART AT THE SEAMS

MATTHEW LOOKED at Michelle and wondered what the future held. He wasn't sure whether he could accept a life without fighting but it was in his thoughts.

'I kind of just want to go to Alaska and live a quiet life up there,' he told his wife. 'I just want to move there and live a quiet life, where nobody really knows me and they just leave me alone.'

But it didn't happen.

They had money, they could have sold Jenkintown, Michelle's parents had a successful commercial and residential painting business, and Matthew could have made a living there, if he had needed to top up his pension fund.

'If he could have unified the title, and even if he didn't [but he'd had the chance] I think he would have felt better about retiring because it would have been easier to say, "We were both champions and we duked it out and the best man on that day won,"' Michelle said.

But as time went by Matthew, still only 28, listened to others. Some of them contended Matthew had become too domesticated, softened by wealth, marriage and his baby son. Michelle didn't see that and argued if that was the case, it would have happened when they were newly in love and he would have been distracted earlier.

Matthew felt he could beat the other light-heavyweights bar Braxton and by the end of the year, he had made his mind up to give it another try.

Matthew and Mustafa Ameen drove up to Detroit to see Emanuel Steward at the Kronk Gym, where the former world light-heavyweight champion was put on trial, but Emanuel – who had been a staunch Saad Muhammad supporter – refused to work with him.

Matthew failed to impress in sparring sessions and Steward feared he didn't have anything left to offer.

* * *

The big unification fight took place in Atlantic City on 19 March 1983, and a week later, a much smaller bill in the same city featuring Matthew attracted considerably less fanfare.

Dwight Braxton, following a pattern at 175lbs, changed his name to Dwight Muhammad Qawi. Spinks out-jabbed Qawi over 15 rounds to unify the title for the first time since 1974 in what many called the biggest light-heavyweight title fight in history.

Spinks had accomplished what Matthew had dreamed of doing, completed the final piece of the puzzle that had eluded not just Matthew but Galindez, Johnson, Conteh and Eddie Mustafa. Still, only around 7,000 turned up at the 14,000-seat Convention Hall in Atlantic City. The fighters were supposed to have made $1.2m each, but Butch Lewis told sources they were making $2.1m apiece.

Qawi complained and thought he'd won, that Spinks had 'run away'. 'It was more like a track meet out there,' Qawi spat. But not even Qawi's own people believed he had done enough. His co-trainers, Quenzell McCall and Wesley Mouzon, thought Spinks was victorious. McCall admitted, 'Dwight didn't do anything.'

Spinks was where the money and glory was in the division.

It wasn't with a fighter named Eric Winbush, who was born in Boston, lived in Manhattan and was a social worker who helped pensioners.

The idea was for Matthew to ease himself back in, get a feel for fighting and winning again and to give him some confidence.

It was a rebuild. It was a step back up the mountain, a fight closer to Spinks and the opportunity to win both belts with just one fight.

Winbush was safe, then heads would turn towards someone like Oscar Rivadeneyra. A win over the Peruvian contender would give Matthew a ranking with the WBA.

Fearing a mismatch, fight officials in New Jersey almost called the Winbush fight off.

Steve Traitz was gone, and Matthew was at Marty Feldman's Gym at 63rd and Market Street home in Philadelphia. As he tried to restart his championship mindset, Matthew reckoned his offence would be his defence.

'I'm going to prove to the world and myself that I can still do it,' he said, loud enough so a few could hear but not loud enough to convince many. Matthew cautioned that after eight months out his timing might be off, but Spinks was still in his sights.

His announced manager at the time, old friend Salim El-Amin, hoped Eddie Mustafa would be next, leading to Spinks.

Winbush, a late starter to boxing with no amateur pedigree, talked a cliched game and admitted he had chosen not to study tape, of Matthew but said he was coming to fight. Eric's trainer, John Bowman, didn't sound quite so confident when he said: 'With the good Lord, hopefully we'll make it.'

Around 800 filled Claridge's in Atlantic City to watch Matthew go through the motions, including Eddie Mustafa, cheering him on again. Winbush started well enough, firing out his jab and moving off his back foot. He wasn't an aggressive type and had only scored three stoppage wins in 15 fights.

Matthew was off the pace, trying to warm to the task, looking for big right hands but missing by a long way. In round three, Matthew was caught by a sudden right hand and startlingly unravelled. He desperately tried to clutch on but he was badly hurt, and Winbush unceremoniously tossed him to the canvas. Matthew struggled to pull himself up by the ropes, but Winbush hammered away with glory, Matthew's No. 3 ranking and money in his eyes.

The crowd screamed. This is what they'd paid to see. Matthew was hurt, here is when he'd roar back.

Not this time. Not again.

His legs wobbled, his nostrils bled and, with Winbush landing at will, New Jersey's boxing commissioner and former world heavyweight champion Joe Walcott got out of his seat and ordered referee Zach Clayton to end it.

Winbush wheeled away, in shock as much as celebration. A stunned silence descended on the venue. It was a colossal upset and reinforced the opinion of those who had thought Matthew had reached the end of the line.

Matthew was placed on his stool and had an awful lot to absorb.

Winbush had only laced up gloves for the first time four years earlier.

'I didn't see Walcott at all,' Clayton later said of his decision to end the fight. 'I stopped it because Saad Muhammad was receiving too many combinations, all to the head.'

Some said the initial punch that appeared to do so much damage didn't seem hard, but Matthew's resistance had crumbled. Winbush wasn't a puncher. The fight had been a gimme, to see what Matthew had left – and it showed everyone watching what was left in his dried-out tank. The magic had gone and only a nostalgic shell remained.

Jeff Chandler and Eddie Mustafa consoled Matthew in his dressing room. 'You don't need this shit,' said Eddie. 'You've got enough money.'

'Eddie sometimes has good opinions,' countered Matthew to a journalist later in the evening. 'If he feels I should get out, I don't feel that way. The best thing I can do is try one more time.'

But Eddie wasn't alone. *Ring* magazine went in hard, saying Matthew had been 'smeared all over the ring', adding, 'There was general concern for his well-being. Now there should be outright alarm. He was pitiful.'

'I'm embarrassed,' Matthew sighed. 'That's very bad for me.'

One reporter said the meagre $20,000 payday would not come close to softening the blow to his pride.

The fighter in Matthew argued that Clayton should have given him more time. Then, reaching, Matthew theorised it was a set-up. He just couldn't understand it. 'Maybe they paid the guy off. I think it was a dirty deal,' he charged, making unfounded allegations about the commission and Joe Walcott. But nobody had been paid off and there had been no dirty deal.

The queue of people wanting to see the ex-champ fight was shortening. They knew the miracles had run out.

Manager Bilal Muhammad considered it could be all over. 'I'll let him sleep on it and see if he wants to fight again,' Bilal said.

'It is not a pretty epitaph for a man who started lower than hell, then rose to the heavens of his profession,' wrote the *Daily News*.

Those who knew Matthew's mileage realised the time had come. He had to stop.

'Everyone knew,' said Russell Peltz, who worked as a co-promoter on the Winbush bill. 'Winbush only had a handful of knockout wins in his entire career. Saad was coming apart at the seams.'

Winbush, by the way, who'd been called little else but a nobody beforehand, now thought it was his time to take over. His $5,000 was double what he'd ever made before. 'These other guys have been fighting too long, they're all punched out,' he smiled, looking at the war-torn 175lbs landscape.

Boxing News thought the curtain had been pulled down on Matthew's career. 'Sad Saad bows out with a real beating', they headlined.

The *Philadelphia Daily News* agreed it was all over. 'Winbush puts an end to Muhammad', they wrote. 'Muhammad went to the mountain, and it fell on him.'

The Winbush ambush saw the underdog hijack Saad's spot in the ratings. Matthew plummeted.

'It'll put me way back,' Matthew admitted. 'But I'm definitely not going to retire.'

New Jersey, the scene of so many of his glorious battles, was now hesitant to sanction his fights and considered withdrawing his licence.

But Matthew fought again six months later, topping the bill against Larry Davis at Madison Square Garden in New York. Davis had won 12 but lost 25 and had been outpointed by the in-form Winbush in July, three months after Eric had defeated Matthew. Saad

Muhammad–Davis was a live TV prelim fight for a Miami card that saw Aaron Pryor defeat Alexis Arguello in a classic.

Janks Morton, who had trained Sugar Ray Leonard, was working with Matthew and told journalists he could take Matthew back to the top. 'It's amazing how little Matthew was taught,' Morton asserted. 'He accomplished everything on native ability and heart. I don't understand how Saad got as far as he did. Not with the lack of defence that everyone thought was so exciting. The man went a long way with a big heart.'

Matthew's sparring partners included former opponent Pete McIntyre and Robert Folley, son of former heavyweight contender Zora.

Davis, by the way, was originally rejected by the New York State Athletic Commission, deemed unsuitable because of his patchy record. However, after learning that he'd won three of his last four, officials thought he would be okay.

Matthew's defence was tight early on, but as soon as he was caught a few times, he dragged Davis into the trenches. Davis was ultimately stopped by referee Joe Cortez after 27 seconds of round ten, but he'd enjoyed plenty of success as the damage Matthew acquired mounted further.

'I knew I was a little stale tonight, but personal problems and a long layoff have taken their toll,' Matthew conceded. 'I will improve and I am back on my way to the light-heavyweight title.'

He promised he wasn't finished, even though Morton wasn't happy with the display.

Matthew couldn't shake the belief of many journalists. He might have won but he would have iced Davis years earlier. There was a legitimate concern he had already taken a lifetime of punches.

Almost as bad, Davis was still standing by the end, having eaten up Matthew's biggest shots.

'His power has gone,' said a concerned Harold Lederman, who'd been a judge for several of Matthew's big fights.

Matthew appeared on ABC's *Superstars* multi-sport show, along with Aaron Pryor, but neither fighter covered themselves, or boxing, in glory. Pryor finished last out of 12 athletes; Matthew was just one place higher and that was mostly because he'd been able to beat Pryor in several events. They took part in an obstacle race, a 100-yard dash, a half-mile run, a half-mile bike race (and a quarter-mile version), golf, bowling, rowing, weightlifting, tennis and swimming.

Sprint hurdler Renaldo Nehemiah won overall, but the question most asked Matthew was why he was still boxing. With a fortune in the bank and an adored legacy intact, what did he have to gain or prove?

'I don't believe it's all over,' Matthew stated.

Matthew was telling reporters he was destined to get his titles back. He had become friendly with the *Inquirer*'s new boxing man, Mike Bruton, who had covered the sport in San Antonio before moving east. Matthew would tell him the belt was only being borrowed.

'He was a really good-natured guy; he was a very nice guy,' said Bruton. 'It was amazing, the violence you saw from him in the ring, he was just the opposite as a person.'

But Bruton had been around and wasn't naïve to the fact that Matthew was not what he had been.

'There was a concern,' Bruton admitted. 'As much as people loved to see him fight, people also feared the worst. There was a feeling that he couldn't just keep doing that. He couldn't keep taking that punishment. If you watched carefully, in '82, '83, '84, some of the fights he had, you could see the wear and tear had caught up with him and it became a thing where you loved to see him fight but you'd spend your time grimacing or gritting your teeth. It was like a guilty pleasure.'

Undeterred, Matthew headed out to Phoenix for more work with Morton. He knew he was missing something, he just didn't know what, so they went looking.

After a few weeks in Arizona, Matthew admitted he'd lost his hunger and desire, and that he'd been side-tracked in a materialistic world.

'I started enjoying life and forgot about boxing. I just settled down,' he sighed.

Matthew alluded to personal problems at home. He and Michelle were at odds, in part because she didn't want him fighting any more and she was still unhappy with some of the faces who remained in the team.

Tony Green was no longer needed for sparring and the paycheques no longer covered the likes of Paul Trace and Lana Shabazz. Bilal had let Trace go after the Braxton fight. Matthew's 'white shadow' was gone.

'Bilal told me that he couldn't afford to have his own personal photographer,' Trace recalled. 'When you're the champion, you can afford to do that. When you're not champion, you're not making that kind of money.'

Mustafa Ameen had also gone. He moved to Seattle but could see the carnage unfolding. Ameen had known how long he was going to stay with Matthew since they were in Muhammad Ali's hotel room after 'The Greatest' had been drubbed by Larry Holmes in Las Vegas.

'I knew he [Ali] didn't want to fight Larry, but his crew, his entourage, they wanted the payday,' Ameen stated. 'They wanted the excitement and they helped convince him to fight Larry so I promised myself that when the time came for Saad, that I wouldn't do that and I would walk away. And lo and behold, I was put to the test the night of the second Qawi fight and I remembered my promise to myself. I wouldn't grease Champ up any more and I walked away.'

He also knew of the problems between Michelle and Bilal.

'I served Saad to the best of my ability but there was so much I didn't know that ended up being harmful,' admitted Ameen. 'Like the thing with Michael Spinks, walking away from $2.5m and me not saying, "Hey, man, F you. Champ, this is the right move to make." Something I'd say today, and pulling the trigger on it.'

Religion was also a bone of contention. Some of the 'brothers' thought Matthew wanted Michelle to embrace Islam, and when she didn't, that created a gulf.

'Religion was never a point of opposition for either one of us,' Michelle insisted. 'He knew I was not converting to Islam, and I wasn't expecting him to convert to Christianity but we loved one another enough to co-exist without any issues. I did Ramadan with him, but he celebrated Christmas with me, and he said he wanted his children raised Christian.'

But she knew all too well what Bilal thought about her. 'Bilal never liked me,' she said. 'I don't say this with arrogance, but I wasn't their typical Philly girl. I didn't come from a broke background, my parents worked hard and were very successful. I was a graduate and I went to college. I just didn't go back because Matthew and I started having babies.'

But Matthew didn't have the education that would have allowed him to understand legal and financial paperwork, so Michelle wanted to keep an eye on things. She would ask questions Matthew wouldn't have known to ask.

'Keep your wife out of your business,' Bilal would tell Matthew.

'It's our business and he's my husband,' she would counter.

'He felt very contemptuously about me, and I felt the same about him, because I just felt, "You don't care about him. All you see is a person to make you money,"' Michelle said.

She wanted Matthew to be a father and a husband but those who had been on the payroll saw the money drying up.

The $20,000 Winbush purse wouldn't have gone far.

'Matthew loved me and I loved him and maybe Bilal didn't trust me to stay in a woman's place and stay out of Matthew's business,' Michelle continued. 'My parents were very astute and saw through a lot of things as well and I'm sure Bilal knew they read him from the moment they met him.'

Michelle also realised she was not the only woman in Matthew's orbit and couldn't understand not only why Matthew didn't stand up to the 'brothers' in the camp but how they assisted him looking elsewhere rather than his home.

'Not blaming them, but by them being older and supposedly so holy, why would you not encourage him to be the family man that he had signed up to be?' Michelle said.

She added: 'We tried. Matthew made promises and when you come into a marriage, you bring all your stuff, all your baggage with you and I made a promise to myself before I met Matthew that I was not going to be that girl that the guy's just running around and she looks stupid. He's a public figure but I'm the little wife he keeps sequestered up Route 611 in Jenkintown? It was a pride thing for me, that I'm not going to let you do that to me. Everybody's laughing, and your camp is laughing, and I just felt very alone and very alienated.'

By now Matthew's focus had shifted to Willie Edwards, who he was preparing to face in Detroit in February 1984. Just weeks before the bout, Michelle and Matthew found out they were expecting a second child, but their future didn't look good. Things were so poisonous behind the scenes that Bilal was telling Matthew to get a paternity test.

'I'm going to stay with you and have this baby, but I don't think we're going to make it,' Michelle told her husband.

Ahead of Edwards, Jerry Stokes was working the mitts with Matthew as part of the team.

'Saad is coming back,' Stokes promised. 'He's got himself together. There are a lot of things we've changed. Defence mostly. He's not going to be a punching bag anymore.'

Matthew revealed that he had sparred 190 rounds in preparation for the tough Detroit fighter and he'd run more than 200 miles. He wouldn't even entertain the usual Spinks questions even though he thought the demand for a mega-fight was still there, but said even if he won, there were other avenues away from boxing.

Mutual Edwards opponent Pete McIntyre was again a sparring partner and tipped Matthew to beat the person they called 'The Sandman' who, despite being a pro for just a couple of years, held Matthew's old NABF title. McIntyre was the only man who'd beaten Edwards, who was 17-1 and had avenged the McIntyre loss.

Matthew fumed that he was being written off and took the detractors personally.

'I turned around and got beat in the third round by this bum named Eric Winbush and everybody's acting like I'm all washed up,' he snarled. Then, turning his attention to Edwards, he went on: 'I wouldn't call it a do-or-die fight. I don't like that kind of wording.

I hope I don't die. But you can say that it is essential that I win this fight. I shall be champion again. I give myself one year to do it. I'm 28 now. If I haven't got the title back in a year, I'll retire.'

There was bad blood, too, from a Detroit sparring session a few months earlier.

Matthew didn't sound quite so bullish talking to the newspapers before the fight.

'I'm willing to take the chances,' he predicted. 'That's what this is, a game of chance. I just hope that one day that chance won't land me in a hospital.'

It started to go wrong again when Edwards rocked him in round three. Matthew had his nose bloodied in the next session and then absorbed more steady punishment through the following few rounds. Finally, in the 11th, Matthew was clipped by a left hook and came unglued. His legs trembled and sagged, causing him to hit the ropes. Edwards ploughed in, destruction in his mind and chaos in his gloves.

Referee Max Harnish intervened, saving Matthew from further punishment.

Again, Matthew disputed the stoppage. Saad felt it had come too early and argued he should have been given a standing eight count. The majority of ringsiders felt the stoppage had come too late.

In the ring, Edwards jumped up and down excitedly and punched the air. Matthew walked towards him. Edwards was willing to touch gloves and leave their feud behind, but Matthew attacked. He planted his feet and started throwing punches. Edwards was cut by his eyes and fired back, and it got ugly as team members raced to either separate them or join in.

Once, twice, three times Matthew had to be restrained from going at Edwards again. It got so wild that the fighters were made to leave the ring at separate times. Matthew was clearly frustrated, perhaps by the officiating and the fight being stopped, but maybe because he was no longer who he once was.

After a chunk of time passed, Edwards went into Matthew's dressing room to squash the animosity, but Matthew wasn't having it and they had to be pulled apart again.

'Why should I shake his hand?' wondered a distraught Matthew. 'He comes over here talking about shaking my hand ... He hit me [after the fight]. What would I look like shaking his hand?'

There was a chorus of writers who thought that was it for Matthew and they were not alone. 'It's just not there anymore,' said Top Rank promoter Bob Arum, bluntly. 'As far as I'm concerned, he's finished.'

The Ring, so often a supporter of Matthew, couldn't condone his actions. 'He lost more than his talent,' read their report. 'He lost any class he had and can no longer accept defeat.'

As the months went by, Matthew started taking acting lessons in Greenwich Village. Three days a week, he'd travel up to New York to take classes with Jack Waltzer, hoping to follow the veteran coach's former clients Al Pacino and Robert DeNiro into movie roles.

As always, there were stories of a film or book about Matthew's life. It was just that, however. Talk. Matthew said, however, he wasn't looking to play himself in the film. The ideal candidate was Howard Rollins, a star of both stage and screen.

'It doesn't have to be somebody who looks like me,' Matthew explained. 'But this guy is a fine actor.'

As time wore on, Matthew's love for the sport that had made him wealthy and had given him an identity was dimming. He stayed away from going to fights in case it gave him the urge to lace the gloves up again.

'I really don't like to go,' he insisted. 'It's like a fire within me that makes me want to do it again, so I just stay away.'

On 12 November 1984, he was pictured in Hahnemann Hospital with Michelle following the birth of another son, Michael, and later that year Matthew was on a team of boxers playing against the cast of *Cats* at stickball in New York, raising money for charity. His team included Rocky Graziano, Jake LaMotta and rising heavyweight Tim Witherspoon. He'd found a level of contentment and perhaps now agreed, finally, retirement was for the best.

Even non-boxing people were able to see that he'd hit the end of the line.

Former Boston Celtic draft pick Ollie Johnson talked about Matthew in an interview, and said: 'I'm a boxing fan. I thought Matthew Saad Muhammad was a great champion. But when I first saw him, I said he would not stay champion more than two years. Here's a fighter who came back from the grave too many times. Be bloody and battered and in the 14th round and you'd say, "Don't worry, he'll find a way to win." Well, when he went, he just went.'

* * *

Perhaps things would have been different had Matthew, Michelle, young Matthew and baby Michael moved to Alaska.

There was a lot of heartache on both sides when the Philly glamour couple eventually formalised their split. They had been kids who had fallen in love, ill-prepared for the challenges of fame, the politics of boxing and all that went with it. Both had done an awful lot of growing up, but Michelle had been unable to tolerate Matthew's indiscretions.

'If you're losing fights and you've got women that are telling you, "You need to fight for the championship again …"' Michelle recalled, as part of what she was going up against. '"No, the hell you don't. I wish you'd stop. Just stop."'

'I wasn't telling him what he wanted to hear, and others were. I filed for divorce. Matthew wouldn't sign those papers for almost a year and finally he did. It was hurtful for both of us. Had we been a little more prepared, and had we had a more supportive circle, maybe … if we'd had people who cared about two people that cared about each other.'

'Looking back, I realise how difficult it must be to be monogamous when everyone is throwing themselves at you. But it's doubly hard when those people who are not only your management, your cronies, but also your religious "brothers", too, encourage and condone … Matthew and I would probably still be together if some things had not happened.'

Michelle moved out with the boys to South Street. Matthew was in the home when she left. She took the children's furniture

– a crib and a couple of bureaus – her record collection and her clothes.

'I did not take anything from him,' Michelle said. 'I took what I came with and I'm out. If you take care of the kids, okay. But if you don't, they're not going to starve. The day I left him, I loved him. The day I left, he loved me. It was just a trust thing. At the end of the day, it hurt us both a lot.'

* * *

Early in 1985, Matthew couldn't believe what he'd done in his career and all that he'd achieved. Seeing his wild brawls was like looking back and seeing someone else fighting. He also reflected deeply about what had come and what had gone.

'The wars are over,' wrote the *Inquirer*'s Elmer Smith. 'He [Matthew] has climbed off the floor for the last time. Never again will he have to make a living wiping his own blood out of his eyes or trying to ignore a punch that threatened to drill a hole from his stomach to his spine … And yet you can't help wondering if, when he is alone with his fearful memories, he doesn't shiver just a little bit.'

There was an undercurrent of belief that Matthew had given too much of himself and that the beatings might have come at too great a cost, but you couldn't tell on the surface.

In late April, Matthew did a ten-mile charity run – the Trevira Twosome – around Central Park in an hour and six minutes. Paired with one Ellen Hoffman, he left the likes of Mark Frazier [Joe's son] and Tim Witherspoon for dust. 'Smokin' Joe actually ran three miles, but then hailed a cab and met them at the finish line.

In early May disaster struck. Matthew agreed to an exhibition contest, a move-around with novice pro Jesse Goodmond, to help Sam Solomon improve the gate at his West Philadelphia fight club's monthly show at the Mayfair Ballroom.

Matthew's body was still lean and rippled with muscle and he was only a pound over the light-heavyweight championship limit but, wearing headgear, the 30-year-old ex-champion was dropped in the third round. Goodmond, a club fighter with a soft 10-4 record, was on the receiving end afterwards, but it was another sign that Matthew couldn't take a shot any more because he had taken too many.

After the exhibition, though, journalists discovered Matthew had been pursuing a licence to fight again. He'd passed some physical tests and his brain scans were clear.

Solomon admitted Matthew had called to ask about a return. The trainer made him go to a doctor and then said: 'We have to bring him back slowly.'

'It's a possibility,' Matthew eventually concluded of the comeback. 'I still need to go in the gym and see what I have left in this boxing game. I'm glad he [Goodmond] knocked me down, because that means I have things I need to work on.'

Matthew boxed another exhibition in August for the Montgomery Boys Club, in a star-studded show with Bennie Briscoe, Pinklon Thomas and Mike Rossman also appearing, but by then the comeback was on after he made headlines nationwide.

* * *

Where had all the money gone? How did it happen? Matthew had no answers and never really knew, but his fortune had evaporated. Worse, the Internal Revenue Service said the bankrupt former champion owed them $239,076 that he didn't have.

The six-figure purses, the eight title defences, the wars … they'd funded a lavish but unsustainable lifestyle.

On 14 June 1985, newspapers around the US announced 'Ex-boxing champion is bankrupt'.

Matthew's attorney, Jeffrey S. Toaltoan, said Matthew hoped to negotiate a repayment schedule based on the amount he owed for his taxes in 1980, back when he had a business manager and was hiring an accountant to look after his fortune.

'There have been some problems in filing, yes,' announced Toaltoan.

To make matters worse, Matthew's earning capabilities had dropped phenomenally. Records indicated he made just $30,000 in 1984.

There'd been several bad investments and ventures that hadn't worked out, but Toaltoan was unable to explain to reporters where the funds had gone.

Tim Crawford, who had represented Matthew for years, said, 'He's a fighter. Apparently he did not prepare himself for anything other than fighting.'

No one wanted Matthew to box anymore, but he didn't have anything else to do. He could no longer afford the acting lessons, everything had to be sold piecemeal, the cars, the piano, the home … gone. All he had left was his name and all he knew how to do was fight.

* * *

Beating Matthew in Atlantic City was as good as things got for Eric Winbush. No sooner was he in the rankings than he was out. He lost to Larry Davis in his next fight – who Matthew incidentally then beat – but became an opponent and lost six of his final seven fights to the likes of future champions Evander Holyfield and Virgil Hill. In later years, he moved to North Carolina where he was surrounded by his supportive family.

'All I know is I was in the ring with Matthew throwing punches and I did my jogging so I wouldn't get tired and I'd be able to punch with him and I did the training that I was supposed to be doing,' he said in 2021.

In retirement, he trained boxers and worked regular jobs, driving trucks for supermarkets and Coca-Cola.

'He's a wonderful man,' said Mickey Dunne, one of his boxing students. 'I can't tell you how many of us youngsters he helped along the way. No cursing … No acting up … He taught us to be men.'

Winbush, who also became a preacher, continued: 'I knew Matthew was up there [as one of the best]. I was really just coming into boxing but I knew he was someone big. It was the biggest win of my career and I thought it might lead to a title shot. It was a huge shock. I enjoyed my career, travelling around the world, taking trains and buses. I always got my wife a souvenir from wherever I went. I missed it when I retired but I've been blessed and highly favoured.'

Things went badly for Willie Edwards, however. By 2011 he lived in a Detroit homeless shelter. The money and fame had gone, he shuffled when he walked and showed symptoms of Parkinson's syndrome.

At one point, against Bobby Czyz, he'd been just about one punch from the light-heavyweight title but lost and retired at 26-5-1.

He worked in the kitchen at the shelter as he didn't like to go out.

'He's the sweetest man, but it seems he is confused and scared of life out there – not in the ring or in here but on the outside,' said one of the employees at the centre.

'What's happened is nobody's fault,' said Edwards.

CHAPTER 18

THE CRASH

THE AMERICAN dream had become a boxing stereotype.

The crash had been sudden, dramatic and ruthless. The June 1985 announcement that Matthew Saad Muhammad was broke was shocking.

Three years earlier there had been the Rolls-Royce, the nice house, the entourage and now they were all gone.

Matthew faced the music alone.

Michelle had moved out before everything had come crashing down and when the IRS came calling, it was out of nowhere. Matthew thought he had paid his taxes and that everything had been taken care of.

'You take a kid out of the ghetto who's never had a quarter and now all of a sudden you're giving him $100,000, $200,000, $500,000 ... with no education,' stated Matthew's old promoter Russell Peltz. 'Education is the key. You can give anyone a million dollars but if they're not educated, they're going to piss it away. That's what happens to fighters. They're not educated enough to be able to hold on to their money ... Matthew wound up broke, and the Muslims abandoned him, and he lent them money and he never got it back ... It was sad to see him sell his robes, his trophies, his belts, his awards. When you're at that point, you have nothing.'

Peltz, as with a few others, feared it might only be a matter of time. He had gone to a party at Matthew's house and left thinking, 'Who was advising him, to spend that kind of money?'

But Matthew was not listening to many people, and Peltz didn't think he could get through to his former fighter.

'Matthew was so brainwashed by those guys that you just couldn't talk to him,' Peltz added.

Now there was no tread left on the tyre. 'He was beginning to slow down, and he was beginning to wear out,' said the *Inquirer*'s Mike Bruton. 'He'd just taken too much punishment.'

'The human body can only take so much,' agreed Tony Green. 'He took a beating for seven or eight rounds and then he'd come on. You can't do that in the fight game. You can't keep taking those beatings.'

Some close to Matthew urged him to wrap up his career.

'Russell, although he would love to have seen him go out as champion, he was definitely in the group of people saying, "You need to get yourself squared away because you can't fight forever,"' Bruton recalled. 'There were people also who did him no good. I don't think it was on purpose, I just think he had too many "friends". There were people around him … who as far as spending money and needing to fight, especially in later years, when he just needed the money … It was just not good.'

Not only was Matthew running out of options in boxing, he found himself running out of friends.

Salim El-Amin, his old friend from the projects, was still around, but he was powerless to help. 'All hell broke loose with the IRS, and they took his money and his house because he didn't pay his taxes and people around him weren't taking care of the business like it should have been taken care of,' El-Amin alleged. 'He had accountants. You always have to take care of the IRS because they will take your cars, your money and your house. Bilal was a manager, he did what he had to do … Made sure they got the fights, talked to the entourage and they were supposed to be taking care of business. After it was over, there were some difficulties. [Matthew] didn't have no money. People were looking out for him and they buried him. We were Muslims, we all believe in the same thing, but other people have their own ideas.'

Others in the team were no longer around. Paul Trace had to go back to work, running his photography studio in Woodbury, New

Jersey. Tony Green took a job working for the Roofers Union. Ameen, who'd had a cash row with Bilal at the end of 1984, was in Seattle and most of the gang had moved on.

There was also a bitter split between Bilal and Matthew. The boxing community collectively shook its head at what was happening to the former hero who had given them so many thrills over the years.

Matthew's old manager Frank Gelb thought Matthew should have just stayed with him. 'I had a lot of other fighters, and you saw what happened,' Gelb said. 'Matthew didn't have anything after a while.'

'I'm not saying everything was above board at any time, but the Muslims got most of his money,' reasoned Nigel Collins. 'So, would he have been better off with Frank? He probably would have been. Today, all fighters should have lawyers. Back then, not so much, and sometimes the manager was a lawyer. It's a corrupt world and boxing is no exception. That's pretty much par for the course. I figured it was going to happen to Matthew. Eventually the taxman's coming. That's inevitable.'

Matthew's fall looked inevitable to Paul Trace, too. 'I could see that when it was happening in real time,' said Matthew's loyal photographer. 'Obviously I couldn't say anything because it wasn't my place to say, but they were draining him for everything he had.'

It was a sad story, even if it had been on loop in boxing. Matthew's smile, his personality, those fights, no one wanted it to happen to him, not least Tony Green. 'He lost everything,' sighed Green. 'It all was gone. When the taxman and the IRS came, he lost everything. Then all his so-called friends abandoned him. They abandoned him, man. That's how it went.'

'We didn't think that would happen,' reflected Murad Muhammad years later, 'because his manager was able to make sure he had the necessary things.'

'I felt horrible,' said Michelle, watching the fall. 'My parents helped him as much as they could but the people who were, "my brother this" and "my brother that" were the ones who got them in the whole tax situation to begin with.'

Bilal had hired Michael Alexander as Matthew's accountant, but Matthew's lack of education meant he didn't know what he was signing or what questions to ask. He had hired them to make sure he was financially stable. An adviser, a business manager and an accountant should, between them, have been able to handle a client's finances.

'Unfortunately, Bilal was in over his head,' claimed Ameen. 'Mike Alexander was supposedly responsible for paying the taxes and, in addition to paying the staff after each fight, we would meet with the bank and the accountant and go over the finances for the fight and the accountant would specify how much he'd need to pay the taxes to make everything work. But there should have been another set of eyes because Bilal the manager was expected to perform fiduciary duties, but who's going to police the police? Bilal should not have had independent control of Matthew's finances. Matthew should have had his own folks advising him. Should Matthew have had responsibility? He shouldn't have had sole responsibility; he didn't have the education. He couldn't have managed his own finances but with the right understanding, he could have empowered people to act on his behalf other than blindly. And I don't mean mistakenly, because I don't believe – except for a couple of mistakes he made – Bilal deliberately misled Matthew.'

Regardless of what Ameen thought, plenty had been living their best life off Matthew when he was riding high. When the crash came, he couldn't find them.

Ameen was then only the same age as Matthew, late twenties, and admitted he didn't understand the intricacies or the economics of boxing, that he didn't have a full grasp on the business.

'I'm just a great friend and an administrator that can carry out certain administrative functions, but I didn't have any real understandings of the real big picture so I look back and just wish I knew then what I know now,' Ameen said.

There are plenty who were not so forgiving about who had done what to Matthew and left him high and dry, but not many blamed him. He trusted those around him and just didn't know any better.

And although Matthew and Michelle were no longer married, they remained close and had Matthew and Michael to look after. She had been there when he found his family and saw how his heart had been broken by people he didn't know; now, his heart had been broken by people who he did.

'It was almost as profound a hurt as the family, because at one point he looked at these guys as brothers,' Michelle said. 'And for them to do to him as they did – and Bilal was the ringleader because he brought everyone into the camps and introduced Matthew to all these people – it was like a second devastating hurt.'

* * *

'I'm not coming back just for financial reasons,' Matthew insisted, attempting a positive spin not many bought into while trying to explain why, almost two years after the Willie Edwards hammering and having lost four of his last six fights, he was returning to the ring.

'A lot of that was misunderstood,' he insisted. 'I didn't file bankruptcy because of my personal finances. It was one of my corporations. I was just looking over the light-heavyweight ratings and it made me laugh. I don't see anybody out there who can give me trouble.'

Now 31, he surveyed a landscape that was wide open after Spinks had moved up to heavyweight. When both Eddie Mustafa Muhammad and Marvin Johnson tossed their names into the ring for the vacant belts, Matthew thought 'Why not?'

Eddie Mustafa had lost in a bid for the new IBF title held by Slobodan Kacar in December of 1985 and two months later, Johnson began preparing for a surprise shot at Jamaica's Leslie Stewart.

Sam Solomon, who was back on board, said Matthew had spent much of the last year in the gym while Matthew again tried to play down that exhibition knockdown against Jesse Goodmond.

'He can take that to the bank now, I guess,' said Matthew. 'But it was nothing but an exhibition to try to raise some money for some people. It didn't mean anything.'

Matthew, however, admitted a training trip to Florida would give him an indication of what he had, his reflexes, handspeed and footwork, and whether he could still count on the legs that had started to all-too-willingly betray him.

Matthew liked Miami so much he settled there for a while. He claimed his personal problems were behind him, but acknowledged he wasn't ready for the likes of Marvin Johnson – his old opponent who'd resurfaced as a top dog after 14 wins since losing to Spinks – and Jamaican Stewart. He thought he was about six months away from them and he could get first-hand knowledge of Stewart because he was working out in the same Florida gym as him, where he was training to face Johnson for the vacant WBA title.

Hallandale Athletic Club's Stu Kaufman was the man financing the comeback. He and business partner Phil Vasta paid Matthew's bills while he trained at Beau Jack's gym. The idea was three comeback fights, then maybe face Lottie Mwale again, who was rated No. 7 by the WBC.

'We'll find out fast if he has anything left,' said Kaufman. 'His face is unmarked and his speech is fine. He looks like he's never been hit.'

It sounded ominous.

More than a decade earlier, Frank Gelb wanted to know what he had. Now Kaufman wanted to see what was left.

The Florida papers covered Matthew's return bout against Orlando journeyman Chris Wells at Hollywood's Diplomat Hotel.

'Because of my age, there will be obstacles to weave around,' Matthew confessed. 'Foot speed will be the biggest. It's the first thing that goes. I know a lot of state commissions have said I'm too old and shouldn't be boxing. But that's just the politics. I've always worked out, even when I haven't fought. They said a boxer shouldn't come back after he retires. But who said I ever retired? I never announced anything. I just stopped fighting for a while.'

He reiterated that money wasn't his motivator, though he owned up to 'bad business decisions', 'mismanagement and being misled.'

Dapper Matthew was known as a smart dresser (Paul Trace)

Philadelphia boxing icons Matthew and Joe Frazier on a night out (Paul Trace)

At the height of his fame, Matthew was friendly with another Philadelphia star, singer Teddy Pendergrass. Both would suffer different but tragic declines (Paul Trace)

The search for Matthew's family was marred by sadness. He's pictured here with his sisters and brother, Rodney, who had abandoned him as a toddler (Paul Trace)

Matthew and Ali get a sweat on sparring in Deer Lake (Paul Trace)

L-R Matthew, Muhammad Ali and Eddie Mustafa Muhammad were good friends (Paul Trace)

Matthew perches nervously
on Bombay for a publicity
shot in Atlantic City
(Paul Trace)

Saad Muhammad
jabs his way in against
lanky Vonzell Johnson
(Paul Trace)

Saad Muhammad's split bottom lip dangles loosely following a Sutherland uppercut
(Boxing News) and right (Paul Trace)

Matthew, in green trunks,
trades bombs in a
battle with Jerry Martin
(Paul Trace)

Matthew's team would swell in size. There was a core group, but when fight week came around the numbers grew. Among those pictured (back row) Sam Solomon, the masseuse, Milt Bailey and (far right) Paul Trace. Bottom L-R Mustafa Ameen, Tony Green and Bilal (right of Matthew) (Paul Trace)

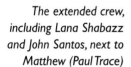

The extended crew, including Lana Shabazz and John Santos, next to Matthew (Paul Trace)

Before a flight to Alaska, Matt visited the pilot's cockpit and asked Paul Trace to photograph him. Then he was announced on the plane (Paul Trace)

The team steps out in Jacksonville to prepare for Braxton, but Trace (centre) realised there were problems when Saad Muhammad bought his new (inset) cherry red Rolls-Royce Corniche while in training camp (Paul Trace and The Ring)

Matthew sizes up Dwight Braxton as Murad Muhammad looks on (Paul Trace)

A blood-soaked Braxton ends the title reign of the great Saad Muhammad

The fall – Saad Muhammad crumbles a second time to Dwight Braxton as his career begins to spiral

Matthew points to his plaque at the International Boxing Hall of Fame after his 1998 induction (International Boxing Hall of Fame)

Matthew wound up having a sad 'No Holds Barred' fight in Japan when he could no longer get licensed to box (Mike Altamura)

Saad Muhammad and Frank Stallone meet again on the set of Rocky Balboa (Frank Stallone)

Old foes reunite – Marvin Johnson, Yaqui Lopez and Eddie Mustafa attend Matthew's induction into the Pennsylvania Boxing Hall of Fame (Larry Tornambe)

Matthew takes the microphone to talk at a fundraising event for the homeless in Philadelphia, and is flanked by Larry Tornambe (Larry Tornambe)

Matthew, on the streets of Atlantic City, with his friends Ralph and Willie (Author's collection)

Matthew and 'Sharkey' visit Joe Frazier's Gym to talk about an event that failed to materialise (Author's collection)

Rocky stories – Chuck Wepner laid claim to being the motivation for Sylvester Stallone's movie, while Matthew auditioned for the Rocky III role of Clubber Lang (Author's collection)

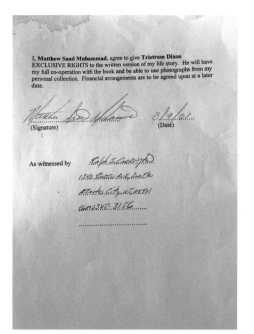

The provisional contract between the author and legendary fighter after they agreed to write this book in 2001

The note Dwight Qawi left by Matthew's bedside as Saad Muhammad fought for his life in hospital (Paul Trace)

Matthew and the author in Atlantic City.

(Inset) Saad Muhammad trains Dixon in the Atlantic City Police Athletic League Gym (Boxing Bob Newman)

The headstone that John DiSanto from Philly Boxing History raised money for so Matthew could be remembered is in Ivy Hill Cemetery (Author's collection)

A limousine business his name was attached to had folded and another venture Matthew wouldn't discuss had resulted in Chapter 13 bankruptcy. Friends said he'd lent people money to open the businesses and they had just taken off with it. He was back boxing because modelling and acting were too slow.

Matthew fought Wells with four days' notice. That's where his career was. The memories of long training camps in Deer Lake were forgotten.

Despite Saad saying he was only at around '60 per cent' of where he needed to be, he had too much for Wells, who took four counts in the first five rounds before being hurt and stopped in the sixth. A crowd of around 1,200 cheered Matthew's every success.

'It's still there,' Matthew contended. 'You saw the punching power there. I just have to get my coordination together. I wouldn't say I'm happy. I'd say it was okay.'

Things started to change quickly; Kaufman's partner Vasta was not all he was making himself out to be.

'Boxing attracts them all,' read the *New York Daily News* when Vasta hit the headlines. Vasta had signed other boxing talent, including Doug DeWitt and Anthony Fletcher, and he had even offered heavyweight Carl Williams $125,000 to work for him. Then he bought half an interest in Jimmy Glenn's Times Square Gym only to be arrested and charged as the kingpin in a narcotics ring.

When Vasta was caught in a sting in a car park, he had no idea that he'd been tracked by DEA agents for months. 'How long were you guys following me?' he asked. 'How did you get into the restaurant parking lot before I did? I don't understand how you knew I would be there ... was the other guy I met with arrested, too? ... you don't have to tell me anything, but you never know when a favour can be returned ... Do you follow boxing? Did you ever hear of Saad Muhammad? I just signed him ... great fighter.'

More than $5.5m in cash was found at Vasta's home in Mineola, New York. There was also 13lbs of heroin (worth $7m in 1986), 14lbs of cocaine ($800,000), seven weapons and drug paraphernalia.

They found $12,000 in cash, a bulletproof vest and a stun gun in his car.

'He seemed like a real nice guy,' said Jimmy Glenn.

Authorities announced it had been 'the largest seizure of cash ever made from an individual in the United States'.

Just when Matthew had thought he'd seen and heard it all, boxing could still surprise him.

* * *

Old warrior Marvin Johnson was the champion once more. He'd upset unbeaten Stewart on 9 February 1986, to capture the WBA title, becoming the first-ever three-time world light-heavyweight champion. He'd stopped Stewart on cuts in the old Market Square Arena where he'd lost his WBC title to Matthew seven years earlier.

Back in Florida, Miami promoter and manager Chris Dundee wasn't sure what he had with his young stud Uriah Grant, but he knew the Jamaican had something. Grant could crack with both hands and could take a shot.

One way of road-testing his prospect was to put him in with a fighter who still had name value but didn't have the same ability he'd had years earlier. Matthew took the call. On the flipside, a win over a nine-fight novice would take Matthew a step closer to contention.

Six weeks after fighting Wells, Matthew faced Grant before 1,500 fans at the Galt Ocean Mile Hotel in Fort Lauderdale. Matthew told writer Elmer Smith he'd been able to focus in Florida, adding that he was in much better shape for Grant than he had been for Wells. He had dropped around 10lbs.

'I don't know nothing about him,' Matthew said of Grant. 'I don't want to know nothing. I'm just going to kick his behind.'

He wanted to win a world title and then face his old opponent Marvin Johnson in a third fight, to finally unify the titles. 'I want to bring something [a title] with me before I fight Marvin Johnson. I don't want to come naked. I am a champion. *Ring* magazine announced me as one of the best champions of my time, so therefore I want to come back in with the championship and then maybe fight Marvin. I will be worthy and it will be a multi-million-dollar fight.'

He was far from that and he knew it. You could tell he had been humbled. The bright lights of the casinos in Atlantic City were a long way off, and so were the purses that ran into hundreds of thousands, but Johnson's unlikely victory had given Matthew hope. He thought a trilogy bout with Johnson would be 'Superfight III'. 'If Marvin can do it, I can too,' he reckoned.

Then Matthew lost to Grant on all three scorecards – and he was damaged throughout the fight. The Florida press wrote that the youngster had 'all but ended' the comeback, having cut Matthew above both eyes and caused the old champion's face to bulge with swelling.

'Physically, he was stronger than I was, he hurt me several times in the fight, but I was conscious,' Matthew conceded. 'I knew what I had to do, but his style was confusing to me.'

One headline said it was a 'Saad, Saad situation'.

Even Kaufman lamented, 'Grant was a fighter he should have beaten.'

The glory days were slipping further away for Matthew, but not for Michael Spinks. He had beaten Larry Holmes to become the world heavyweight champion, ending the great Easton man's unbeaten run at 49 fights.

It actually turned out that Grant was a legitimate prospect. He went on to win the IBF world cruiserweight title. Years later, Grant said he had no idea he was facing a legend before he got in the ring with Matthew. 'It was a local show, there was no press, it was just an event, with no real money behind it, no one really cared,' Grant recalled in 2021. 'They put the fight on because they wanted to get me a fight ... I was the new kid on the block. I had no idea about boxing, who was involved, who was great, who was not. In those days, I just had the desire to do something with my life. Only after the fight, I learned who he is. I learned he was a gentleman. I can't take anything away from his credibility, he was a wonderful man, a guy who devoted his life and career to the game. [He was] a fighter with that determination and mindset who deserves some credit.'

The Florida experiment was over for Matthew. He headed back to New Jersey.

Trouble followed in June 1986 when he was pulled over by police for doing 85mph in a 55mph zone on the Garden State Parkway. As he reached into his glovebox for driving documents, the officer saw a .25 calibre handgun. Matthew was charged with possession of a concealed weapon. He had a permit to have one in neighbouring Pennsylvania, but not in New Jersey. He was released on $1,000 bail.

On 2 July, there was more sad news when John Santos, Matthew's adoptive father passed away. He was 85 and had travelled with Matthew until old age prevented him from doing so. It was another blow for Matthew. He and Michelle went to the funeral together. They sat in the car and had a heart to heart.

'My dad's gone,' cried Matthew. 'I'm really all alone in the world now.'

Michelle's heart broke for him once more.

In the summer, Matthew returned to Kaufman in Florida hoping for another fight. He was desperate. A few weeks after losing to Grant, he had also reached out to Don King's step-son, Carl, a fight manager, and asked him to get him a bout. Kaufman still had a three-year contract with Matthew in place.

'He wants to fight again,' said Kaufman. 'There's a lot of questions about how serious he is. I want him in the gym for at least a month before I get him a fight.'

In October 1986, Matthew's name appeared on posters in North Dakota, advertising a fight with 1984 Olympic silver medallist and novice pro Virgil Hill. The *Bismarck Tribune* said Matthew 'backed out' of the contest at the Civic Center two days before the bout. Matthew had suffered an injury while sparring in Pleasantville, near Atlantic City, on 1 October. It would have been a cynical mismatch, a young prospect using a veteran's name to get some rounds under his belt while handing out a steady beating to a legend.

Hill hoped the fight would be rescheduled but Eric Winbush stepped in to take Matthew's place, losing a decision over ten rounds, getting dropped twice in the process.

Hill's 1984 Olympic team-mate, Evander Holyfield, was also making waves in the pros, and had captured the WBA cruiserweight world title in a 15-round thriller over Dwight Muhammad Qawi in July 1986.

In November, Matthew and Leslie Stewart, who was now being trained by Sam Solomon, crossed paths as they shared a bill at the Jean Pierre Sports Complex in Mucurapo in Trinidad and Tobago. Matthew beat Colombian Tomas Polo Ruiz over ten rounds, while Stewart stopped Fulgencio Obelmejias in four to put him one fight away from a Marvin Johnson rematch.

But as 1987 opened, Matthew moved even further away from any kind of contention when he dropped a ten-round decision to local fighter Pat Strachan in Nassau. Sure, Matthew won a fight in the Bahamas with a victory over an obscure novice named James Coakley, who lost three of his next four and then retired, but Matthew's career trajectory was going in one direction. It wasn't a healthy one.

In between those fights, Matthew was indicted by a grand jury for illegal possession of a weapon based on the Garden State Parkway incident. He faced as many as five years in prison and was given the chance to enter a pre-trial intervention programme. All charges would have been dropped had he completed a supervised probation period and 60 hours of community service. He didn't, and then he failed to attend a 1 April hearing and was canned from the programme, with a bench warrant issued for his arrest. He told authorities he planned on turning himself in but he was looking for a New Jersey lawyer to represent him.

Things took another turn for the worse when the jury was told about his previous convictions from earlier in his life, when he was charged with aggravated assault and battery and aggravated robbery as a teen under the name Matthew Franklin. The earlier charge could add a further 18 months onto the possible five years.

By now, Matthew's former trainer, Steve Traitz, was serving six years in prison on racketeering charges in the aftermath of a bribery scandal and for intimidation while head of the Roofers Union.

Retirement still wasn't an option for Matthew, but he did receive some positive press more befitting his championship days when, on 31 October 1987, he was on the scene with a passer-by who helped save children and parents from a fire in Atlantic City. A newspaper reported on its front page that a huge fire engulfed an apartment block on Arctic Avenue, and Matthew and Arthur Johnson scaled the walls to rescue screaming toddlers. Firefighters said lives might have been lost if Matthew and Johnson hadn't shown up when they did, helping people down from the roof as sirens rang out.

A smaller piece on the cover was titled, 'Rescue Normal for Heroes'. Matthew modestly played it down. 'That was normal for me,' he told the newspaper. 'It's natural just being human to help another person. Maybe someday someone will save my life.'

'Saad Muhammad went home to train,' wrote the *Press*.

Two months later, in December 1987, Matthew showed up in Weirton, West Virginia, and won a ten-rounder against Bobby Thomas at the Millsop Community Center. While in town with trainer Solomon, he was a guest on Larry Tornambe's radio show. It just so happened that Larry was a boxing guy and his favourite fighter of all time was Matthew Saad Muhammad.

Tornambe was wary about meeting a hero, but his concerns were put to the side by his guest.

'It was a sobering time for him,' Tornambe said. 'He understood he wasn't fighting a world contender, but he did not denigrate the man [Bobby Thomas], the opponent or the situation. He was so gracious, he spilled his whole story out there for me and we talked boxing.'

In April 1988, Matthew boxed Lee Harris. Harris had lost the only contest he'd had. They headlined a bill in Mechanicsville, Virginia. Matthew squashed Harris in 30 seconds, and Harris never fought again.

But the darkest days of Matthew's descent were just beginning and there'd be only one more win in his next, and final, ten fights.

It was a horror show. When one thing went, everything went; the skills, the power, the punch-resistance, the title, the house, the family, the friends, the possessions, the lot. Just a proud man remained and there was just one thing Matthew Saad Muhammad knew how to do. He bit down, planted his feet and took his licks.

CHAPTER 19

SCRAMBLING

WHEN YOU'RE scrambling around for a cheque it's not easy to produce quarter of a million in back taxes. There was talk of some sort of financial plan for Matthew to pay back what he owed and when the bankruptcy news first hit, Matthew tried to put a positive spin on it.

He said he'd 'accepted responsibility' but really, he questioned how his team could have let it happen. He felt betrayed. He'd been paying people to look after his affairs.

Everything he said he didn't want to do, he would now have to do. He didn't want to fight on too long. He didn't want to have to go around the gyms and spar for a few hundred bucks. He didn't want to have to take on more damage because he knew he'd already had his fair share. But he was in a financial pit and there was no other way of escaping.

'I was just signing cheques,' he sighed, clearly regretful of his generosity. 'Yes, it's my fault, but I had people who basically did my work for me, supposedly paid taxes for me, because I did not have the knowledge to go about paying taxes. That's why I had a manager and an accountant.'

According to best guesses, more than $4m had gone.

Throughout 1987, Matthew was earning money as a sparring partner, working with Emanuel Steward's team of Kronk fighters from Detroit, training with the likes of Tommy Hearns and Michael Moorer.

Back in 1979, shortly before Matthew fought Marvin Johnson for the world title, Hearns was an ambitious welterweight who did a few rounds with Matthew in Philadelphia. After seeing Hearns do well, Steward and Tommy felt they could go all the way up to light-heavyweight. Years on, Matthew was now sparring Tommy.

'He looks good, damn good,' Steward said of Matthew. 'With a couple of fights, he could be right back on top.'

It was just what Matthew wanted to hear. Someone believed in him again. The money would be back, so would the fame. Why wouldn't he want to listen to that?

Others in the Kronk encouraged him, too. Hearns, who had used Saad for sparring before he lost to Iran Barkley for the middleweight title, said that if Matthew kept training like he was, he'd be champion again.

'He has that competitive attitude,' said 'The Hitman'. 'Deep down inside he really wants to be back on top, to be a public figure again. Talking to Matthew, it seems like getting back to where he was is the most important thing in his life.'

The problem was, Matthew was just a durable old heavy bag for the burgeoning Kronk squad. He was experienced enough to teach up and comers and robust enough to go rounds with dynamite-punching smaller men like Hearns.

You can't tell how much wear and tear was added to Matthew as a sparring partner looking for pay. One young emerging Kronk fighter was Moorer, a future world champion at light-heavyweight and heavyweight and he was a cold, merciless type. Reports got out that Moorer had bashed in Matthew's ribs during a camp in Phoenix that resulted in Matthew spending time in hospital.

'The doctor thought Saad had been hit with a hammer,' Steward later revealed. 'He didn't believe that a fist in a 16-ounce training glove could cause a break like that.'

Moorer was an icy individual with a glare fixed on the big time. Over the years, he probably felt bad for taking liberties with the legend. Asked who his childhood heroes were decades later, he said: 'Matthew Saad Muhammad. He was always behind in his fights and he was always victorious. I used to train with him in the beginning. A very great, nice man.'

Matthew's mileage clicked well over and above what was healthy for any normal odometer.

'I appreciated the job,' he would say of those Kronk sparring days, wearing the red and gold of the famous Detroit fight club. 'But I want to say that I am not a punching bag and I am not a sparring partner, at least not on a regular basis. I am a past and future world champion.'

It was September 1988. People knew he couldn't perform miracles any longer, but still wouldn't accept what he had become. He was certain he could get back on top.

One man who hoped to see Matthew there was his new trainer, Atlantic City's Cash White.

White and Matthew trained out of the Pleasantville Rec Center in New Jersey. White had boxed as a professional and had a mixed 4-9 record, but he'd fought the likes of Joey Giardello, Bennie Briscoe and Jimmy Hairston. White didn't suffer fools, but he was also hoping for his big break as a trainer.

'Just look at him,' White said of Matthew. 'Does he look like a guy who can't fight anymore? The man is still an athlete. And he's dedicated. And he's willing to do whatever is necessary to make it back to the top.'

White felt it was as simple as Matthew training hard and then getting it all back, perhaps without realising all the damage that had been acquired.

Matthew bounced off White's positivity and said he was a 'new and improved' version of the old Saad, that he was better now because, 'I decided it was all right to duck a punch every now and again.'

Six weeks later, Matthew was annihilated in one round by Frankie Swindell in Newark, New Jersey. It was a sorry night at the Quality Inn Hotel. Not only did Matthew lose, but Eddie Mustafa Muhammad fought for the final time in his life. Eddie was stopped in round three by Arthel Lawhorn.

If there was a miracle left in Matthew, it was that he had somehow managed to get a licence to fight in New Jersey again.

But this was it for him. New commissioner Larry Hazzard never wanted to see him fight again. Having refereed Matthew during his heyday, he saw a different man in front of him. Hazzard had saved Jerry Martin against Matthew: now he was trying to save Matthew from himself.

'It's kind of ironic that I was the referee in a fight when I felt like I'd saved another fighter from the wrath of Saad Muhammad,' Hazzard said. 'Then, years later, when I became a commissioner in New Jersey at the end of Saad Muhammad's career, he tried to make a comeback in New Jersey and I denied it. In many ways, I felt like I was saving Saad Muhammad from himself, because I felt that Saad was well past his prime and I just didn't feel he possessed the skills anymore to make him successful. I really didn't want to see him get hurt and so I denied it. And unfortunately, I think I was proven to be correct because in some of those fights that he took in places where they allowed him to fight, he was not successful, and he could have been seriously injured.'

Tennessee's Swindell was a good fighter. He'd won 14 and lost only two at the time but defeats to Wali Muhammad and Robert Foley revealed he was not quite from the top drawer. He'd won the USBA light-heavyweight title in his previous bout, and he'd go on to lose a couple of times in bids for the world title, against WBO champion Michael Moorer and IBF ruler Charles Williams.

The IBF's No. 3 contender had come in at late notice when Matthew's team and the promoter decided he was a decent fit for the show. Originally Harry Daniels, a limited southpaw from Georgia, was supposed to be in the opposite corner, but the New Jersey commission rejected him as they didn't think he was strong enough. They hadn't realised how badly Matthew had declined, but they learned and would never issue him another licence.

Matthew was hurt every time Swindell landed and shuddered after each punch. Matthew was dropped early by a right hand and beat the count but was then driven into the ropes and shipping punishment when referee Randy Neumann stopped it. Matthew protested, certain there was another comeback up his sleeve.

In the co-feature, Eddie Mustafa Muhammad was knocked down and stopped by Detroit's Lawhorn. Lawhorn had come in for little-known Tim Bullock, and he'd dropped Eddie who, like Matthew, was taking a shellacking on the ropes when referee Paul Venti stepped in.

The $3m bounty the two Muhammads could have split several years earlier was long gone.

'I think that's it for me,' Eddie told Matthew.

'I'm going to keep on fighting,' Matthew replied.

A decade later, Swindell fought Harry Daniels, the man he'd deputised for on that night in Newark. He blew Daniels away in two rounds in Nashville. The man whom Eddie Mustafa had been due to fight, Tim Bullock, retired with a losing record. There weren't any winners from that night in Newark. Not really. Eddie, then aged 36, walked and never looked back.

'I always told myself, before I started boxing, if I were to ever get stopped in a fight then that was my last fight, I wouldn't fight no more,' said Eddie. 'I made that promise to myself. I'd started my family, I wanted to raise my family, I wanted to have fun with my family and I wanted to be there for my family. When I retired, I had a lot of opportunities. I could have kept on making movies, I could have done a lot of other things but I would have had to move to LA and I wanted to stay in Brooklyn. I was in construction, that worked out pretty good. There's a bunch of things I could have gone into and become successful in.'

Boxing would eventually entice Eddie back, but from the safe side of the ropes, and he did eventually move west.

'People said, "Where you been? Everyone's been looking for you,"
he recalled. 'They would tell me about the knowledge I had in the game and so I said I'd spread that. When I made up my mind that I wanted to do that, my first fighter was Iran Barkley, who was on the downslide. I was here in Vegas and I saw Iran running, doing roadwork, and it had to be about 120 degrees and he was running with heavy clothes on and I was thinking, "Who the hell is this guy?" It was the height of noon. "This guy is nuts." We started talking and

he said he was trying to make a comeback. He had eye problems, he was broke, and he said, "I'm trying to get my career back on track." He'd been a world champion but he'd lost everything and he asked if I'd work with him. I said I didn't do it anymore but if he listened to me, I would, and I would make him world champion. Now he thought I was fucking nuts. "Me, be world champion again? I'm at the bottom of the totem pole." I said, "All you have to do is listen." He listened, he became three-time world champion.'

There would be more champions for Eddie, who became a prominent trainer working with Michael Bentt, Hasim Rahman, Badou Jack, Johnny Tapia, James Toney, Chad Dawson and Zab Judah. In 2003, he worked with the Teamsters and James P. Hoffa to form Joint Association of Boxers (JAB), a union for fighters and by 2008 more than 2,000 boxers had signed up.

'This is my legacy, the union,' Eddie said. 'When fighters can no longer fight and no longer hear the roar of the crowd, the fighters will still have their medical and health benefits.'

It was a wonderful idea, but boxing has never been able to sustain anything like that.

A union could have provided a vital safety net for someone like Matthew.

'It looks like the end of the line for Saad,' predicted one report after that Swindell defeat.

But Matthew wouldn't even contemplate retirement. Worse still, he wanted a rematch with Swindell.

Hazzard said no way. Not in New Jersey.

'We didn't fall out,' Hazzard later recalled. 'He respected my position. He wasn't happy about it but he respected it. We had a good relationship. He always greeted me warmly, was always very respectful and I think he always appreciated my position as a referee and as a commissioner.'

In December 1988, two months after Swindell, Matthew was in the papers for the wrong reasons following the 'theft' of a car.

'Ex-champion pleads guilty to theft', read the *Atlantic City Press*. He'd borrowed a car from a woman on the agreement that he'd buy it from her. The woman was transferred in her job out to California and Matthew couldn't buy the car. She asked him to take it to Pittsburgh and hand it over, but he didn't.

He was put on probation and made to make payments of $1,200 he clearly didn't have but his defence attorney, Albert Mills, said if he paid up before mid-February the charges would be reduced to 'that of a disorderly person'.

There was talk of Matthew facing Darnell Wingfield, 17-0, in Ohio in January but Matthew was replaced by Elvis Parks. In July 1989 there were discussions to match him in Toronto with Willy Featherstone as part of a WBO 175lbs tournament with the winner getting a shot at new WBO light-heavyweight champion Michael Moorer.

The fight delays probably didn't help him, but Matthew managed to get a date in Australia, and he was soon back to being used as dog meat by world-class fighters.

Jeff Harding, WBC light-heavyweight champion – owner of Matthew's old belt – decked Matthew twice in sparring as they trained for their respective bouts on the same Brisbane bill, a Bill Mordey–Top Rank co-promotion on a Tuesday in October 1989.

Matthew had hooked up with Harding in Atlantic City where he helped the champion with sparring before his fights with British duo Tom Collins and Dennis Andries.

In the other corner from Matthew, Kevin Wagstaff was an average left-handed cruiserweight who outweighed Matthew by about seven pounds and took him eight rounds before a majority draw was announced. Wagstaff, originally from Nottingham in the United Kingdom, had won 24 of 40 contests, losing 13 and drawing three.

Throughout the fight, the commentators lamented how far Matthew had fallen as Wagstaff mauled forwards and outfought and outpunched the former great.

Aussie fighting legend and three-weight world champion Jeff Fenech encouraged Matthew from ringside, but Matthew couldn't do a thing, even though Wagstaff spent most of the fight right in front of him.

The spectacle, at the Brisbane Entertainment Center in Queensland, was another sad one. Even though Matthew gradually improved in the fight's second half, he was done as a fighter and shouldn't have been doing it anymore.

In Matthew's corner, Aussie cornermen Manny Hickman and Peter Mitrevski told Matthew he was ahead with one round to go. Matthew and Wagstaff flew at each other to kick off the eighth, swinging to almost a standstill and crossing the finish line with a sporting touch of gloves. Matthew celebrated, Wagstaff raced to his stool to recuperate. Matthew wanted to show everyone, particularly the judges, that he had plenty left in the tank, so he moved around the ring shadowboxing in one last desperate plea to sway them but it was not enough. He'd managed just a draw and he had plenty to think about on the 28-hour flight home the next day.

By now, people in the sport were feeling sorry for him. Mordey's agent and matchmaker was American fixer Don Majeski. He'd tried to get Matthew to go out on a win.

'"Matthew, that's the end," he told him. '"You shouldn't fight any more. You didn't lose."'

'But he continued,' Majeski added. 'I don't know who was putting him in and he could always get fights as an ex-champ. Value for money, he was one of the most exciting fighters who ever lived – he was like Arturo Gatti but he was better than Gatti. Those fights with Marvin Johnson, Yaqui Lopez ... unbelievable. But I couldn't get him to go out with a win. I said he had to pack it in but, unfortunately, he continued to lose. There was always someone out there willing to put him on.'

Everyone knew what Matthew couldn't afford to accept. Years later, when one Australian matchmaker stumbled across the Wagstaff–Saad Muhammad tape in his collection, he had to check the speed of the recording as he originally thought the years had slowed it down. It hadn't. Matthew had lost his snap, his power, his reflexes. It had all gone.

As 1990 dawned, a decade on from the highest highs Matthew had experienced, the slow disaster continued to unfold. Broke, bankrupt and unlicensed in New Jersey due to concerns over his health, he lurched from one dire payday to the next, staking his future health with every outing and every concussive loss.

'Battered Saad hits a new low,' read the *Boxing News* headline after 2,300 fans filled the Sporthalle in Hamburg-Wandsbek in Germany to see the shell of a legend get chewed up and spat out in three rounds by Markus Bott. Bott was a decorated amateur while 'Muhammad performed like all shot fighters perform,' wrote Andreas Lorenz, who was ringside in Germany.

Up at cruiserweight, Matthew was put on the canvas in round two; his night was ended in round three by a big right hand.

'I think I'm still part of the title picture,' said a deluded Matthew. 'But at light-heavy. I still have the heart – he just caught me cold.'

Matthew was hiding from reality but even he had started to see what others saw. Someone asked him about the New Jersey suspension while he was in Germany and he replied, 'They just won't let me fight anymore, because in their opinion I've had too many hard fights. After this result … maybe they're right.'

CHAPTER 20

REALITY CHECK

BY THE summer of 1990, reality was unavoidable.

Aged 36, Matthew boxed on, but another year went by between contests, from the Bott fight in Germany to a sad homecoming in Philadelphia.

It's hard to track Matthew's whereabouts apart from where he was on fight nights during his descent. He cropped up here and there sporadically; sometimes he was in New Jersey and sometimes in Philly.

He somehow passed his physicals in Pennsylvania and was, according to sources, 'begrudgingly given permission to fight'.

It was a horrible decision. Everyone bar Matthew hoped he'd stop trying to hunt the meagre paydays.

He was being looked after by Pat Doran, a New Jersey civil engineer who was not a fight figure. Doran had his own business but worked with amateurs in a local gym and he was thrilled that he'd got to meet the former WBC world champion.

'I was a tiny, tiny part of Matthew's career, but I knew him well over that period of time,' Doran stated. 'I met him in 1990 and I knew him for the rest of the time. He was a great guy. I was lucky.'

The first day Doran walked into a boxing gym, Matthew was there and the old champion asked him for a lift to Brigantine. Matthew's car had been towed to a lot and Doran's brother was a police officer who managed to get the car released.

'I'd brought this kid to the gym and Saad said, "I'll train him for you,"' Doran smiled. 'All of a sudden, I've got a young heavyweight who wants to fight, Saad who wants to train him and it was like, "Wow." Saad was still fighting, but that's when nobody wanted him to fight anymore. I think he had lost his last couple of fights. It was 1990, so he trained my young guy and I watched him work out.'

Doran knew Matthew was at the end of the line and hoped he would retire but stay in the gym and train more amateurs. Doran thought the once-great champ could pass his knowledge and experience on and inspire a new generation of warriors.

Matthew was always in the gym anyway, and he was more than happy to oblige Doran, but in return he wanted Doran to help him out and get him fights. With Matthew helping Doran out, Doran wanted to return the favour.

'Who the heck am I?' said Doran. 'Here was Saad Muhammad, a world champion, and he was such a nice guy. Yeah, I was helping him out with a couple of dollars here and there. I brought him in to my house, brought him to meet my friends and I'm a little skinny guy who was never a fighter but for me I had a talent working with one kid, not a team but one person. All my confidence came from being around Saad, learning how to set these fights up, but at the same time I knew the situation – but at least I thought I was taking care of him as best I could. My justification was that if I didn't do it, somebody else was going to really get him hurt. And nobody came after me, at least that I knew of, as far as [saying] "You better stop doing this …" I heard all the talk yet nobody said, "You better not do this, you better not do that …" But nobody else was helping Saad. Nobody was helping Saad. In any kind of way. Saad had to live, too. He had no other means of income, he'd gone through all his money, he was living in a little lot in Egg Harbour Township.'

Matthew had remarried and his second wife, Elaine, was a reservations manager at the Trump Plaza Hotel and Casino. She was concerned Matthew couldn't find anything to do but fight, and that was stopping him from committing to training fighters full-time, too.

'He wants quick money,' she said. 'But he should start realising that these 20- and 30-year-olds can beat him. I happen to love him and I want to grow old with him. I don't want him taking any more punches than he has up to now. I worry every time he steps in the ring. Will it be the last time I see him? Or will he survive today and become punch-drunk tomorrow? I've said all this to him, but he says a man must do what a man must do. But to me he is endangering his health and tarnishing the championship he once held.'

In the ring Matthew tried to recreate the magic, but the only miracle was that he managed to get licensed in Pennsylvania again. All *Boxing News* could say of his bout against Ed Mack was that it was a 'Saad affair'. Everyone knew that. Fellow Philadelphian Mack beat Matthew in front of his own fans in Philly in an eight-rounder with a young ambitious pro called Bernard Hopkins on the undercard.

'The depressing saga of Matthew Saad Muhammad continued,' wrote Nigel Collins in the trade paper. 'The once-magnificent warrior refuses to accept the fact he is flirting with disaster by continuing to box.

'Unfortunately, the only way that's going to happen is if he absorbs another uncompromising beating. The Mack bout wasn't that. Saad was game enough to fight on, even though he didn't come close to winning. His legs trembled from time to time, but they never completely let him down,' added a dejected Collins.

Fans, still hopeful but becoming increasingly upset by what they were watching, yelled, 'Come on, Champ! You can do it!'

It was hope, not expectation.

'I gave him too much respect,' assessed Mack, who won by margins of 77-74, 77-75 and 78-75. 'At one time, he was one of the best.'

Matthew thought the Mack outcome wasn't that bad, that it could have been worse.

'Matthew Saad Muhammad is not washed up,' he insisted, with denial one of the few layers of self-preservation available to him. 'I'm going to keep on trying like an old war horse. I thought I had an edge, maybe a draw. If I'd been more active, I would have won this fight for sure.'

His self-assessment was grim, but a more realistic perspective came from Dwight Qawi, his rival ten years earlier.

'Looking at Saad, I realised how good he once was,' Qawi said. 'For someone who has no legs at all, he put up a helluva fight. He did some nice things. He still has the heart of a lion. But I think he should walk away.'

Matthew made just $1,800.

His fights were dropping off the radar as his relevance plummeted. A few weeks later, his name appeared on an English fight poster as the opponent for Swedish hope Roland Ericsson in a bout for the European super-middleweight championship, but the British Boxing Board of Control refused Matthew a licence.

West Ham puncher Mark Kaylor was brought in and handed the Swede his first loss.

As much as it's a game of snakes and ladders, boxing is a sport of trapdoors and loopholes.

But if England wouldn't allow Matthew to fight, someone else would so he travelled to Serbia and lost an eight-rounder to 6-0 Anton Josipovic. Southpaw Josipovic had won gold at the 1984 Olympics and would only have three more fights, losing two of them.

Three months after that, Matthew was back in Europe where he beat Govoner Chavers in Marbella. The Spanish city was known for its lax licensing regulations, and the outcome provided a lone island of hope for Matthew. They say the last thing a fighter loses is his punch, and Matthew threw the last good shots he would ever throw, a left hook and a wrecking ball overhand right that put Chavers flat on his back, earning Matthew courteous applause from the small crowd. It was the final win of Matthew's career.

There were more fights. Some never made it on to his official record but he punched for pay in Aruba, St Maarten and Trinidad and Tobago after the spell in Florida had not worked out, and there were a handful of fights in Portugal around the time of the Chavers victory.

However, it would prove to be only respite for Matthew. When he went to capitalise on the win in Woodbridge, Virginia, two months later, Matthew lost over eight rounds to three-fight novice Michael Green.

Matthew had become a 'shot' fighter at 27; now he was almost ten years older and virtually a sitting duck.

His opponent was only 2-1 but still managed to beat Matthew, having his 56th fight. Green never won another bout, losing his last four before retiring.

Matthew was just a pound over his title weight but the body had slowed and the lights were dimming.

The Green farce was worthy of only a line in a *Boxing News* roundup section, but around the same time, the late boxing writer Joseph C. Tintle caught up with Matthew for *The Ring* and the resulting interview was heart-breaking.

Matthew tried hard, unsuccessfully, to convince Tintle that he was ready for the likes of Michael Moorer, Jeff Harding, Virgil Hill and Prince Charles Williams. 'They know I still got it,' he contended, discussing the new era of champions.

Then Tintle brought up the Markus Bott fight and Matthew just said his head wasn't in it.

Around that time, Matthew was transitioning into becoming a boxing trainer, and according to the piece 'a low paid' one. He was with Tintle at Joe Mari's Boxing Gym on Atlantic Avenue, a couple of blocks from Atlantic City's Boardwalk. He was driving a Volkswagen Jetta, and Tintle reflected on the Rolls-Royce, the Mercedes, the BMW, the mansion in Jenkintown and all of the other trappings that came in those glory years.

Matthew was working with heavyweight journeyman Robert Colay who had a short-notice fight coming up with Riddick Bowe. Colay wasn't expected to win a second of a round. 'I tell you the truth,' said Matthew. 'I'm kind of embarrassed bein' in his corner.'

Matthew and Tintle traced the highs and lows, and then Matthew told Tintle that the well-publicised bankruptcy was courtesy of a faltering limousine service and a seafood restaurant.

'They fell through because I had people stealing from me,' he said. 'I was never around the businesses much because I thought everybody would be nice and wouldn't be stealing. In a lot of ways, I guess I'm my own worst enemy ... And I couldn't offset the money problems I was having at the time. I'd spent, spent, spent and had paid every one of my 17-member entourage $500 a week for a couple of years. That, plus tax problems, led to bankruptcy, and eventually I lost my home in 1984.'

He was too proud to ask for help and too proud to own up to what was happening, so he returned to boxing to set things straight.

'My self-worth was hurting something fierce,' he explained. 'I so wanted to be successful again. But I thought the only way I could do it was through boxing. After all, I was once a great warrior and great champion, all of which made me a wealthy man. And I wanted to be all those things one more time. So, once again, I put on the gloves.'

It was his identity. He wasn't just Matthew Saad Muhammad the boxer, he was Matthew Saad Muhammad the warrior. How could he go from that to packing groceries, labouring, delivering mail or working a 9 to 5? How could he transition from celebrity to civilian while maintaining his dignity?

'I don't think he has a firm grip on reality,' said Philly boxing writer Bernard Fernandez. 'Not from the standpoint of that he's whacked out; he just remembers himself in the way he was, and he just doesn't want to see the way that he is. Sure, he looks good and he sounds good. But watch him fight. There's nothing there.'

Nigel Collins agreed. 'With him these days it's a matter of self-delusion. In that way, he can hold on to his sanity.'

Tintle asked Matthew to describe the contests he'd fought in Trinidad, Australia, the Bahamas and West Virginia. It caused Matthew to think. Then a sharp dose of reality surged through him.

'I don't like fighting in tank towns,' Matthew confessed. 'But you got to do what you got to do.'

Then, thinking back to what he had, his voice cracked. 'All that is gone now, but I block it out because if I thought about what I've lost, I might just start crying.'

But Matthew wouldn't finish the interview on a downward trajectory. 'Can't think negative,' he smiled softly. 'Got to think positive and never give up on myself and the title shot.'

* * *

Brave, careless and insensitive matchmaking saw him face decent contender Andrew Maynard next. The hook was that Maynard had taken 12 rounds to beat Chavers. If Matthew did a better job, surely he and Maynard made sense and the fight would be competitive, right? Wrong.

Maynard was ambitious, hungry and a 1988 Olympic gold medallist who was tipped for the top. He'd only lost one out of 18 fights, and that came when he was moved too quickly into a match with Bobby Czyz.

There was a cursory mention of Maynard–Matthew in *Boxing News*, likely because it was on the undercard of heavyweight Riddick Bowe, who stole the headlines on a depressing Tuesday night for boxing at the Convention Center in Washington DC. Bowe and former sparring partner Elijah Tillery had a grudge match that concluded when Tillery kicked Bowe and an ugly melee ensued. Afterwards, gunfire broke out in the venue as 7,000 fans dashed for the exits and three were injured. One had been shot in the head.

Earlier in the evening, read *Boxing News*, 'in a sad light-heavyweight affair, poor Matthew Saad Muhammad was stopped in 20 seconds of the third round by world-ranked Andrew Maynard'.

One of many damning lines in a ringside report was, 'Though Saad looks physically fit, he just can't get out of the way of anything.'

It had never been his strongest suit, but he was now boxing in a fog; the haze of more than a decade of bloody wars had slowed him.

Frankly, Maynard beat the shit out of him. He worked over Matthew's body and head as the veteran fighter retreated to the ropes. But Matthew's legs weren't under him; the slaughter could and should have been stopped in the second.

'Do you know where you're at?' asked a concerned doctor between rounds.

'Of course, I do,' Matthew snapped, spent and confused. 'I'm in America, man.'

'I'm in er … I'm in er …'

'DC,' assisted his corner team.

'Maryland,' confirmed Matthew. 'DC, Washington.'

Not satisfied, the doctor probed further.

'What's your name?'

Matthew clucked and rolled his eyes, embarrassed, realising just how bad the fall was.

'Matthew Saad Muhammad.' He urged the doctor to get out of his face.

Maynard came out bombing in the third, and Matthew tried to block and cover while doing neither.

Matthew protested when the fight was stopped, but it was his stubbornness and pride, not an argument based upon any kind of reality.

* * *

Back in New Jersey, Doran prayed Matthew would become a full-time trainer, working with amateurs at the Brigantine gym.

'I think he'd be great at it,' Doran went on. 'He's like a Pied Piper at the gym, anyway. He leads all the kids in exercises.'

Doran admitted it had been a challenge to get Matthew licensed in Maryland, and that part of him wished that he had not been given the all-clear for Maynard. Doran worried about his friend if he had nowhere else to turn but admitted he'd have to sit Matthew down and discuss his options.

There had been five fights in 1991, four losses and the quick Marbella win to raise false hopes.

By the time Matthew fought Jason Waller on 21 March 1992, in the Colonial Theater in Fredericksburg, Virginia, you couldn't find Matthew's fight reports even in the most hardcore boxing magazines. Many probably didn't know he was still going. His nose was beaten flatter, the scar tissue around his eyes would slice open easily and hapless Waller stopped him in two rounds.

That was it for Matthew. He left the sport anonymously, the door slamming behind him on the way out.

'I wish I had a magic wand but I didn't and I wasn't a millionaire,' said Doran of his friend and his time with him.

Doran had been asked whether he felt bad being involved in Matthew's final fights. 'It's not like I could just set him up for life but I didn't see anyone else [trying to help] ... You know the stories, fighters have money and then they lose it, they all kick 'em to the kerb after that.'

Doran, who would admit to not knowing a lot about the boxing business, was not an enabler in the back-slapping sense. He was trying to help Matthew, and he was trying to keep him safe.

'I knew these little promoters putting on shows,' Doran explained. 'Probably fights that Saad could be okay in, you know. Then he went in with Maynard in Washington on this big card down there with Rock Newman and these guys, they took care of him. As soon as he got hit one time, they stopped it ... Which was good. He could have gotten hurt there. I don't know. Who knows? The point with me was I tried to look after him as best as I could because I knew somebody would try to put him in a big fight and take advantage of him ... I wanted to satisfy his desire to keep training and fighting but we did our best to try to take care of him. Anything can happen in any fight but eventually he retired, and that was good. He just had such a heart of a lion. He was just a true fighter.'

But after Waller, that was pretty much that for Matthew Saad Muhammad. There was nowhere else to go.

'He just kind of faded away,' said Doran. 'At that point, I was not trying to get him fights anymore and then he kind of accepted it. It just ended there. I don't think there was anyone trying to get him fights anymore. I kept pushing him to train the guys, "Be a trainer, Saad, don't fight. You're done."'

CHAPTER 21

HALL OF FAMER

'HE WOULD come round once in a while,' recalled Pat Doran of Matthew and his gym visits in his life after boxing. 'He was such a great guy. Everyone was friends with Saad. I'm not saying I knew everything about him, but to me he was the greatest thing in the world. After the fighting was done, we stayed in touch.'

In early 1992, the great ring announcer Michael Buffer told thousands at an Atlantic City boxing show that the brilliant former light-heavyweight – Matthew Saad Muhammad – was ringside. Matthew watched as the crowd rose and cheered. He soaked in the applause and then went to the fridge to grab a drink.

He was watching on TV at home.

'I heard my name announced,' Matthew laughed. 'I don't know how that happened.'

It was a rare high for Matthew, who was slipping further and further out of the consciousness of fight fans.

His slow descent continued as he reeled from fighting Jason Waller in Virginia in March of 1992 to clashing with Kiyoshi Tamura in Japan on 5 August 1992 at the Yokohama Arena. Matthew was still desperate to fight, to reclaim past glories, when a new, enticing door opened.

He needed the money, too, of course. One fighting payday, whether it was for thousands or, by now, hundreds of dollars, would equate to several days of work in a regular job, so it was easier just to pick up some paydays than get into a 9 to 5.

Besides, old foe Lottie Mwale was calling out Virgil Hill and Dwight Qawi was still fighting. But it wasn't the roaring 1980s any longer. Marvin Johnson had retired after losing a rematch to Leslie Stewart in 1987. Eddie Mustafa Muhammad had gone in 1988, Yaqui Lopez's last fight was in 1984 and Michael Spinks had retired on a pile of money in 1988 after a 91-second blowout loss to a rampant Mike Tyson.

Matthew was still trying. He still hoped. And in Japan, organisers believed his former world championship status would help sell tickets to one of their new events, a mixed martial arts shootfight, in what was a precursor to the Ultimate Fighting Championship.

The days of headlining Atlantic City, the big paydays, the hero-worship, it was all gone. The former matinee idol was on his own in Japan. He didn't know what he was doing and he didn't know what he'd signed up for. He had travelled to Japan with his name and his heart but there was nothing else left.

Pre-fight TV vignettes of the UWF International martial arts show were filmed with Matthew going through the motions on a punchbag, jumping rope and working on the pads. Physically, he could still do the things he needed to do to bluff a commission. But he sounded off. There was a slur in his words.

Kiyoshi Tamura boasted a 6-2 record in shootfighting, and he had fought the likes of Pat Miletich, Renzo Gracie and Frank Shamrock. He knew what he was doing and what he was getting into. Matthew was out of his depth, and he didn't speak the language of either the country he found himself in or the sport he'd signed up to take part in.

The Japanese had used several high-profile but greatly diminished boxers to build their emerging brand. In December 1991, Trevor Berbick, former WBC heavyweight champion and Matthew's sparring partner, went over, confident he could handle himself in a mysterious world. He ended up complaining that he was being kicked during the fight. Kicks were legal. Like Matthew, he likely didn't read or understand any small print. He was in agony from the leg kicks. Mid-contest, he pleaded with the referee, and then Berbick was kicked in the head by Nobuhiko Takada. A few minutes later, Berbick fled from the ring. Debris flew as the erratic Canadian protested loudly that he didn't know the rules. It was a tragedy, really. The fight clip was viewed more than 200,000 times on YouTube.

Meanwhile, a video of an old, pudgy Roberto Duran – wearing a tracksuit – losing to Masakatsu Funaki by a headlock in an equally sad sight from April 1992 has racked up about 50,000 views. The best boxers at the height of their careers were too expensive; the ones who needed the money, who couldn't make much from boxing any longer, were prime targets. Organisations like the UWF could claim their best would beat boxing's best, that they were superior. It wasn't just a case of chess and checkers; they were markedly different sports, and the fighters who went over had nowhere else to go. They were at the end of the line, commercially and physically, but they could be repackaged into major, fresh attractions in Japan.

'The world knows that I have a good right hand,' Matthew said, trying to hype the contest. 'But you can't just rely on one punch. I have to land a series of punches … He's very crafty, he's sly. I will catch him and I won't let him get close to me.'

Matthew's boxing record was announced as 38-11-3 when it was 39-16-3.

It was 8 May 1992, and in Yokohama Matthew put his right hand on his heart as they played ' The Star-Spangled Banner'. He waited to try this unusual form of combat in a foreign land.

As it was, the introductions and anthems lasted longer than the fight. Matthew was 38 and the younger, determined Japanese fighter came out of his corner with a high guard wearing red trunks and red knee-length boots with his knuckles bare. Matthew wore boxing boots, white shorts and boxing gloves.

Within seconds, Tamura kicked Matthew in the leg, which instantly unsettled the fighter, who tried to fend off the same kick once or twice before Kiyoshi landed one cleanly, scooping Matthew's lead left leg from under him. Matthew dropped on to all fours, Tamura jumped on his back and started to choke him. Matthew couldn't even attempt to prise himself free because he had boxing gloves on. His legs straightened. He faced down towards the mat and he tapped out, surrendering with his right glove.

In just 34 seconds, Tamura had beaten the former world light-heavyweight champion; he could boast the scalp of the great Matthew Saad Muhammad to all and sundry, as could the promoters. Matthew's name had been bought and paid for.

Worse, it was likely a double cross, with Matthew thinking he had to go through the motions of a fight like an act, only to find his opponent was a 'shooter' who took advantage of his naivety.

'It's almost certain it was a double cross,' said one MMA industry insider, who thought Matthew would have made in the region of $20,000. 'Matthew didn't know – he was blocking with his hands for low kicks and you don't do that. He would have thought it was like Rocky against Hulk Hogan in *Rocky III* but really Tamura was part of the promotion. It was in a crazy period when UWF kind of morphed into Pride [a new MMA organisation]. With Saad, it was little more than them taking advantage of a big name who was at their mercy. They could *shoot* on him, get him to the ground while he was wearing gloves and from there choke him out and finish a boxing legend in short time, make themselves look like the toughest guys in the world and *legit* fighters. For a country that prides itself on honour and all that bullshit, they've always done this and the UWF was notorious for it.'

Worse still was that Matthew had quit. Tamura celebrated like he'd won the world title. The veteran fighter groggily rose, knowing it was the end. Never would Matthew Saad Muhammad, the man who would never give up, quit. But he had.

* * *

Dwight Qawi retired in October 1992, losing to Nate Miller over ten in Philly. He would be back briefly in the late nineties, but he, too, was effectively done. He hadn't just gone up to cruiserweight and won the title there, but his lifestyle and excesses even saw him go up to heavyweight where he was absolutely swamped by a returning George Foreman in 1988. Despite being so small for the weight, he was still a handful, and he knocked off a couple of contenders. Had he been disciplined he would have still been at light-heavy, certainly no more than cruiser.

In March 1995, Matthew was part of a Muslim delegation that travelled to Indianapolis to meet with Mike Tyson on his release from prison. Matthew's group was going to try and steer Tyson away from re-signing with Don King. The convoy included Akbar Muhammad, Bilal Muhammad and even Harold Smith, who said he had $45m for Tyson if he promoted his comeback bout. But they were all ejected by Don King's security detail before the press conference started.

One report said Matthew was upset and embarrassed.

He had visited Tyson in prison and said Tyson had called him his idol.

'Why do I have to leave? They know I'm a big influence on Mike,' he argued.

Akbar and Bilal had worked with King before, back in the 1970s, and they thought King was trying to isolate Tyson.

'He's still in prison, still doing time. Not one thing has changed,' said Matthew, after Tyson was released in to King's custody. 'Obviously Don King felt threatened by our presence.'

In April 1995, Nick Belfiore passed away, and Matthew's world was shrinking.

Unable to get a break on the East Coast, he headed south with Elaine. They moved out to New Orleans and Matthew helped out at the Neutral Corner Gym on Magazine Street.

Between around 1994 and 1995, he toyed with the idea of fighting again, but by now he was 39. It was more about having nowhere else to turn and it being the only thing he knew, but he sparred in the gym and other fighters raved about how fit he was. He was still in great shape.

His wife was working at Harrah's Casino, but after a while they hit a rough patch and Matthew was thrown out.

'He had a good heart, but all those punches and the streets affected his good common sense,' said a friend from the time.

Gym owner John Carmody loved having Matthew around and helped the old fighter make a few dollars through training.

Around that time, heavyweight champion Riddick Bowe was doing his strength and conditioning work with Mackie Shilstone, who worked out of the same gym. 'Matthew lived in a part of town called Algiers,' said the friend. 'It's just a typical suburbia-type middle-class neighbourhood, nothing fancy. Normal. Average. He was arguing with his wife one day and he was down and out. He asked me to give him a ride after the gym to the YMCA, which is where he was staying. He had asked me not to tell anyone. I gave him that right. I was so honoured to have him around and I had grown up in boxing and I'd watched him on TV.'

Years later, Matthew would claim a lot of his memorabilia was in a storage unit in New Orleans – robes, belts and so forth. There was an overwhelming feeling that they'd all long since been sold, but he'd told several friends his treasures were still there.

'He had mentioned to me about having valuables hidden somewhere but I never asked him about it,' said a New Orleans gym-mate.

Occasionally Matthew would get down to the local fights. He was at a card headlined by club fighter Bobby Crabtree – best known as the comeback fall guy for an old George Foreman – against Terry Ray for something called the WBU Continental Americas cruiserweight title.

On the bill, England's Jane Couch fought Andrea DeShong and the Bristol woman spent time with Matthew.

'He was sleeping in the gym they took me to,' said Couch. 'On the night of the fight he was with a few shady characters but he stayed with me most of the night until I went to bed, then I never saw him again. I was going to give him some money after my fight but the promoter didn't pay me. I was gutted for Matthew. We never got to say goodbye, either. It was a pretty rough place. He never left my side all the time I was there and always made sure I was okay.'

Matthew was ringside at Larry Holmes–Anthony Willis in Mississippi. He was cheering on Holmes when a pretty blonde woman approached and asked him for his autograph. 'You're Riddick Bowe, aren't you?' she asked.

Matthew said he wasn't but that didn't deter her. 'I know you're someone famous,' and she implored him to sign, which he did.

Like the Florida move a decade earlier, this one also did not work out so Matthew drifted back East. You couldn't say he settled, because he never really did, but he was living in Philadelphia and occasionally in Atlantic City and was sometimes spotted at events, including a fundraiser for a Boxing Scholarship Foundation's Boxers' Ball, with Larry Holmes, Boogaloo Watts, Harold Johnson, Joey Giardello and an emerging star called Arturo Gatti.

Gatti had turned pro in 1991 and won his first world title in 1995. After several high-profile wars, and then making his fighting base Atlantic City, the parallels with Matthew would come thick and fast as generational warriors who guaranteed excitement, often coming from behind to win fights in the most dramatic of ways.

And for a while, things seemed to look up for Matthew as he gradually accepted his role as a trainer. With nowhere left to turn, he laced on the pads rather than the gloves. He was still physically fit even if his own fighting reflexes were shot. He could still see if a fighter was good to go, even if he struggled to admit he no longer was.

On 17 January 1998, Matthew's thrilling contemporary Gatti fought Angel Manfredy at the Convention Hall in Atlantic City and Matthew was ringside. A month earlier it had been announced that he was going into the International Boxing Hall of Fame.

'He looked good,' said Nigel Collins, of seeing him at Manfredy–Gatti. 'Everybody was coming up and congratulating him and he was really happy to be in the Hall of Fame but behind the scenes I didn't really know what was happening and I feared the worst.'

Collins was right to think that. All those wars had started to cost Matthew and his health was faltering. He bumped into former Philly reporter Mike Bruton in the nineties and Bruton instantly noticed changes.

'He did not have the slur in his speech as much as someone like Joe Frazier and some others,' said Bruton. 'But I always worried about him. If you knew him, sometimes he would hesitate when he was talking, like he was searching for the next word and he'd come up blank. That gave me some concern in the mid- to late-nineties. It was particularly sad. It's always tough if you know any boxer over a period of time and then see them deteriorate but in his case, he was such a friendly, amiable guy, it was very sad to see him slow down. He was trying to be Matthew with that bubbly personality and it just didn't work as he began to slow down.'

A fighter becomes eligible for induction into the International Boxing Hall of Fame five years after their last fight and Matthew was a rare first-ballot inductee. Sometimes top fighters spend years on the ballot before going in.

In June that year, Matthew Saad Muhammad was enshrined in Canastota in upstate New York in a class that included Puerto Rican star Miguel Canto and promoter Lou Duva.

Michelle's parents, Matthew's former in-laws, were there, along with Matthew and Michael.

'I'm so happy,' Matthew smiled. 'This is like winning a world title again. I have to thank God for making it all possible. I'm so honoured to be here. Thank you, Boxing Hall of Fame for bringing me here and making me an inductee.'

He was interviewed by a local paper in Oneida and when asked whether his sons would follow in his footsteps, he smiled, 'There are no more fighters. I'm the only fool in this family.'

A star-studded cast was on hand to watch Matthew's induction speech. Former heavyweight champions Joe Frazier, Ken Norton and Floyd Patterson were there, along with Archie Moore, Bob Foster, Marvin Hagler, Alexis Arguello, Aaron Pryor, Joey Giardello, Carmen Basilio and Emile Griffith.

There was an awkward moment when, after Matthew had been presented with his Hall of Fame ring, he couldn't get it over any of his huge fingers bar his pinkie.

Still, he didn't have the ring too long. He needed the money.

CHAPTER 22

ROVING

MATTHEW WORKED with emerging Philadelphia light-heavyweight Will 'Stretch' Taylor, who he thought had potential. Matthew coached the fighter in gyms around Philadelphia, New Jersey and Delaware.

'When Will stays in shape and concentrates on what he needs to do, he can become a world champion,' Matthew, whose own coach Sam Solomon had died at the end of 1998, predicted.

But Taylor couldn't stay disciplined and couldn't stay out of trouble. He lost to two-time world champion Reggie Johnson in 2001, was consumed by the streets and never fought again. He had won 19 fights and lost just four, all in good company.

Matthew also had spells working with former WBA heavyweight champion Bruce Seldon and India's ex-Olympic heavyweight Guru Singh.

But the real world had come biting and Matthew got work with Union 30 as a roofer. Steve Traitz was the president and Tony Green had already joined. Traitz had helped many boxers transition to civilian life, giving jobs to the likes of Tim Witherspoon, Curtis Parker and Anthony Fletcher.

'All the fighters of Philadelphia wind up on the roofs,' joked Green.

In a twist of fate, Matthew and former light-heavyweight Rossman – who had come close to splitting a record-breaking million dollars some 20 years earlier – worked together.

It was a hell of a fall for both, and Nigel Collins would hear snippets about what Matthew was doing.

'Then he was working as a roofer, then he was training boxers,' Nigel recalled. 'I knew he was fighting overseas, but for people who had been around with him, it was just an overflow of sad news. It's not like somebody dying but it was this recurring nightmare of this guy being a shadow of himself and really taking it bad.'

* * *

Matthew's alarm would go off on weekdays at around 04:30. He'd get up with no complaints, sit on the side of his bed, wrestle with his socks trying to line them up with his feet and wearily get dressed. He'd breathe heavily, nasally, move slowly and step deliberately but unsteadily towards his front door. The process needed a lot of concentration.

He'd make his way to his beaten-up old Cadillac, slump behind the wheel, sigh, pull away and head to work.

He'd arrive at headquarters of a union where they dished out day shifts to roofers.

Among things Matthew had to do was lug heavy rolls of roofing felt up tall ladders and then lay it. Given his faltering motor skills, it was astonishing how he could complete the tasks. Matthew made it look almost effortless, apart from the sweat that would glisten on his brow and the damp areas that would appear on his T-shirt in the sweltering Atlantic City sun. Sometimes, he wore a T-shirt that had been given to him by the WBC with 'WBC champion' printed across it. It was white with a picture of their famous green and gold belt. The title he used to wear.

Sometimes fate would make him work on the new casinos that popped up or underwent refurbishments. It wasn't lost on Matthew that he was one of the attractions upon which the now-weary fight city was built.

His bout with John Conteh was the first that set in motion decades of championship fights that headed to the Jersey Shore. Now he was helping rebuild it in another way.

He'd pause on the roof at times, look out to the ocean and appear pensive. Was he thinking of his parents? His childhood? His fortune? His fights? His fall?

It was like the scene in *The Shawshank Redemption* with the inmates on top of the old prison block. Matthew looked free up there, with his thoughts, away from the bullshit, away from the struggle and what his life had become.

He was usually tired when he got off work, and hungry. He might go to a friend's house and smoke some weed and soothe his aching body and relax his overactive mind. He'd had a lifelong fight with depression and welcomed an escape. There were a couple of spots he could go to for free food, but he was always wary about outstaying his welcome. One was a few blocks back from the bustling Boardwalk. Matthew could go in there and be left on his own while he caught a late lunch or an early dinner. The old owner would exchange pleasantries; Matthew would mumble back and slowly eat his food, alone. There was a signed picture of him in a frame on one of the walls. Each time he motioned to pay as he left, reaching for his pockets. The owner would wave away his gesture. Matthew would then go somewhere to spend the rest of the day. He would say he had his own place on the outskirts of the city and maybe he did but more often than not he'd stay with friends. Ralph, who was one of them, had an apartment in a rough area off Baltic Avenue and Willie lived in a skyrise block for veterans across the street.

Crime was on every corner. The apartments were not too far from the Atlantic City Police Athletic League gym where Matthew would drop in to share his wisdom.

Fighters, like future lightweight champion Leavander Johnson, and welterweight contender Shamone Alvarez, would listen.

The old timers and trainers, including Cash White who trained young hopefuls there, would welcome him, saying, 'Now this was a fighter.'

Matthew would smile shyly, play it down and express gratitude when people spoke to him about the wars with Lopez, Johnson and the others.

Then it was back to see Ralph or Willie, to crash on their spare beds or sofas.

They didn't know who Matthew was, not really. They certainly didn't know him back in the day, but they were there for him when he needed them. They didn't want anything from him, they didn't care to talk boxing – they didn't know much about the champ at all, even though they'd call him 'Champ' sometimes, when they didn't call him Saad – and their doors were permanently open to him. They were good guys, unemployed and living at home, watching sports on illegal cable while spending most of the day smoking blunts. Matthew hid away with them, unrecognised and anonymous. Just another face in the struggle.

Matthew never complained. He was grateful. Summer nights were hot and stuffy and they'd keep the windows open. Old, yellowed curtains with cigarette burns ruffled in the dark breeze.

The bright neon lights of the Trump Plaza, Bally's and Caesars Palace would flicker in the background, and the past, the scenes of his huge wins over Conteh, Martin and Sutherland were there as permanent reminders. He was in the real world now. Sirens would blare outside. Wheels would spin. Guns would be fired. Matthew's alarm was set for 04:30. He had to work in the morning.

* * *

Boxing would welcome Matthew back with open arms if it could use him. If it didn't need him, it didn't give a shit. Basically, if someone could gain something from Matthew, they'd give him a leg up, but if he couldn't help, he was of no use.

Smaller fry would give him the red-carpet treatment because they could claim they were hosting an International Boxing Hall of Fame legend, such as one night in Kahunaville, Delaware, where he was given a ringside seat to watch a club show featuring the last fight of Tracy Patterson's career. On other occasions, his fame, celebrity and the dues he'd paid held no currency.

Don King had no use for him. Late September in 2001, a few days after the Kahunaville show, Matthew drove up to Madison

Square Garden in his rickety Caddy. It was astonishing he made it. He appealed to people in the box office to let him in to watch his fellow Philly great Bernard Hopkins meet Puerto Rican Felix Trinidad. Matthew wound up in the bleachers, stuck in the cheapest available seat, watching the fighters – who were like ants to the naked eye – on the screens hung above the ring. Matthew had worn a T-shirt with his name on it. It made him easily identifiable to fight fans who knew a Hall of Fame fighter when they saw one. For $25 and a loose-fitting lumberjack shirt, Matthew sold the shirt off his back and then proceeded to listen as fighters including Iran Barkley, Jake LaMotta and Gerry Cooney were introduced as ringside guests. Matthew buried his head in his hands. He was yesterday's man.

A few months later, however, at the Trump Taj Mahal, Matthew was hamming it up for pictures ringside with former heavyweight contender Chuck Wepner and former New Jersey State Athletic commissioner Larry Hazzard as he prepared to take his seat to watch Ray Mercer get pummelled by Wladimir Klitschko in a fight for the WBO heavyweight title.

'Now this guy,' said Wepner, humouring Matthew and pretending to be awestruck. 'This guy was a real warrior.'

Matthew grinned. He was modest, but he was also only too aware about his fall.

He scrubbed up beautifully in a cream suit. He looked a million dollars and wearing that, wherever it came from, helped put a little swagger back into his stumbling steps. He belonged again. The despair from the Garden had been replaced, for now at least. He was off boxing's treadmill but life was still a roller coaster, from one high to the next devastating low.

Sometimes he'd get mail from Las Vegas and it would be Eddie Mustafa Muhammad sending him some cash. Matthew was always grateful.

'At the end of the day, I knew Matthew would wind up in trouble with his fighting style,' Eddie said. 'I would try to reach out to Matthew on varying occasions because you'd hear things, that he's not doing good, and when I'd reach him I'd say, "If you've got to call me, call me collect. If you need something, I'll be there for you, no problem." He was more than a friend. He was a good dude. I tried to look out for him because he was my brother.'

* * *

Sadly, Matthew was ripe for the picking. He needed help and he wasn't above asking for it, even if he did so reluctantly. Unfortunately, with a Hall of Fame name and as a former world champion he was exactly the type of man chancers and opportunists could use to get ahead. He made 'friends' with guys who felt he could give *them* a leg up, who thought they could capitalise on *his* fame.

He once showed up at the International Boxing Hall of Fame with a guy known simply as 'Sharkey'. Sharkey was a 6ft 4ins, 300lbs lump who'd driven Matthew up to Canastota in upstate New York from Atlantic City in his mid-size Nissan. Matthew got free transport from New Jersey and in exchange Sharkey got to hang with Matthew over the weekend, rubbing shoulders with the likes of Sugar Ray Leonard, Marvin Hagler and George Foreman as almost an equal. He tried to get Matthew money for signing his name from fans, possibly on a percentage basis, and he managed to vicariously live a life – if only for a weekend – that the trailer park he lived on in New Jersey didn't afford him. Sharkey was an 'entrepreneur'. He started coming up with ideas as to how he could make money out of Matthew, and one was to host a celebration banquet in Atlantic City as a fundraiser.

Copying a bunch of ideas from the International Boxing Hall of Fame, he produced flyers for an event that didn't exist in a venue that hadn't been agreed upon on a date he was unsure of. He started selling advertising to local businesses. There were different packages, including sponsorship in a programme that was pie in the sky, awards for categories he hadn't thought of and tables of celebrity guests he was certain he could fill.

He would go around and collect cash or cheques from New Jersey establishments. Some advertising packages were sold for about $2,000. Matthew's sad story helped sway anyone who was on the fence. If that failed, Sharkey was big enough and unstable enough to intimidate people into parting with more money than you'd believe.

Matthew was a passenger. Sharkey emailed a few boxing dignitaries to get them involved and several tentatively agreed. The problem was that Atlantic City was a shithole and didn't host many major fights anymore. No one really wanted to go there. The lack of actual details for this speculative fundraiser was also a stumbling block, although Sharkey wasn't fussed about those particulars as he pressed ahead, coining in money from local businesses.

Another issue was that Sharkey had a drug problem. And he was addicted to gambling.

One day, high as a kite on some shit he'd snorted, or perhaps injected, he was involved in a fender bender. He'd cut up an elderly man who, on seeing the size of the man people knew as 'The Land Shark', pleaded for forgiveness.

Sharkey had this white Nissan and there was a whole chunk of damage that would have run into thousands of dollars. The pensioner didn't want to use his insurance so he asked if he could cut a deal. That was music to Sharkey's ears. The man had $200 on him. Sharkey nabbed it, drove to the casino in his nobbled Nissan, lost the lot in five minutes and was then stuck with a car that was no longer road legal.

Some days Sharkey would gamble this 'free' programme money and win thousands.

Sometimes, he would lose everything. When he bottomed out, he'd go to supermarkets, fill up trolleys of food, mostly fresh meat, and leave without paying. He'd then go to Atlantic City restaurants selling steaks, burgers, lobsters and filet mignons out of his trunk in the unforgiving sun and by the time he'd been to all of the major eateries he'd go to the less-popular hangouts. If there was anything left, he'd go to the poor neighbourhoods, pull up his impromptu meat wagon and sell anything he could to whoever he could for whatever he could. By the time he reached those neighbourhoods, the meat had been in the back of the car for hours, but they always seemed to be grateful for a $5 lobster tail.

Sharkey wasn't a fundamentally bad guy, he just wanted to get rich quick and the faster the better. He had been busted for theft and assault before and he'd done some time. He claimed it was down to his addictions, which was probably partly true, and he was often put on intervention programmes. He had to take tests with some regularity, making sure he was clean. He was never clean. He preferred to live in a parallel universe, where he was a boxing mover and shaker. He would find friends or even acquaintances to go with him to the meetings, have them wait in a car and then pop out through a window with a jar and make them pee for him. Then he'd be off to the supermarkets, high, ready for another day of crime with the congratulations of his none-the-wiser counsellor ringing in his ears.

Meanwhile, he was trying to build this fundraiser for Matthew, which had some potential as an idea but no logistical backbone.

With Matthew in tow one day, he drove over to Philadelphia to see George Benton, the legendary Philly middleweight and coach, and George said he would show up for Matthew. Sharkey then drove to Joe Frazier's Gym to see the heavyweight great. Frazier said he was in, too, but that all bookings had to go through his agent or manager. Matthew sat uncomfortably as Sharkey pleaded poverty.

Frazier occasionally would fire in a cursory nod as Sharkey unveiled these grand plans. It was at the baseball stadium in Atlantic City ... There'd be a gala dinner ... Frazier would be Matthew's guest of honour ... Frazier and Matthew embraced at the end, and Sharkey and Matthew got in the car. A few minutes later, Smokin' Joe's agent called to say his old friend would, of course, help him out. The price was $25,000.

That might have been all of the 'programme' money but that had already all come and gone.

Ultimately, there was no programme, no guest list and no benefit night for Matthew.

Matthew never knew that money was being made off his name on the sly, and it's better that way. He would have been ashamed, but he may have wanted a few of those dollars, too.

For a while, the 'easy come-easy go' nature of Sharkey's income allowed him to live the life of an erratic high-roller.

When he was high, he could be the nicest guy in the world, strolling the Atlantic City Boardwalk with his one-eyed Pekinese dog on his shoulder, but within hours he could be violently punching holes in his trailer, paranoid, depressed and ashamed.

As Sharkey's life spiralled out of control, he was in and out of prison. He and Matthew lost touch.

That was for the best.

'He's crazy,' Matthew would say.

* * *

In a 2003 *Boxing Digest* article, Matthew said he was living in Pleasantville, New Jersey, and he was happy to remember the good times. 'When I lifted the belt over my head, it was the greatest moment of my life,' he recalled.

He added that both fights with Marvin Johnson were 'devastating' and said the losses to Qawi came at 'the end of my career' even though there was another decade to play out. He didn't like to talk about what had come after.

Asked who the hardest puncher he faced was, he replied, 'Well, I took a lot of punches.'

He said his best friends in boxing were an eclectic mix of trainer Emanuel Steward, his former coach Janks Morton, Muhammad Ali and Hector Camacho.

Asked how he'd like to be remembered, he said, 'As a gentleman, a stand-up gentleman with a nice personality.'

* * *

Matthew's smile could still light up any room. He never lost that. He remained a handsome man, even though he had lost confidence behind the smile.

One day, while surrounded by fans at the Hall of Fame, he was asked whether he had any regrets. 'I wouldn't change a thing,' he said.

Asked the same question behind closed doors in a friend's Atlantic City apartment, he thought long and hard, breathing heavily. His nose had been battered flat and there was thick scar tissue around both eyes. He must have known his motor skills were faltering and he said slowly, 'I wish I'd been a singer, or an actor, then perhaps I wouldn't be like this.'

His increasingly depleted state concerned him. He didn't know what was happening or why. He hadn't realised the wars had caught up with him. But whatever havoc was going on inside his brain from all of the brutal battles and the punches to the head, Matthew was still a big, muscular man. He had huge hands, a thick chest, wide shoulders and shifting all the roofing materials had maintained his strength. Even in his fifties he could jump rope, hold the pads and punch the bag like a man half his age.

But life's high points were becoming fewer and fewer. There were occasional trips to the annual induction weekend at the International Boxing Hall of Fame and he'd make it to a fight card occasionally. Then there was real life and work, facing harsh realities each day. On 15 May 2005, he had another of those priceless days in the sun that ex-fighters get sparingly. Not only was he being inducted into the Pennsylvania Boxing Hall of Fame but his friends and old rivals Marvin Johnson, Eddie Mustafa Muhammad and Yaqui Lopez were on hand to celebrate with him. Eddie flew in from Las Vegas, Lopez came in from Stockton and Johnson travelled from Indianapolis. It was an emotional night for everyone at Romano's Caterers in Northeast Philly.

They were almost a quarter of a century removed from their glory days.

'It was great that we all came,' beamed Johnson, who'd become something of a recluse in Indianapolis, where he'd had a long post-boxing career in the prison system, creating programmes for inmates. 'It was a much different atmosphere to when we were all fighting, because then it was all about business. This time it was just a happy occasion and a time of celebration. We were all there to support Saad Muhammad and it felt really good. I haven't seen those guys in so many years. I'm glad I went because Matthew's a nice guy and he deserves it.'

'It was fantastic,' smiled Lopez. 'It brought back so many memories, it was like being in the seventies and eighties. It's been 25 years but they all look pretty good. When I saw Matthew, nice guy, we talked to each other, we hugged, there were my tears and his tears.'

'I hadn't seen Marvin since I knocked him out,' Eddie joked. 'We all went back to the past and everyone was getting teary-eyed. It was magical. It really was.'

It was Matthew's big night and he couldn't believe his three rivals had made it there for him.

'Man, it was great,' he grinned. 'Marvin, Eddie and Yaqui being there was one hell of a surprise. It was a great feeling. I totally enjoyed myself.'

* * *

Matthew was ringside at the light-heavyweight championship bout between fellow Philadelphian Bernard Hopkins and Antonio Tarver in Atlantic City in June 2006 but it was exhausting being Matthew and living with uncertainty about where he was going to be from day to day. The roofing work was becoming scarce, too. Still, he seemed to find a rhythm and faced up to it. It was what it was, he'd often say, but life was a rough routine of trying to scratch together money to live off, finding places to stay and trying to hold down work.

That stupid bashed-up Cadillac ended up costing him dearly. To make money, he needed to drive to work, but the car wasn't roadworthy, and he kept getting pulled over. He got ticket after ticket, fine after fine. His licence was probably taken a few times, then he'd get stopped for driving without one, but he often found sympathy. He had to work.

Plenty of the local cops knew who he was and didn't want to make trouble for him.

'I was an ardent fan of Saad Muhammad's,' said one New Jersey police officer. 'On and off duty. I always had a soft heart for him, and looked to give him the benefit of the doubt anytime I could. Every time I saw him, I'd slip him some cash. On one occasion, when he was stopped for a motor vehicle violation, I gave him cash to make the necessary repairs to his vehicle rather than the officer write him a summons. He would always promise to pay me back but never did. I never wanted anything back from him, nor would I have ever taken it. I just cherished the fact that I was able to share positive experiences with a fighter I idolised and adored.'

Matthew was roving. He and Elaine were no longer together and he was in different gyms, but he made a particular impact in the Gladiator Boxing Gym in Forked River, New Jersey, which was run by Shawn Darling.

Darling was a corrections officer and ex-boxer who opened the Gladiator in 2005. He'd been teaching clients how to box and decided to open up his own place. Of Matthew, Darling said, 'We were friends, we'd hang out occasionally and I'd pick him up and take him to the fights.'

Matthew started helping in his gym in around 2006 and was a regular for a couple of years.

'He was there all the time, he lived right down the street from the gym and everybody loved him,' Darling recalled. 'He was a gentleman. He was fantastic. He helped everyone, the amateurs and regular people and he actually brought in Guru Singh, his professional, and he brought him into my gym when he was training him for one of his fights.

'I remember he lived in a little apartment in Mays Landing, he lived in a trailer with guys in Egg Harbour Township, and I actually moved him up to Lacey in '06. I got him an apartment near the gym and he was living up here helping me out.'

Around that time, it was in the news that Matthew's old world title belt was being sold on eBay.

'Matt, did you hock your belt? How did this stranger get your belt?' asked Darling.

Matthew told him it had been stolen. Darling wasn't so sure, but he knew he wanted Matthew to have something to show for his career so he messaged Mauricio Sulaiman at the WBC. Sulaiman was the son of the late Jose and had become the figurehead of the Mexico-based organisation.

'I said, "I've got the champ Matthew helping me out, is there any chance you can send him out a new belt or a replica because he doesn't have any belts anymore?" And they said, "Yes sure, we love Matthew, he's one of our greatest champions," and they shipped it from Mexico to me and I gave it right to Matthew.'

Matthew had some pictures with his new belt and the smile came back, if only for a while.

Another of Matthew's crowning achievements, the red North American title belt, had been donated to the International Boxing Hall of Fame by a collector where it was displayed in a glass cabinet inside the museum.

While Matthew helped in the gym, where he felt at home, his health faltered. Every day was a struggle.

In the 2000s, as the wider world learned through the NFL's concussion crisis that repeated head trauma in sports causes damage over time, it became obvious the fighter had paid a price. The miracles had come at a devastating cost.

'I knew the wars were going to catch up with him,' said Nigel Collins, who had been there for so many of them. 'What I didn't know was it would catch up with him after he'd stopped fighting. I thought it would catch up with him like it did when he fought Qawi, you know, he'd lose it, he'd get the shit beaten out of him and that would be it – the whole miracle run would be over. I didn't think of the whole long-term effects.'

The Matthew of the mid-2000s was considerably slower than the Matthew who had that devastating unbeaten run from the start of 1977 to the end of 1981.

'He wasn't really good at taking care of himself,' Darling remembered. 'He really needed to be helped. He couldn't pay his bills, couldn't handle money, couldn't keep an apartment, it seemed like he just crashed at whoever would let him crash at their house.'

Henry Hascup, who ran the New Jersey Boxing Hall of Fame, would see Matthew once in a while and they would talk.

'He would come to a lot of amateur shows, especially in South Jersey,' Hascup recounted. 'Shawn Darling would bring Matthew and introduce him and everything but Matthew was quiet and subdued at the time. You could see he wasn't the Matthew Saad Muhammad he once was.'

Matthew had met the owner of the PhillyBoxingHistory website, John DiSanto, through the 2000s and they had swapped numbers, but on the few occasions they saw one another, Matthew was up and down.

'Sometimes you'd see him and he'd be doing great and he'd seem really well and other times you'd see him and he was really down and he was struggling,' DiSanto remembered. 'It also seemed like his life was getting extremely hectic because that period of time I'd call him and leave a message and then he'd call me at like 2am and it was funny because it was Saad Muhammad, who was like a hero to me, so it was exciting. But it was in the middle of the night, and there were times they were showing his fights on ESPN Classic when I'd call him and say, "Hey, you're on TV."'

CHAPTER 23

HOMELESS

IN 2006, Matthew was at California's World Boxing Hall of Fame in Los Angeles. He travelled with fellow Philly great and old friend Jeff Chandler and recounted some of his career highs and lows.

'Being beaten by Dwight Braxton was the worst thing that ever happened to me, everything went down from there,' he lamented. 'I remember the beatings, but things are looking good for me now. I'm getting ready for a movie to be made of my life story, I'm talking to a couple of people from HBO, just a lot of good things are happening. I'm working in Forked River in a boxing gym in New Jersey and helping the youngsters there.'

At the end of the year, Sylvester Stallone was in Philadelphia promoting the new *Rocky Balboa* movie and Matthew spent time with the Hollywood idol. 'Now this is a real fighter,' said Stallone, pointing at a thrilled Matthew.

But few knew what Matthew's life had become.

They'd see him, he'd smile, act like everything was okay, too proud to say otherwise, and perhaps after making someone's day, he was back on the road, rebounding from apartment to apartment, from place to place, with no fixed abode.

But by 2009 Matthew was on the floor. The *Philadelphia City Life* wrote about him in an article headlined, 'From champion boxer to down and out'.

He met with the publication's Tim Whitaker, who wrote, 'For the past hour, the 57-year-old former light-heavyweight champion of the world has been running down his life story to me in a flurry of free-form, loosely stitched-together anecdotes, each more devoid of context and detail than the last. It goes like this: I ask the champ a question, and in response I get a series of unrelated thoughts, one dissolving into another without resolution, a litany of rambling biographical excerpts that include punching and getting punched in memorable bouts, memories of having wads of cash in his pockets and a nearly 50-member entourage to help empty those pockets, gauzy descriptions of the dream house he once owned and the many sweet rides he cruised around town in, including a \$275,000 Rolls-Royce.'

'Boxing is no good,' he told Whitaker. 'Why would anyone let himself get hit in the head? I still feel some of those punches.'

Matthew sighed at how many had robbed him, how he had given so much of his fortune away because he wanted people to like him and to be accepted.

For more than a decade, Matthew had been living like a cat. He had nowhere to go and nowhere to be.

'Most distressing is how Saad simply disappears for stretches of time,' Whitaker went on. 'While I was reporting this story, for example, promised meetings and tours of the old neighbourhoods never quite materialised.'

But Matthew and Michelle were still in touch as their boys grew up. Matthew's ex-wife was concerned about his health. He'd sleep over to spend the night with Matthew and Michael and she was worried when she heard the former champion sleep because it was as if he'd stop breathing.

His nose had taken so much punishment from boxing it had given him sleep apnoea, but he would still confide in Michelle.

'I remember him saying he almost wished he hadn't had it [wealth and fame] because then he wouldn't know what he didn't have anymore,' she said. 'Matt wouldn't see the boys as often as he wanted to because he would say it was too painful to be with them and not have us all together.'

* * *

Matthew finally went home to Philadelphia. He no longer crashed from place to place in Atlantic City. The roofing work was gone, he wasn't training fighters and he was homeless, but his old South Philly friends were pleased he was back, even if they wished circumstances were different.

Some of his old friends didn't see him much, and his constant phone changes made him almost impossible to pin down. But Salim El-Amin said Matthew knew where to find him in South Philly.

'He knew where I was and whenever he needed me, I was there,' insisted El-Amin. 'But he never really let me see that he was in difficulty.'

Mustafa Ameen said he never changed his phone number so Matthew would always be able to reach him.

'He never complained,' said Ameen. 'He never told me, personally, he was homeless. He never told me about the bad things that were happening, he never asked for money, not once, never asked for a dime.'

But back on the streets of Philly, the legend of Matt Franklin and Matthew Saad Muhammad lived on even through his daily struggle.

'We still loved him,' said Eddie Everett. 'Matt came down and I remember I was at a gas station one time and he'd become a street person and the guy at the counter said, "This guy came up telling me he used to be the champ."'

'"What guy?" And Matt came over and said, "Eddie, tell him I was the champ." And I said, "Yeah, this was Matthew Franklin, the champ." And that hurt me, that a guy came up to me and said, "This bum here came up to me saying he used to be the champion."'

Eddie and Stephen Chandler were happy to occasionally bump into their old friend.

'There were those who were there when he had all the adulation and were patting him on the back,' said Chandler. 'None of them were around.'

One person who was around was Neil Gelb, son of Matthew's old promoter Frank. Neil, a lawyer, had helped Matthew get jobs and apartments and had helped him with transport.

Another was Joe Johnson, one of John and Bertha's kids who had known Matthew since he was seven. Joe had always tried to get investment into a documentary about Matthew's life, but in a pre-Netflix and streaming service era, takers were few and far between. Everyone said it was an incredible story. Nobody took the next step.

'He really does have Matt's best interest in mind and heart,' said Larry Tornambe, of Joe. 'Matt has told me about his old entourage being "unavailable". Joe is definitely an exception. Matt said he couldn't find those guys even if he wanted to, but if he did find them all they'd want is money anyway but to think about what some of his so-called friends have taken from him just really ticks me off.'

In June 2010, Matthew Saad Muhammad went to the homeless shelter on North Ridge Avenue in North Philly, about 20 minutes from his old Jenkintown mansion. Needing an escape from the real world, and with nowhere else to go and nowhere left to be, he didn't leave the shelter for four months.

Initially, Matthew was terrified of being recognised, but he knew he needed help. He'd been roving, moving, surviving for too long. Surrounded by others needing or praying for a second chance, Matthew could at least rest awhile.

There he met Kevin Roberts, who edited the *One Step Away* newspaper, a publication that covered homelessness. Roberts found Matthew a place to stay on Diamond and 17th, and they worked together on raising awareness about the plight of homelessness in Philadelphia.

But Matthew still struggled. He was endlessly having cell phones cut, a regular theme over the years, because he wasn't paying the bills. He was lost in an old world, a seventies star who didn't understand modern technology.

'Rent, food, electricity – the choice of what to pay and when becomes very tricky when you're down like this,' said Roberts. Despite being the person closest to Matthew, Roberts would still lose track of him for days.

Sometimes he would stop by Matthew's place and he'd be gone but Roberts had been told Matthew had been living like that since the end of his boxing days, even if no one knew where he went.

That's why so much of his life after boxing and even through his wilderness years post-Qawi are difficult to trace.

The transition from boxer to ex-boxer is stark for every former fighter, even more so if that was your sole identity. Matthew was the all-action hero who gave the fans everything. Now he had nothing left to give.

But he felt a real purpose in raising awareness about homelessness, and he wanted to help others, even though the punches and the wars had got to him. He was slurring his speech and his balance was going. He appeared on Art Fennell's Philadelphia talk show to discuss an upcoming homeless fundraiser and admitted, 'A lot of things, I've forgotten.'

But Fennell was deeply sympathetic to Matthew's plight. He was patient, compassionate and held his hand, metaphorically, throughout their interview. Matthew actually sounded better than he had in years and told his story, his origins and his rise. Then came the story of the descent.

'What happened to the money?' Art asked. 'What happened to the people who were around you and supporting you when times were good?'

Matthew looked down and ruefully shook his head. The question still hurt him. He had no idea where those people were. He composed himself and then stumbled for the words. He didn't want sympathy or to sound like a lost cause so he tried to spin it as best he could. 'I just gave it away. I was friends with people but in order for them to be around I guess I had to give them some money and that was it. I gave money to people who I thought needed it and it ran out. It just ran out.'

Then, he bit down and – with Fennell's help – he fought on. 'I had the courage to bounce back,' he said. 'I could have stayed down but I didn't want to stay down. I wanted to get back up, I wanted to be something. I wanted to do something, I wanted to represent people, period, regardless of race, creed or colour I wanted to show people that once they get knocked down, they can get back up, wherever it is, however it is.'

Fennell asked whether he felt embarrassed, whether the boxing community had helped in any way or if it had reached out while Art tactfully worked with Matthew and acknowledged his greatness along the way. Matthew wanted to spread the word about the KO Homelessness charitable movement but he didn't want to dwell on the negatives. 'There's going to be a lot of good times coming up now,' Matthew said, trying to believe it. 'I believe that HRD [he meant RHD, Resources of Human Development] is going to work with me, that other things are going to come to me, and I've just got to believe in myself, believe in the programme and believe in what we're going to do today.'

Matthew thanked Fennell, flashing that memorable smile from behind his tired eyes. The cameras faded to black. Matthew was back in the real world once again.

It was a sharp contrast, but one he understood. He'd been at each end of the financial spectrum, from poverty to wealth and back again.

'I've been both, you know,' he said. 'A guy with mansions and millions, and a guy sleeping under the freeway.'

At the first annual Knock Out Homelessness charity dinner at Chickie and Pete's, Joe Frazier was on hand to support Matthew, and so was Phillies baseball star Darren Daulton. It was a success but Matthew would have been uncomfortable knowing everyone there was aware of his fall from grace, from the top of the world to the bottom of the pile.

Frazier, by the way, was on hand for no charge. 'We were so thrilled to have Joe Frazier, who literally did it because Matthew asked him, because it was for Matthew he agreed to show up and we were incredibly gratified,' said event organiser Roberts.

'He always is happy, and smiles at everybody,' said Frazier of Matthew. 'I will be damned if I know how he does it, with all the shit that happened to him in life.'

Whitaker, the journalist tasked with chronicling Matthew's plight, covered the event: 'Near the end of the evening, I spot the ex-champ [Matthew] wandering alone at the edges of the crowd. He's smiling, but his head is down, and he's staying on the move. He's not looking anyone in the eye, ducking interactions where he can, searching for a quiet place to be, hoping, above all else, to avoid contact.'

Matthew was still proud, even though that pride had been knocked over and over.

When he first found himself at the homeless shelter, he asked the authorities to keep the news of him staying there private. He didn't want people to know. Eventually, however, he felt he might be able to help others and an early interview with the *One Step Away* newspaper led to wider coverage in the news and, a few months later, he was again living on his own in Philadelphia and working for the development organisation as an advocate and spokesperson.

'He was great at connecting with people, and he had a simple message: You can be down but you can get back up,' Roberts said. 'He was a gem. We loved him.'

'We loved Matt, we grew up with him,' said Eddie Everett, who had gone to the Chickie and Pete's fundraiser with his brother Mike and Stephen Chandler to lend support to Matthew and to donate.

'He turned Muslim, then all these people came in, that's where he messed up,' said Eddie. 'None of them were at the fundraiser when he was homeless. When he fell, he came back. The ones he truly loved and respected were the ones he came back to after the fall.'

Matthew was passionate about helping and it gave his life a new purpose. He would host the Knock Out Homelessness each year from 2011 to 2014.

Larry Tornambe, who had segued from radio host in Weirton, West Virginia, to a ring announcer had been friends with Matthew since they had met in the late 1980s. Tornambe went to help support the event and wound up being the MC.

'The first year Matthew was the host of this thing and Matt was expected to speak, he didn't realise he was supposed to speak,' Tornambe smiled. 'Matt stuttered a bit, stammered a bit, he was just nervous. He's not a public speaker, he's a boxer. The second year, he sounded great. In 2013, he sounded like a professional speaker. He sounded fantastic. He remembered everybody, he thanked everyone he was supposed to thank, I looked at him and said, "If I ever quit ring announcing, you've got a job."'

Matthew and Kevin Roberts were close, and Roberts could see Matthew trusted Tornambe.

'He's been scorned so many times by people who led him down false avenues,' Roberts told Tornambe. 'He trusts you.'

After one of the shows, Matthew tried to give Tornambe $100 for working the event.

'I felt Matt always did care about me as a friend but he had this, "Alright, I trusted a lot of people over the years and it didn't do me much good,"' said Tornambe.

Matthew thrived in his work for the homeless, raising awareness at every opportunity. He was given space in the *Philadelphia Inquirer* in April 2014 for a lengthy first-person story.

'It hurts me to see people who've lost that,' he said, broadly talking about hope. 'I wanted to give people some inspiration, a sense of worth, of dignity. I wanted to give people some hope ... I trusted the wrong people with the money I made when I was champ, and I've had some tough times. But I'm still getting back up. I'm sure not alone – look around. People are having a tough time out there. They're not lazy. They're not stupid. They're not bad people. They've just lost hope. They've stopped fighting in life, because they've lost hope for something better. They've taken a fall somewhere, and they think they can't get back up. And that's how we'll Knock Out Homelessness. We'll help people help themselves. We'll help people get back up. Together, we can help people have hope in their hearts. A homeless kid can become champion. A champion who's fallen can rise again. People can better themselves. Even if you've had a hard time in life, you can succeed. You have to have heart, and be strong.'

CHAPTER 24

THE END

MATTHEW SAAD Muhammad was hospitalised in May 2014 from complications with Lou Gehrig's Disease. He had been diagnosed with the illness, also known as ALS, in March at the Pennsylvania Hospital.

On 21 May, a Tuesday, one of Matthew's daughters, Zakiyyah, called Michelle and said that if her son Matthew wanted to see his father, he needed to do it immediately, because time was running out.

The disease was named after the baseball star who was famous for his incredible durability, which included an unbroken run of 2,130 consecutive games. Gehrig died in 1941, aged 36, but decades later a 2010 HBO programme about the links between ALS and contact sports revealed Gehrig's record-breaking streak saw him play after several violent head traumas. On one occasion he returned to the field having suffered a brain injury and for one game his head was so swollen from being struck by a ball he had to borrow a cap from Babe Ruth as his wouldn't fit over his head.

HBO researchers located an image of Gehrig being helped from the field after being nailed by a 'bean ball'; he'd needed smelling salts to bring him round. He played on. There was another picture of him out cold on second base being assisted by team-mates. HBO discovered that he'd suffered at least six serious head injuries, including one that saw him lying motionless on the field for five minutes.

The 'Iron Horse' was as tough as they come but his toughness came at a cost.

It was Matthew's story all over again. The stars paid a high price for immortality.

In recent years there's been scientific links between ALS and head trauma over time, with several high-profile NFL stars being diagnosed, including former Oakland Raider Steve Smith, Dwight Clark of the San Francisco 49ers, Rickey Dixon of the Cincinnati Bengals, Derrick Jensen of the Oakland Raiders, Wally Hilgenberg of the Minnesota Vikings and another 49er, Eric Scoggins.

Matthew's stories of boxing hundreds of rounds in training camps, fighting through hazes in the violent brawls, then having equally ferocious fights a few weeks later, made him a candidate for neurological illnesses, as did his failure to quit more than a decade before he finally did.

The ALS decline is horrendous and irreversible. It's vicious and progressive and there's no recovery. The only question is how long it will take to shut the body down to the point that it stops. It attacks the voluntary nerve cells until talking, eating and walking go from difficult to impossible. Breathing becomes a challenge. Then a permanent darkness finally consumes the patient. Ezzard Charles, another great light-heavyweight, had it. Minnesota heavyweight contender Scott LeDoux also died from it.

That Matthew died aged just 59 spared him from an even worse decline than he'd experienced, hard as that is to imagine.

Matthew became unresponsive in the Chestnut Hill Hospital, breathing through respiratory equipment.

Mourners travelled from far and wide to see him.

'Before that he had gotten in touch with me,' said Dwight Qawi. 'He had the programme helping the homeless and we got together a couple of times and I was trying to help and one day he told me to come up and see him to help him. I went up there and they told me he was in a coma and it shook me. It hit me. It hit me in the gut. I didn't want to hear it. He had the heart he had and you just couldn't believe it, but I went there in case he woke up.'

Matthew was motionless. He did not have long left.

The 'Camden Buzzsaw' left a note. 'Saad, Qawi came to see you. Allah, love you for the sake of Allah, Muhammad Qawi.'

He was praying for him.

'He was a kindred spirit,' added Qawi, who looked at Matt and regretted the brutal nature of their fights.

'I just wish it wasn't so hard, you know? I'm regretful for that,' said Qawi. 'I wish it wasn't so hard. I hadn't considered all that, that he would end up like he did because he took a lot of punches. If I had to do it again, I would have done it different, boxed him more, but I did what I had to do.'

Well-wishers came and went, but what many were actually doing was saying goodbye.

Trainer Steve Traitz visited him. Paul Trace, his old photographer, went to see his friend.

'It was a devastating shock to me, the physical difference from when I last saw him at the Boxing Hall of Fame in Philly,' said Trace. 'He'd had an incredible body, was in tip-top shape and lean and mean and then I almost did not recognise him.'

Tony Green, former sparring partner, visited. He called Mustafa Ameen to tell him Matthew was facing the end.

'Tony walked me to the room and Saad had some equipment hooked up to him and he was comatose and I started talking,' recalled Ameen. '"Alright champ, enough rest, it's time to get up. Roadwork. You know what to do."'

Michelle went to see her former husband. When she saw Matthew, she couldn't control the emotions.

'It makes me tear up even now,' Michelle said. 'Everyone left the room when I went in. I got real close, because he wasn't responsive and I whispered, "You didn't even tell me [about your diagnosis]" and I started singing "Yes! Jesus Loves Me" and the ALS had constricted his body so he couldn't really move but he opened his eyes and I said, "I'm so mad at you. You really thought you were going to leave and not even say goodbye? How could you do that? But it's okay, because I'm going to live right so I can go to heaven too." And there was a tear that came out of one of his eyes and that was the last time I saw him on this side. I will love him until the day I die, as he did me. Although we redefined it, we couldn't go back to what we were, he was the man who made me a mother and he was my first real love.'

Michelle was heartbroken. She wondered if things might have been different for them but also wondered why Matthew had been dealt such a bad hand.

Matthew had spent a lot of time alone over the years. He did not want to be a burden to anyone, but he would always wonder why things had turned out the way they had.

'Matthew struggled lifelong with depression,' Michelle said. 'He masked it very well but he struggled. He self-medicated but that man went to his grave just wondering, "What was it? What was it about me? Why? What did I do?"'

Matthew Saad Muhammad suffered a stroke and died on 25 May 2014.

* * *

Eddie Mustafa Muhammad, Matthew's old friend and foe, called Russell Peltz to tell him the sad news.

A slew of obituaries were written in newspapers, magazines and online, documenting Matthew's terrible beginnings, his glorious reign and the inglorious descent. It was for Hollywood, they said. Matthew had hoped it would get there one day but it never did.

Mike Tyson tweeted, "Condolences to the family of #MatthewSaadMuhammad. He was a warrior in the ring. He won't be forgotten."

Matthew's funeral was held at the Enon (West) Tabernacle Church on Coulter Street in the Germantown part of Philly. A number of fighters including Mike Rossman, Tim Witherspoon, Buster Drayton, Eugene 'Cyclone' Hart, Nate Miller and Boogaloo Watts attended. Old opponents Richie Kates, living in Vineland, New Jersey, and Yaqui Lopez, who travelled from his home in Stockton, California, were there.

Asked why he felt it was important to attend, Yaqui could not hide his emotions.

'Because, er,' Lopez paused as he wept. 'He was a good guy. When we finished fighting, we talked sometimes, we'd talk about the past, and then when he passed away, I felt so sad, like I was on my own. He was my buddy, you know. I loved him like a brother. I didn't want him to go.'

Traitz attended, so did Peltz and Larry Hazzard.

Philadelphia was no longer the same old fight town, though. Not one current pro went to pay his respects.

With Matthew's casket in the church, ten bells were tolled. Afterwards, old warriors exchanged stories of the fighter, who was buried at Ivy Hill Cemetery.

But the sadness wasn't yet complete. Matthew's body was placed in an unmarked grave and he lay under 'a soggy unmarked patch of grass just past Joe Frazier's impressive tomb'.

He was just as anonymous as he had been on the streets of Atlantic City or even on the Ben Franklin Parkway.

Philadelphia boxing historian and founder of PhillyBoxingHistory. com John DiSanto wanted something better for 'Miracle Matthew' so he started a GoFundMe account, hoping to raise $5,000 for a headstone.

John had started a gravestone programme, trying to make sure that the city's boxing legends could be remembered, having discovered that the late Tyrone Everett did not have a headstone. He did the same thing for Gypsy Joe Harris, then Garnet 'Sugar' Hart and Eddie Cool.

'Saad Muhammad was certainly one of my favourites – growing up I saw him at the Spectrum, and you know the story – and his career had been once in a lifetime,' said DiSanto. 'If he came along now, none of those fights would have happened. They would have been stopped before he made his big, storied comebacks. He passed away, and I was never close with Saad Muhammad but there was a time in the 2000s that I ran into him, I had a number for him and he had my number, and we talked for a while and we'd see each other at the International Boxing Hall of Fame and things like that. Then, all of a sudden, he kind of disappeared and he was sort of out of what limited public view he was in, and then I heard that he'd passed away.'

In a statement released to appeal for help, DiSanto said, 'Saad Muhammad gave us indelible memories to cherish and relive for the rest of our lives. Now it is time for us to return the favour.'

DiSanto was happily stunned at how quickly the money poured into the online fundraiser, with more than $6,000 raised.

'He was the easiest one ever because everyone loved him so much,' he continued.

The headstone was in place around a year after Matthew passed away.

'It's a beautiful stone,' DiSanto said. 'It's a laser-cut image into black granite and it's just up the lane from Joe Frazier's.'

There had always been someone somewhere trying to do something with Matthew, someone hoping they could use his incredible story to get their break in movies, in TV or in boxing. One wonders if any serious proposals made it to any serious players in Hollywood but the story should have made it there and so should he.

Matthew should have had so much more, his life should have been a best-seller, his likeness on billboards advertising his movie or a Netflix special. He wound up in an unmarked grave, but history would remember the man, the fighter, as brave as anyone who'd ever stepped in a ring.

He'd never made it to the big screen. He wasn't immortalised like Rubin Carter or Jake LaMotta. He waited. He hoped. Everyone said it would happen. The call never came but Matthew Saad Muhammad's story was over.

* * *

'I think what my father taught people is that even though you fall down in life, just know that you can get back up,' said his daughter, Zakiyyah Mitchell. 'You can get back up from anything that can knock you down.'

You can say Matthew was defiant against all odds, that he'd stared down bankruptcy, homelessness, poor health and that although he'd lost everything he was still fighting. You can say he found the answers to the questions he otherwise would have spent a lifetime trying to learn, that he knew who he was and where he had come from and had satisfied those long-burning questions. But, in truth, there were three very ugly decades after the second loss to Qawi.

Life was hard and it had been for years. If only he could wind the clock back. If only he could be the champion again. If only he'd kept the money. If only he could have had a fresh start. That's what he wanted and that's what he needed.

One day, in around 2005, he received some mail and opened it. It was a new driving licence. Perhaps he'd lost the previous one, or been banned for erratic driving. Neither would be surprising. His face lit up and he held the new licence aloft as if it were a championship belt. There was his picture along with the name on his new ID. It belonged to Maxwell Antonio Loach. That was him. He wasn't Matthew Franklin the orphan or Matthew Saad Muhammad the warrior. His life had gone full circle. He was back to being who he was at the start. He had nothing, had everything and went back to having nothing again. He'd been Maxwell Antonio Loach, Matt Franklin, the great Saad Muhammad and the ID said he was Maxwell Antonio Loach again. He looked at the new licence and smiled. It was as if the story had run its course. His search was over.

CHAPTER 25

IDENTIFICATION

MATTHEW AND Michael LeViege are the two sons Matthew Saad Muhammad had with Michelle in 1981 and 1984 and they had different relationships with their father. What they had in common was the pride they had in their dad and how they idolised him.

'The last time I talked to dad was when he was in Atlantic City and I'd broken up with my girlfriend of eight years and I said, "Dad, I need to see you. I really need to get away,"' said Matthew LeViege. He wasn't doing too good. We were really close but he ended up moving around and I went to Atlanta, Georgia, for about seven years and then I moved to Orlando, Florida and now I'm out here.'

Meanwhile, in Atlantic City, Michael was being trained by his father to box, often going to the Police Athletic League gym.

'The last couple of years I was in touch and in tune with my father,' Michael said. 'My father was phenomenal.'

Boxing was a common bond.

Michelle didn't want Michael to fight because of the damage it inflicts and the toll it takes.

'My dad wanted me to fight,' said Michael. 'He knew I could have done it. He would say to people, "My son is the next one. My son is the next champ."'

That was despite Matthew saying in interviews he didn't ever want his children to fight. He loved the commonality it gave them and how they could bond over it.

'He said that to me before [about not wanting Michael to fight] and he used to always say this, "I love it." And he knows that I loved it. I loved to fight, I loved the competition, I loved the adrenaline and ego I got out of it. My dad said, "You've got to love it" and I loved hitting people and getting hit. I wanted to do it for my dad. Everything I did, it was for my dad.'

Michael is in his late-thirties now and left to wonder what might have happened had he trodden in those Hall of Fame footsteps, if he'd been announced to the world as Michael LeViege Saad Muhammad. At one stage, after a boxing camp in Ohio, he had caught Don King's eye and Michael believes he could have been a success.

'We're not living paycheque to paycheque but I could have guaranteed us a better life at that time, for sure,' Michael said. 'Her [Michelle's] fears are, and her being a mother ... you can't fear. You have to let your children live their life. What my parents did for me, I'm not going to do for my son [Michael John].'

'Michael hits like his father,' said Michelle. 'And I begged my son, "Please don't do this. Your dad did what he had to do because that's all he had, but you've had far more opportunities and I want you walking on your whole foot, I don't want you walking on your toes, I don't want you walking on your heels, okay? And I just don't want your brains rattled around."'

'He wanted to go the boxing route,' Matthew said of his younger sibling. 'I had a lot of anger issues. When my dad was a pro, he carried me in his arms everywhere, I didn't walk on the ground, and when that stopped and my parents broke up it made me have a psychological breakdown as a youth, so that kind of made me go into BMXs and find stardom through that to try and show him. My father was my idol, but also he was my rival. Growing up, I wanted to emulate him and be great so I did the BMX riding and I would travel all over. He followed me, but I'd be in Texas and California so I wasn't around too much ... He's not a father to me, he's an idol, he's a superhero.'

Matthew and Michael have both heard the story of the rise and the fall, but neither were old enough to remember being around when their father was on top of the world. Matthew wasn't worried about missing out on the wealth and extravagance, and certainly has no ill will for his father losing the fortune.

'I never was angry at that,' he said. 'I was really more hurt because I didn't understand what was going on. Money is nothing to me. I came from money, great money, but it was a pain as far as, "You're my father and I looked at you as a hero so how did you disappear from my life, like vanish into thin air?" I have his pride and I cloak my feelings like he did, but as a youth I didn't understand that. Now I forgive him.'

Michael also has no hostilities about the life he and his family could have had rather than the one they had.

'When I think about it, I was privileged because I was in a Rolls-Royce, I was in a Benz, I lived in a nice house with a piano in Jenkintown,' he said. 'Do I remember it? No. Have I heard the stories? Yes. But I think I was privileged. Was I around for the glamorous stuff? No. But I have a glamorous life now, I'm happily married, got a wife and a son and I'm happy. It's crazy my father overcame all the obstacles he did. He went through a lot, and then some. Regardless of him and my mother going their separate ways, he was always there for me, and he always did everything he could for me. My dad didn't have money, and when I think about it, I've literally seen my dad give his last to me and he had to do what he had to do to get some money. He did a lot of favours for people, too.'

There were 'favours' and there were others who took advantage of the former champion. Saad told Michael about those who had done him wrong.

'He gave so much and people just took advantage of him and it boils my blood,' Michael said. 'Allah knows best and what's due to come will come. I wish no harm on anyone. My dad told me about everyone who took advantage of him and it's only facts. Because when it's all said and done, my dad knows who did it. They're all fake. All of them are fake. I've got some bad blood. I don't know them … I lean up to God now, because I have a son. I can't go off emotions.'

Michelle said Matthew was always protective of their boys, whether he was in a relationship or whether she was.

Matthew had other children, Jamar, Tenile, Sheena, Rashida and Zakiyyah. Michelle had another son and he and Matthew had a great relationship, too.

As Matthew lay in bed in hospital, Michael was preparing to get married in Chicago. The great ex-champion was being kept alive on a ventilator but after Michael was wed, his son Matthew thought it was time to let their hero go.

'I called Zakiyyah and once my brother tied the knot it was as if Michael said, "Hey dad, you're here with us in spirit, you're here on this earth with us, I got married,"' said Matthew. 'I made the call for him to be at rest.'

'My dad did his best,' Michael concluded. 'He did more than his best in my eyes. Just being around my father, money couldn't buy what he had to offer. Man, I wish my dad was here.'

* * *

'Being in most-exciting lists … They put me in there … that's something I was really happy about.' Matthew Saad Muhammad would smile, content in the knowledge that he had left his mark. He'd been announced in *The Ring* as one of the 100 Greatest Punchers of All Time and No. 10 in the top 20 light-heavyweights of all-time. From his same, hard-knock era of great boxers, Michael Spinks was at No. 3, Galindez at 11, Qawi at 15 and Marvin Johnson was 20. Ezzard Charles sat at No. 1 and Archie Moore at No. 2, Tommy Loughran was No. 4and Bob Foster closed out the top five.

'I see greatness,' Matthew replied when asked to look back over his era. 'I see greatness and I was just happy to be one of them. I'm so happy that I made history and my life went the way it did. Then it was my time. It was just my time. I would have loved to have fought Galindez, Rossman, I wanted to fight Michael Spinks. I should have fought Michael Spinks.'

Matthew had regrets depending on the day. Up in Canastota at the International Boxing Hall of Fame where he was admired and idolised for his wild back catalogue of fights, he would say he regretted nothing. When he was back in Atlantic City or in the struggle, he'd regret trusting certain people and even being a fighter.

There was always an internal struggle.

John DiSanto wondered how such a likeable man could have been involved in such punishing brawls, whether dishing out or taking the pain.

'I always thought he seemed like the sweetest and warmest person but the violence of his career and how savage the battles were, these unbelievable battles, and you'd see this sweet smiling guy afterwards,' sighed DiSanto. 'It was an interesting conflict. He was just a great guy.'

Russell Peltz recalled Matthew getting surly with him for a time after they'd split and Matthew had undertaken new management, but they did manage to put the ill-feelings behind them.

'Years later, when it was over and he was down and out, we became friendly again and the year he died we were walking downtown in Center City [Philadelphia] and he was riding in a car which was stopped at the light and when we turned the corner he said, "Russell, Linda [Mrs Peltz] ..." And he jumped out the car and hugged us and it was like he was a kid again. But it was like that with a lot of fighters. "Oh, Russell, why did I give you such a tough time back then, if only I knew?" That was the last time I saw him.'

Peltz described Matthew as 'a loveable kid' and one of the most exciting fighters of all time, certainly of his time.

'He was like the light-heavyweight Arturo Gatti,' Peltz asserted. 'So many of his fights could have been stopped. If you watch the first fight with Marvin Johnson, you wonder how the fight went 11-and-a-half rounds. Marvin was hitting Matthew with uppercuts that were snapping his head back. Even the "Dynamite" Douglas fight, the Richie Kates fight, people thought the Douglas fight should have been stopped in Douglas's favour ... None of that did Matthew much good later in life but I don't believe fighters get ruined in the fights, I believe they get ruined in all the sparring in the gym and the way they live when they leave the gym. You're a professional fighter, you probably go in the gym six days a week and take one day off and if you've got a fight coming up, you're sparring three days a week at least so you're getting hit in the face 12, 36, 45 minutes every week, that's what does it to you.'

Inquirer writer Mike Bruton saw another boxing similarity for Matthew, and it reached into fictional realms.

'When people look at the character Sylvester Stallone played, Rocky, if you saw Matthew fight you would think that was the model that Rocky was based off,' Bruton said. 'That's the kind of fighter he was. He would take whatever he had to take to get his punches off and often he would end up on the carpet but he got up – and it was amazing. Of all the fighters that I saw in the years that I covered boxing, I can't think of another who is an action boxer from the time the bell rings until it's time to sit on the stool. He was amazing.'

Bruton saw Matthew at some points in the 1990s, between jobs and after the money had gone.

'But he was just as happy as you could be,' Bruton recalled. 'That's just the kind of guy he was. I think a lot of his outgoing personality came from wanting to belong. Sometimes he was happy that you'd stop and spend time with him.'

There was always a sense of wanting acceptance. From the start, Matthew didn't have a family. Then he joined the gangs and would fit in with them. Then he experienced the camaraderie of the gym. Then came Islam. Yet despite the different groups, his real lasting identity was the one he carved out for himself.

'I think he liked being known as a warrior, but I don't remember him ever bragging about it,' said Nigel Collins, years after one of his favourites had passed away. 'Most fighters and entertainers feed off a crowd. For some of them, that's the only time they're at peace, when they're in the ring. He was just a happy guy in an unhappy sport and he could punch and he could take a punch. That's all it was. He could box but he really totally abandoned it, it wasn't like I'm going to go after this guy and that guy but hold back on the next one. It was always full steam ahead.'

At the height of Matthew's fame, after that fight of the year war with Lopez, Steve Farhood visited him at the Jenkintown house for a long interview. It was the one Farhood left thinking that life couldn't get any better for Matthew.

'I fight very hard,' Matthew replied, when asked how he hoped he'd be remembered. 'The remembrance of Matthew Saad Muhammad would say that I had to take a lotta shots, but I was a damn good fighter.'

While Matthew didn't like talking about the fights post-Qawi, there were a lot of them and he struggled to remember many of them. Then he breathed heavily through his flattened nose, walked unsteadily and showed progressive signs of CTE.

Peltz was asked whether, back in the late 1970s, he was concerned with the damage Matthew was taking.

'No,' he answered. 'I know it sounds cruel but this is the business we're in. It's a hurting business. I'm much more conscious of it today. Today I might say, "He's not fighting for four months …" "He's not going to spar in the gym …" But I was so caught up in the excitement of my profession and seeing these great fights. That was July 26 of 77, the first Marvin Johnson fight. Normally after a fight like that I'd say "maybe we'll fight again this year". But boxing was different then and within two months he's fighting "Dynamite" Douglas at the Spectrum and he [Matthew]'s on the floor. They could have stopped that fight. Douglas really drilled Matthew in the fourth or fifth round.

'And Matthew was getting pounded on the ropes and in the next round or a couple of rounds later, he's pounding Douglas. Seven to eight weeks after the most brutal fight you could imagine, he's in with another monstrous puncher. Two months later he's back again, three months later he's back with [Richie] Kates. But that's what boxing was like back then.'

* * *

While never outright saying he was promoted by the Mob, and without naming names, Matthew alluded to links with organised crime.

'I was the last of the Mohicans,' he said when asked about Philadelphia and South Jersey boxing and the Mob. 'I was the last one. I was the last big-time fighter and they treated me well. I can't say nothing bad about them ...'

'The people who read this, they'll know,' he said cautiously in 2001. 'I've been around and I know. I have to be very careful with what I say because there are lives at stake. I don't know, all I know I was involved with a lot of killers and I didn't even know. I didn't even know.'

Peltz was surprised Matthew would say that and not only did not think it was right but that it was simply not true.

'No, absolutely not,' Peltz said firmly. 'He was managed the first couple of years by Pinny Shafer, who was head of the local bartenders' union, and did Pinny know Blinky [Palermo]? Sure, because I met Blinky for the first time in Pinny's office, but Blinky didn't get out of jail until about 1975 or 1976.'

Frank 'Blinky' Palermo was one of the two Mafia men who had ruled boxing through fear and intimidation in the 1940s and 1950s. Along with Frankie Carbo, a Murder Inc gunman, they fixed fights and owned boxers. Mobster Palermo's rap sheet included the following: aggravated assault and battery, reckless use of firearms, a lottery conviction, assault with intent to kill, statutory rape, gambling, narcotics, shoplifting, extortion and racketeering. In the late 1950s, Palermo was imprisoned for managing boxers without a licence, and in 1964, he'd been sentenced to 25 years and served seven-and-a-half when charged with conspiracy and extortion of former welterweight Don Jordan. Carbo went to Alcatraz. But when Palermo came out in the seventies, he went back to boxing.

Frank Gelb also knew Palermo and claimed their links came through a fish business Blinky was involved in, but Frank also knew another infamous Philly mobster, Frank 'Frankie Flowers' D'Alfonso, on a personal and business level. D'Alfonso was a hitman for Nicodemo 'Little Nicky' Scarfo, who rose to become the boss of the powerful Philadelphia crime family.

Matthew said he had never taken part in any fixed fights or that he'd been asked to throw fights but there were plenty of other links to organised crime in his background. One name that reappeared was Gelb's. In a 1985 Senate investigation into boxing and organised crime in New Jersey, Gelb – who had incredible influence in Atlantic City – was revealed to have ties to Palermo that went back years.

After Palermo got out of prison, he wanted to be relicensed as a manager so he applied to the Pennsylvania Commission. Enter Steve Traitz, who agreed to appear as a character witness on his behalf. After all, according to the investigation, the Montgomery County Boys Club was 'a Palermo hangout'.

Palermo withdrew his application but there were clear links, in the report, between Palermo, the club and its boxers.

Scarfo was becoming *the* major player. In the 1960s, he had been exiled from South Philadelphia for killing a man in a fight, unrelated to gang activity. Angelo Bruno, then the main man in Philly, dispatched Scarfo to the Little Italy neighbourhood, Ducktown, of Atlantic City as a punishment because the resort was dying.

But in 1976, when Atlantic City legalised gambling, the organised crime floodgates opened and Scarfo had a front-row seat. The city's rise coincided with his. By 1981, Scarfo was in charge after Bruno had his head blown off and his immediate successor Philip Testa was blown up by a nail bomb.

When Matthew fought Dwight Braxton at the Playboy in Atlantic City, in December 1981, three mobsters sat behind Howard Cosell near Saad's corner. Nicodemo Scarfo was there with Philip 'Crazy Phil' Leonetti and Lawrence 'Yogi' Merlino.

The assistant attorney general Guy Michael, also the director general of the state Division of Gaming Enforcement, investigated how the three had gotten seats usually reserved for casino high-rollers. The Playboy denied giving them out.

'I didn't comp them, that's for sure,' insisted Arnie Fleischman, Playboy Hotel and Casino president and managing director. 'We had 1,800 people there. We don't screen everybody that comes in.'

Law officials said that while the three men were not on an Atlantic City exclusion list of 56 people who could not get into the city's hotels or casinos, Scarfo was about to be added.

Scarfo was convicted of a triple murder in 1988, having ordered many more hits throughout his brutal regime, and died in prison in 2017.

Leonetti had become a 'made man' by killing for Scarfo, his uncle, and he had earned millions through racketeering, gambling, loan sharking, extortion and skimming from the Atlantic City casinos.

In 1989, Leonetti was sentenced to 45 years when Scarfo was given 55, but Leonetti turned on 'Little Nicky', admitting his part in ten murders which saw him released after five years before he went into hiding.

Leonetti later wrote a book, *Mafia Prince: Inside America's Most Violent Crime Family and the Bloody Fall of La Cosa Nostra.*

Merlino also rolled on Scarfo and was sent into witness protection 'out west', dying under his new government identity in 2001. His body was transported back for burial in Margate, New Jersey, five miles south of Atlantic City.

D'Alfonso, a good earner for the Mob, was killed in a gangland hit when he was shot as he lit a cigarette near his home in 1985.

Palermo died of a stroke in 1996 at a Philadelphia hospital. His death was accompanied by headlines such as, 'Palermo's passing marks the end of a terror'.

* * *

Matthew might have become a boxing stereotype, a flashy champion who had it all but lost it, but his story was far from stereotypical.

'In the beginning he was lost, in the end he was robbed, and he had a lot of money taken and he was back from something to nothing,' said Salim El-Amin. 'His family disappeared, and it was a complete loss. He wanted to know [who his family were] because he always felt lost. Even when he talked about it, you could feel it. All of that really troubled Muhammad, from the very beginning. It was touching. It took so much out of him.'

Although Matthew had grown to prominence in Philly in the epic Spectrum clashes, he became a star in Atlantic City.

'They loved Matt there,' said Tony Green. 'Everyone loved him. He was a nice guy and everyone loved to see him fight. Everyone wanted to get in his business. I didn't stay for the business, that wasn't my place, but Matt had a lot of managers and managerial problems but that wasn't my thing. I was just a sparring partner and a friend. Matt's always been Matt. I'll put it to you this way, you can't take a kid from where he came from and feed him champagne in Beverly Hills. Eventually, you've got to nourish a guy, and Matt was the type of guy that came from nothing and he had millions of dollars and he couldn't believe where he was at. You give a kid a million dollars and you have a kid in a candy store. Matt was generous to some people and a lot of leeches.'

Green has pictures of Matthew on the walls of his home in South Carolina and regretted how open-minded Matthew had been.

'He didn't have the right guidance because everybody was trying to get in his pockets,' Green snapped. 'Everyone tried to get in his goddamn pockets.'

While Tony saw Matthew become an Atlantic City star, Mustafa Ameen always wished Saad had the opportunity to light up Sin City.

'If you look at Saad's record, to this day it bothers me that the great Matthew Saad Muhammad never fought in Vegas,' said Ameen. 'Atlantic City was basically Murad Muhammad's backyard, local New Jersey promoter and we fought everywhere there but we never made The Big Top. We knew that we were at the last option with Murad and had we prevailed [against Qawi] we were going to go to King ... and Saad deserved a better promotional company ... Imagine DK promoting Saad, giving us some Mwale-like defences and winding up with Spinks in a major payday?'

But it was the paydays that Matthew did have and the money that he earned that created the biggest controversy. How was this nice, easy-going guy who everyone liked allowed to go bankrupt? What went wrong?

Of Matthew's relationship with Bilal Muhammad, Ameen said, 'Other things that happened later on [in] their relationship soured very badly, financial reasons. I won't go into details and specifics and say things between the two of them occurred and Saad was always insistent that Bilal always owed him money, and he had this pot of money that was due him and he was very frustrated about it for the last 15–20 years of his life. He would call me and we'd talk two or three minutes and I'd guarantee that within five minutes he'd segue off into his money, what was going on. It was a subject he'd not let go of until his death … some deep financial questions that caused Saad to remain angry until the end of his life.'

The narrative is that a group of Muslims descended upon Matthew and rode the old warhorse until the wheels fell off. They lived the high life, then they disappeared on him.

Asked about that narrative, Ameen said, 'They say the same thing about Muhammad Ali, in that the Muslims used Ali, he gave them money yadda, yadda, yadda and the same thing with Saad Muhammad. Saad made some contributions, like anybody does, whether they belong to the Catholic Church or the Mormon ministry, so Saad was no different than any other Muslim person in Philadelphia or anywhere else. They didn't have this word back in the eighties but it's Islamophobia, a fear of Islam. It wasn't based on skin colour alone, the black Muslims and white reporters, it was just a bad understanding of Islam and what it represented. Not all Muslims are the same. Everybody's agenda is a little different.'

Ameen maintains he was honest with Matthew and that he'd only ever done right by him.

But Michelle is in no doubt someone should have paid for what happened to Matthew.

'Matthew trusted these people, initially,' she said. 'And it wasn't until years later it was like, "Wait, how many years have I got to go back [to paying tax]? You haven't been paying my taxes? You told me this cheque was for it …" Matthew got screwed in the name of Allah.

'There should have been criminal charges for what they did to him. Seriously. There may even be some people that I don't care for that may look back and have regrets on some of the things they did, but that's between them and their Gods.'

She might be right. The Koran says that taking care of orphans is a way to worship, that those who ignore orphans are non-believers and that those who take care of orphans will be righteous in paradise.

* * *

'The thing was, all he could do was fight,' said Nigel Collins. 'That's true with a lot of them but he was a good-looking guy. Models don't have to say anything but he had that body, that great smile, he could have done something but they didn't market fighters back then.'

The light-heavyweights of Matthew's era had mixed fortunes after their paths had all crossed. Dwight Muhammad Qawi battled addictions to drink and drugs but wound up working in the Lighthouse on the fringes of Atlantic City, helping others fight their demons.

John Conteh and his playboy lifestyle caught up with him. He was treated at a London clinic for his fight with alcohol and was 'one day at a time for 31 years'.

'I'm an alcoholic, I got into alcoholism,' the Liverpool hero admitted. 'I got to a point where one drink was too many and 100 wasn't enough ... so if I have one drink, I can't stop.'

But Conteh remained a popular figure in British sport and always had work as an after-dinner speaker, something he thrived on given his Scouse humour and brilliant storytelling. But he harboured no ill will towards Matthew or, more specifically, Adolph Ritacco, many years on. Sadly, Conteh's trainer George Francis took his own life in 2002.

Rossman struggled and wound up on the rooves with Matthew. They were always friendly and had both sampled the unsavoury side of the sport. Rossman lived in an apartment in Atlantic City, and one would have liked to have heard the difference in their conversations given Matthew said, in the late 1970s, 'Someday, after it's all over, I can see us sitting down, talking about the days when there was so much money hanging out there and we couldn't get to it because our managers were quarrelling.'

Marvin Camel, the first cruiserweight champion who Matthew fought in Stockton and then Montana wound up living in Florida, teaching youngsters to box and working in an electrical store. In his own book, he said of Matthew, 'His story makes me think about putting together a boxing federation fund. So many boxers get out of the sport and have nothing to look forward to. The boxing world has never had a pension operation. You leave boxing and you still need to make a wage. Matthew Saad and I have to learn how to work at something other than boxing. So many guys have nothing to look forward to after boxing. Social security is our only remuneration. We have no way to pay bills. I never had to pay one penny for trips out of the state and country. Boxing paved the way in that regard. But I don't have a hill of beans as far as money is concerned.'

Mate Parlov owned a coffee shop in Pula in Croatia and a statue of him was erected in Fazana. He died of lung cancer in 2008.

Marvin Johnson was a sergeant for the Indianapolis Department of Corrections and Richie Kates maintained his job working on offender programmes in New Jersey.

Eddie Mustafa Muhammad would always miss his friend, and he became a successful trainer in Las Vegas. Friendship or not, he always maintained incredible self-confidence about what might have happened had he and Matthew met in that eagerly anticipated rematch.

'The second time, I would have beaten him easier,' Eddie smiled. 'I beat him the first time, in his hometown. If he'd improved, I'm sure I'd improved.'

James Scott was released from prison in 2005. After his enforced retirement in 1981, he was bounced from prison to prison on the East Coast, had his face slashed in 'a buck-50 attack' – getting cut from his ear to his neck – but he educated himself well, earning dozens of college credits as he immersed himself in history, politics and philosophy.

'Saad Muhammad was strong,' Scott admitted. 'I think I had a chance to beat him but he was a very hard puncher and if you managed to get around the punches you had a chance to beat him. I think I was faster than him, he cut easily, he bruised easily. If you can open the cuts, that's it. As you can see, the way I'm talking now, I never took the punishment some of those guys did.'

Scott always felt disappointed that Matthew ruled out facing him in jail and was full of admiration for those who went to Rahway. 'In my opinion, when you become champion the first person you're supposed to challenge are the people who challenge you,' Scott reckoned. 'You're supposed to at least give them a chance. He said in the newspapers that he didn't want to fight a jailbird. That's a cop-out. Who cares where you've been?'

On his release, Scott helped train amateurs at a gym in Trenton but a neurological decline began and 'Superman' died in a New Jersey nursing home, unable to communicate, in 2018. He was 71.

Murray Sutherland, who did have the opportunity to cut up Matthew, lacerating his bottom lip in their Atlantic City battle, read about Matthew's subsequent fall online.

'Somebody emailed me an excerpt from something they'd found about Matthew Saad and I didn't like it too much, he was a tough son of a gun,' Murray said. 'I loved the guy to death. I just feel bad for some of the fighters who end up like that. Fortunately, I've got a beautiful wife and a couple of kids and four grandkids. We're very family orientated. We stick together and we all live in the same town. At certain times, I possibly thought Matthew's mileage was too high to face a young contender like me but I was kind of in awe of him. When I was living in Canada, every Saturday or Sunday or sometimes both, they'd have title fights on the TV and we used to watch these guys. I used to watch Matthew Saad Muhammad any time he fought and to step into the ring with someone like that? It was pretty awesome.'

Sutherland eventually dropped down in weight and won a world title at super-middleweight, having found out the hard way he couldn't hang with big hitters like Saad and Michael Spinks.

'I wasn't a big light-heavyweight,' Murray conceded. 'Guys like Michael Spinks and Matthew Saad … they just firebombed me.'

Vonzell Johnson was helping train youths in Columbus. He'd retired after the back-to-back losses to Matthew and Spinks.

'In the era that I fought in, so many guys could have been world champion,' Johnson remarked. 'You had really good guys. That's why it was taking so long to get title fights, people were trying to make sure they stayed on top but it was a real rough era. If I had been in this era or the era after the one I was in, I would have been champion of the world.'

Yaqui Lopez was one of Matthew's definitive opponents, and his life outside the ring was the exact opposite of his old rival's. Lopez, who never won a world title despite five attempts, remained in the same house he had always lived in, in Stockton, for decades. Along with wife Beno, he grew old gracefully and with his team, Jack Cruz and Benny Casing around him. Father-in-law Jack lived across the street and passed away in old age, but they had shared some incredible memories.

Decades later, Lopez recalled of his fighting days, 'It was hard because there were so many good light-heavyweights in my era. There were about 20 guys, big names, too, from all over the world. I did my job very well. I don't have to be ashamed of anything. I didn't duck anybody, I fought everybody, I went down and I got up. It's a hard game. It's a dangerous sport. In boxing, if you're hurt, you don't tell the coach "I'm hurt will you please get somebody out here" like in football, baseball and basketball. There's no substitutions in boxing … Thank God that I'm alright … I'm very happy I was in that era. I think it was the best era in the light-heavyweight division.'

Lopez opened up the Fat City Boxing Club, not far from his home, and had high-profile visitors, like Mike Tyson, visit to endorse the facility. He also tried to see Matthew when he could as they started to grow older.

'I was sad when I saw Matthew,' Lopez admitted. 'I saw him and the first time he was talking slow, you know? And then the second time, a little bit worse.'

With hindsight, the 71-year-old Lopez would not trade the health he has or the life he has enjoyed for a world title. He's been happy all his life.

'They might have fame, fortune, money, everything. I've not got that but I've got my health,' he said. 'I've got my wife, my family and my friends. The old man is still alive.'

* * *

'I loved Saad, and I watched him back when he was Matthew Franklin,' said Ray 'Boom Boom' Mancini, one of the boxers who picked up Matthew's matinee idol slot after being involved in several thrilling fights. 'I loved watching him, he was one of my favourite fighters. Matthew couldn't help but be in a great fight because of his style and his resilience, his courage, his heart. He was a special fighter. When you watched him on TV, you knew what you were getting. People don't understand, fighters leave a piece of themselves in every fight. It's just how many pieces you've got left, and eventually he didn't have any more to give.'

Twenty-eight years after Matthew and Lopez shared the Fight of the Year, another Philly battler, Ivan Robinson, shared the Fight of the Year with Arturo Gatti, winning a ten-rounder on points.

'Matthew was a great fighter and he was definitely a great human being,' said Robinson. 'He carried Philly for a long time, I was just glad to come up behind him and have great memories of him. Sometimes you've got to be in fights like that and it takes the will and the heart of a lion. You really have to have a big heart to get in there and get the job done and it didn't matter what it took, Matthew was going to get the job done. A lot of fights he didn't have to trade but that was his style, that's how he fought. You can't change a man. That's what he did best. He was a great puncher, a great warrior and he had a lot of skills that people didn't recognise.'

Antonio Tarver would later rule the 175lbs division and he called Matthew, 'one of the greatest light-heavyweights of all time'.

'His battles with guys like Marvin Johnson were legendary,' opined Tarver. 'Those fights really inspired me. Back then, light-heavyweight wasn't a glamour division but those guys had it rocking.'

Tarver would lose his recognition as world champion at the weight to another Philadelphian, Bernard Hopkins. 'B-Hop' enjoyed watching Matthew's fights, but Hopkins was known for his cerebral methodology rather than Matthew's crashing, bashing ways.

'Too tough for his own good,' Hopkins said, with a shake of his head, of Matthew. 'Didn't duck any punches. Didn't try to. One thing about having heart, people get heart mixed up with brains. I'm not saying he didn't have brains but his IQ of the sweet science was set on only one station. It was Channel 6. That means don't duck. Matthew Saad Muhammad was a Philadelphia pride and joy but he didn't get a chance to enjoy his life and he damn sure didn't get the chance to enjoy the fruits of his labour. To me, when you say Saad Muhammad, I say tragedy. I'm hoping that I am a beacon of hope for fighters taking their hard-earned earnings and letting it quadruple in time, benefit generations of their family from their blood, sweat and tears. When you talk about Saad Muhammad, I say tragedy. They used him, they abused him and then they spat him out and nobody cares. Nobody cares.'

EPILOGUE

'Every champion does it his way. I did it my way' –
Matthew Saad Muhammad to the author in 2002

THE FIRST time I met Matthew was at the International Boxing
Hall of Fame in Canastota in upstate New York. It was 2001 and I was
standing near his plaque in the dainty museum when he approached
me and I recognised him. Around that time, as we made small talk
about his career and I did what so many other fans did – praised him
for his wars – veteran English promoter Mickey Duff came over and
the two embraced. It turned out they had quite a storied background.
They hadn't seen much of one another in the recent past, but back in
the day Matthew was an obstacle for Duff, and his fighters.

Mickey had promoted John Conteh, Lottie Mwale and Louis
Pergaud and Matthew gave Duff four high-profile defeats, including
the brace of wins over Conteh. The three of us laughed and myself
and my countryman, Duff, tossed a few more verbal bouquets in
Matthew's direction, which he bashfully accepted, and we took
a picture.

As the weekend wore on, Matthew and I regularly bumped into
one another and attended fights at the Turning Stone Casino. We
went to get something to eat, and he asked me what I was doing
in America. I was actually in the US to try and start a career as a
boxer. As an inexperienced amateur, I wanted to learn from some
of the best coaches so after Canastota my plan was to train with
Kevin Rooney, Mike Tyson's former trainer, in Catskill. Matthew
said that if I wanted to train with him, I could go to Atlantic City

and he would welcome me. He did this while sizing me up, asking what weight I was and likely thinking I had far more to offer than I actually did. I didn't know how seriously to take that offer, given that I couldn't be classed as a serious fighter. However, I did take his number and he seemed adamant that, if I went to Atlantic City, he would be there for me.

A few months later, his phone rang and sure enough the penniless English traveller had wound up in Atlantic City with nowhere to go, nowhere to be but hoping to learn. Over the next few weeks and months, Matthew and I spent a lot of time together. That would turn into long periods at a time over the next three or four years when I would visit Atlantic City as a staple of my trips to America, trying to get involved in the boxing business.

In case you couldn't tell from the book, I was the person who bought Matthew the Team Saad T-shirt in 2001 before we went to the Bernard Hopkins–Felix Trinidad fight at Madison Square Garden. That was an emotional night in more ways than one. Not just because Hopkins, the Philly legend, beat the Puerto Rican sensation, not just because Matthew and I were in the cheapest seats in the arena and he wanted better but, of course, because he sold the T-shirt off his back when I had been for a bathroom break during the undercard.

That led to a frosty journey back to Atlantic City until I broke the silence and asked, 'Where is the T-shirt?' He told me about the offer of a few bucks and the shirt he was now wearing.

There are many sad tales and quite a few funny ones. We went to a show at Kahunaville, Delaware. I was hired as a round-card guy for the women's fight between novices Lisa Foster and Lakeysha Williams. It makes me smile today that, as I climbed the steps for my first taste of abuse and my first ever experience of being heckled, my friends in the front row, including Matthew and Ray Mercer, booed so loudly it became contagious and the whole venue started booing me.

As they mocked my physique and probably how pale I was at the same time, I started to turn bright red and smiled nervously. I couldn't get out of the ring fast enough.

Matthew took me with him to work on the rooves one day. Sharkey told me he would pay me and he was going to get the money from whoever paid Matthew. It was a day rate, and not a good one, which was just as well because I was terrible. I didn't receive a cent but I didn't deserve one. Matthew and his co-worker lugged rolls of roofing felt high up a ladder on the Atlantic City Boardwalk near a Dunkin' Donuts. When I attempted to do the same thing, even though I was fitter, younger and certainly had better neurological coordination than Matthew, I could not get up the ladder. Maybe my trepidation for heights was a factor, maybe I wasn't strong enough. Either way I was with Matthew for the day and I watched him put in the work and I saw him pause, at times, looking out into the ocean, wondering what he was thinking about the past, the present and the future.

Over the years, Matthew and I spoke a lot about his childhood, his upbringing, gangs, fighting and his career.

One day when we talked in the aftermath of the New York terror attacks in 2001, we discussed his religion.

'I wish and pray that things will settle down and get back into their place,' he said. 'I want people to live a natural and pleasant life, I don't want people hurting each other to survive. I don't follow religion but I do have a Muslim name. But Muslims don't believe in that [what happened].'

Matthew never really did like to go in to a deep dive about anything that happened after the first fight with Dwight Qawi. There weren't too many great memories after that.

But I remember we went to Wladimir Klitschko's fight with Ray Mercer at the Trump Taj Mahal and people like Larry Hazzard and Chuck Wepner came up and spoiled Matthew with praise and kind words. I recall him being embarrassed because I think he knew whatever they were praising, he no longer had. I think he was sad for that, and perhaps it only served to make him realise how hard he had fallen.

One day I was leaving Atlantic City via Greyhound bus and Matthew insisted on waiting with me even though I was there and ready to go ridiculously early. He wanted to say goodbye. We waited a long time, and I was using an old sports holdall with all of my worldly goods in it – probably totalling about £100, if you include the bag – and Matthew and I stood and talked with my bag under the timetable by the wall several feet away. At one point, a homeless guy picked up my bag and motioned to leave. I saw it happen, couldn't quite believe what I was seeing, and I was slow to react. Matthew was not so slow. He tapped the guy on the shoulder. He dropped the bag, held his hands up as if to say he didn't want any problems, and walked off as if it was an accident. I remember Matthew waving me goodbye.

In 2005, one of the best things I've done in boxing happened and I wasn't even there. Matthew was being inducted into the Pennsylvania Boxing Hall of Fame and organisers in Philadelphia contacted me via Larry Tornambe, knowing that I had been in touch with a series of Matthew's old opponents for magazine interviews. They knew I'd visited Eddie Mustafa Muhammad, Yaqui Lopez and Marvin Johnson in recent years and knew I had become friendly with that trio of light-heavyweights. They also knew I would do anything I could for Matthew, so when they told me they were inducting him and they wanted those three former friends and rivals to attend in his honour, I said I would talk to them.

I wasn't convinced it could happen. Eddie was possible. He was living in Las Vegas and working as a trainer. Lopez was leading a quiet life in Stockton while Marvin had become a reclusive figure in Indianapolis. I felt he was quite sore at boxing, the sport and the business, and he said it was because he had not made $1m, which had been his career goal, for all that he had given, for all of the hard fights. I called all three and asked if they would consider taking part, without actually asking if they would. I would leave that to the organisers.

With me in the UK, my hands were tied and it was not for me to discuss budgets, flights, dates or any finer details of the arrangements. A few weeks after those calls, Tornambe, a ring announcer on the East Coast who subsequently moved west, took great delight in sending me photographs of the light-heavyweight legends together. Eddie went. Yaqui went. And Marvin went. And Matthew absolutely loved it.

Matthew and I stayed in touch over the years until, I'd guess, around 2007. The further he got away from Atlantic City and Ralph and Willie, the harder it was for me to track his movements. His phones would often be shut off. He was forever getting new numbers. And with me in the UK, if I called him, it would potentially cost him a fortune to pick up, so I was dependent on catching him at places with a landline. It became harder and harder. He was a hard target, often on the move, sleeping from place to place, trying not to be a burden to anybody. Fortnightly calls became monthly. Then it was perhaps every other month. Then a couple of calls a year. Then we didn't talk. I could no longer reach him. But I was always hungry for knowledge, stories and anecdotes from those who did see him. We had mutual friends who could update me on social media and via email if and when they saw him.

I can't recall the last time I saw Matthew. Perhaps it was that time he waved me off at the bus station. I can't recall the last time we spoke, either, or even what it was about.

I do remember reading the stories about him being homeless in Philadelphia and I knew there would be no way for me to reach him. Then I read about the ALS diagnosis. I did not think it would be over so quickly. I thought I would see him again. When he was gone, it was strange. There was closure but it left an open wound that felt raw. Like so many people who are attached to fighters, they feel they could and should have done more.

Matthew and I first talked about writing this book in 2001. In fact, I approached a literary agent who said that if I was going to pitch this to publishers, I would need something in writing from Matthew saying he was happy to take part. I wrote a 'contract' that was several lines long and highly unprofessional but I knew no better.

Back then, Matthew and I were both struggling. I was attempting to embark on a career and his had ended two decades earlier. Turns out publishers didn't want an unknown author to write about a forgotten fighter. Neither of us were in the position to help one another with anything but friendship.

Twenty years on, and after writing several books, this book – my promise to Matthew – has come too late to help him. There had always been talk of a movie, a book, a documentary, an exciting project … It went with him everywhere for the more than 30 years of his life. Like many retired fighters, he hoped that was his ticket out of the world that he had eventually found himself surviving in. Hollywood never came calling. Despite some of the best intentions of some and nefarious intentions of others, it just never happened. Even back in 1979, and having just become the champ, Matthew's story seemed set for the grandest stage. In *World Boxing*, Randy Gordon wrote, 'His life story would be turned down in Hollywood. Too unrealistic.'

I hoped our book was his ticket out. Even after we had talked about it, there were other ideas, scams and projects he would mention that ultimately came to zip. He was always open to other things and the 'contract' – such as it was – was never going to be one I was going to enforce; it was merely to give to publishers to show that we knew one another and he was interested in writing his life story. During the time I was living with Matthew in Atlantic City, I would take regular train rides to Philly, where I would spend days on end devouring everything I could about Matthew's career on microfilm in the old Philly and New York papers in the Philadelphia library. I photocopied everything, reams and reams of interviews, fight reports and previews.

It was during the first lockdown for Covid-19 that I found my 'Matthew Saad Muhammad box' of possessions in storage. In it were microcassettes with hours and hours of our old interviews, the dishevelled contract from 20 years earlier, the cuttings from the Philly library, pictures of us from over the years – including one of me as the round-card guy! – and all of the work I had put in 20 years earlier. Two things came about as a consequence of finding that box and sifting through its contents. First, the emotion was palpable. I was overjoyed at one moment, teary the next. It all felt so fresh and sad.

Second, I started to think it was time to revisit this book. For years, I'd heard how Matthew's was the best story never told and I knew it. Why shouldn't I allow my friend one last day in the sun, provided I could do him justice?

Matthew had long since passed away. He had died in 2014, but going through that box made everything seem fresh, touching and poignant. I opened my laptop and started to write. That took me down several rabbit holes of thoughts, feelings, emotions and stories that I had locked up and thrown away the key to. It had been many, many years since I'd thought about writing the book with Matthew. The last time it crossed my mind was when he was still alive, and when he died, the thoughts must have gone with him. But with Matthew no longer around to tell his story, I felt it was one that needed to be told and that telling it might give me the closure I had not had from not seeing him one last time, from not ever having the chance to say goodbye.

* * *

The day was about as stark as you could imagine in an East Coast cemetery in January.

A biting wind meant standing still was unpleasant and it made it feel like -10 rather than -3.

It was grey, overcast, yet also eerily peaceful. There was a gentle hum of traffic, occasional emergency service sirens, a maintenance truck beeping while reversing, dogs barking, planes flying overhead but you had to close your eyes and really concentrate to make them the first port of call for your senses.

One could see soulless branches swaying on the naked trees but they made no noise. As you walk from the office at the Ivy Hill cemetery, go under the archway and head to Matthew's resting place, you must walk by Joe Frazier's opulent tomb, with accompanying plaque and monument.

'A lot of you guys come to see them,' I was told in the office, when they find out a fight fan wants to pay their respects to the two Philadelphia heroes. 'We know exactly where they are.'

It was nice the legends hadn't been forgotten.

When the book about Matthew is mentioned, the woman in the office mournfully says, 'His story was so sad.'

A few hundred metres on from Joe's, Matthew's headstone stands in a row of others.

It's in good condition, black with a picture of Matthew with his world title over his shoulder.

The headstone reads: Matthew Saad Muhammad – Miracle Matthew – June 16, 1954 – May 25, 2014.

There are houses on the other side of the fence behind his resting place and a concrete path that runs alongside.

I knelt in front of Matthew and the Matthew I knew flashed before me. I didn't know the Saad who rose or rallied against Johnson, Kates, Douglas, Lopez, Johnson again, Conteh, Lopez again, Sutherland, Martin or the Matthew who eventually fell against Qawi.

I knew the one who took me on the pads in the Atlantic City PAL, the one who booed me with my shirt off as a round-card guy, who'd sold the T-shirt off his back, who looked out for me, sat with me in the cheap seats – and at ringside – who would sound buoyed by my phone calls, who would wave the young travelling English kid goodbye from the bus station and who still had the strength to lug heavy rolls of roofing felt up tall ladders. I thought of the laughter and the sadness and the contrasts made me smile through teary eyes.

I thought of my friend. I could see him and hear his voice. I saw that priceless smile that was still talked about as much as his fights were 40 years on, and I told Matthew that I was finally writing the book and telling his incredible story; one that he had told me so much of.

I said I hoped I would do him justice.

And then I said goodbye.

ACKNOWLEDGEMENTS

THERE IS one person who I owe so much to when it comes to writing this book and that is Matthew Saad Muhammad. The hours of interviews we had on microcassette from years ago have provided the spine of *Warrior*. We had the best and the worst of times. He was humbled in front of me, and I was humbled to spend time with him.

I didn't know the Matthew who lived in a mansion, drove high-end cars, hung with celebrities and who had around 20 people on the payroll.

Most of the time I spent with him, it was just the two of us. We would sometimes put his old fights on a VCR and go through them. Other times, we would talk into the night. We went to fights together, trained together, ate together and travelled together. But the only thing that those who knew him in the late 1970s and early 1980s would have recognised was his smile. I felt like we covered a lot of ground ... the fights ... the search for his identity ... of being lost in the first place ... religion ... his fall and his legacy. We never really discussed the women in his life or his children.

I'm also indebted to a number of Matthew's light-heavyweight contemporaries. Years ago, when spending time with Matthew, I became friendly with Eddie Mustafa Muhammad, Yaqui Lopez, Vonzell Johnson and Marvin Johnson. It was wonderful to reconnect with them for this book. Back then, I also met Richie Kates and Dwight Qawi, and they were helpful for this project, as was Murray Sutherland, who was a brilliant interview. It was also good to talk to John Conteh, Uriah Grant and Eric Winbush.

Of course, many of the cast have passed away, including Joe and Nick Belfiore, John and Bertha Santos, Adolph Ritacco, Steve Traitz and several fighters.

I visited James Scott in Northern State Prison back in 2003 and his quotes about Saad from our conversation are in this book.

I'm writing about fights that happened more than 40 years ago and some of the boxers of the era are no longer here and others were far more lucid when we first spoke two decades ago.

We now know much more about CTE and progressive degenerative diseases from exposure to head trauma and the toll it takes on fighters later in life. More than once when I tried to reach an old opponent I was told, 'You better hurry. He's fading fast.'

But I'm grateful to everyone who took the time to talk to me.

Deer Lake has been renovated from top to toe and proudly the rocks with the names of the greats lie around the old Ali camp. Matthew never did get his stone named after him and there is no evidence that he was there. It is a shrine to Ali, and understandably so.

You can't write about Philadelphia boxing without talking to Russell Peltz, Nigel Collins and John DiSanto and I'm grateful to know them.

I had an amazing time in South Philly hanging out and talking with Eddie and Mike Everett and Stephen Chandler. Thanks also to Henry Hascup from the New Jersey Boxing Hall of Fame and Bob Hatrak, former Rahway Prison warden for their memories.

Mustafa Ameen was extremely interesting to listen to and Salim El-Amin didn't care about time zones and was always okay to talk.

Not all of Saad's inner circle are still with us, but Ameen, Tony Green and Paul Trace have been helpful. Thanks also to Paul's son, Doug, for his assistance.

Trace's care for Matthew radiated from each interview, and asked for a favourite Saad Muhammad moment he said, 'It's hard to pick out one or two special moments, because the whole time with him was fantastic. It was the assignment of a lifetime.'

I'm thrilled Paul has the cover picture. I'm sure Matthew would have liked that, too.

Bilal Muhammad did not return calls or reply to messages for this book.

Thanks to some of my journalistic colleagues like Steve Farhood, Bernard Fernandez and Mike Bruton for their help.

I'm also enormously grateful to Michelle LeViege, and Matthew and Michael LeViege. I felt a genuine warmth from all three and it was brilliant to be able to talk to them about Matthew as a husband and father. I hope they enjoy this book.

Thanks to Frank Stallone for everything. He could write his own boxing book and is one of my favourites to interview.

I'm also thankful to the late Steve Lott, Russell Peltz, John DiSanto, Ed and Jeff Brophy and Paul Trace for their photographs and to Matt Christie at *Boxing News* for the use of their archive.

Others I spoke to include Antonio Tarver, Ivan Robinson, Bernard Hopkins, Ray Mancini, Paul Guez, Don Majeski, Mike Altamura, Ant Evans, Al Bernstein, Tim Witherspoon, Clinton Barnes, Jane Couch, John Bertucelli, Shawn Darling, Pat Doran and Larry Tornambe.

Thanks also to Neil Hall and Mark Sim, and my editors who allow me to work on these kind of projects, Matt Christie, Dougie Fischer and Tom Gray at *The Ring* and *Boxing Scene*'s Rick Reeno.

An early phone call from the wonderful Don McRae told me to follow my heart and write this book, and counsel I've taken from Thomas Hauser stays with me every time I open my laptop.

My friends and *Boxing Life Stories* podcast sponsors Lee Blasdale and Derek Andrews are two of the best people I have had the good fortune to meet, and I will always be indebted to them for allowing me to make my passion my work.

And I couldn't have done any of this without Jane Camillin at Pitch Publishing. It's been a pleasure to work with her again on something that means so much to me.

Which brings me to my wife, Johanna Dixon, and my children, Ben and Lois.

They are my constant motivators to be a better author and a better person and their support is always unwavering, regardless of the time of night the phone call needs to be made or how many thousands of miles have to be travelled.

I wish things had been different for Matthew and I wish he'd never known the struggle after he hit the top. I wish his story was continuously uplifting but there are parts that are wholly inspirational, not least the end.

Matthew had hit rock bottom but bounced back hard, working for RHD and trying to help others live a better life. Unfortunately, Kevin Roberts passed away in 2020, but he clearly gave Matthew support and confidence at a time when he needed it and maybe Matthew's final victory was working with others less fortunate than him.

The abandoned kid who just wanted to belong was making sure they wouldn't have the same feelings of rejection and helplessness he had when he had been turfed out and abandoned on the streets of Philadelphia more than 50 years earlier.

MATTHEW SAAD MUHAMMAD

Born – 5 August 1954
Died – 25 May 2014
Record – 39-16-3 (29 knockouts)
5ft 11ins

1974

14 Jan	Billy Early	Philadelphia, PA	w tko 2
25 Feb	Bele Apolosa	Philadelphia, PA	w pts 4
11 Mar	Roy Ingram	Philadelphia, PA	w pts 4
22 Mar	Joe Middleton	Philadelphia, PA	w tko 5
15 Jul	Joe Jones	Philadelphia, PA	w ko 3
10 Sep	Lloyd Richardson	Philadelphia, PA	w tko 4
22 Oct	Joe Middleton	Alexandria, VA	w tko 2
10 Dec	Wayne McGee	Philadelphia, PA	l pts 6

1975

25 Feb	Vandell Woods	Philadelphia, PA	w ko 6
24 Jul	Roosevelt Brown	Philadelphia, PA	w tko 4
21 Oct	Wayne McGee	Philadelphia, PA	d pts 6

1976

13 Feb	Harold Carter	Baltimore, MD	w pts 10
21 May	Mate Parlov	Milan, Italy	w pts 8
17 July	Marvin Camel	Stockton, Ca	w pts 10
15 Sep	Bobby Walker	Scranton, Pa	w tko 4
23 Oct	Marvin Camel	Missoula, M	t l pts 10
3 Dec	Mate Parlov	Trieste, Italy	d pts 10

1977

| 11 Mar | Eddie Gregory | Philadelphia, PA | l pts 10 |
| 21 Apr | Joe Maye | Wilmington, De | w pts 10 |

23 Jun	Ed Turner	Philadelphia, PA	w tko 6
26 Jul	Marvin Johnson	Philadelphia, PA	w ko 12
17 Sep	Billy Douglas	Philadelphia, PA	w tko 6
1 Nov	Lee Royster	Philadelphia, PA	w pts 10

1978

10 Feb	Richie Kates	Philadelphia, PA	w tko 6
19 Jun	Dale Grant	Philadelphia, PA	w tko 5
16 Aug	Fred Bright	Newark, NJ	w tko 8
24 Oct	Yaqui Lopez	Philadelphia, PA	w tko 11

1979

22 Apr   Marvin Johnson   Indianapolis, IN   w tko 8
WBC light-heavyweight championship

18 Aug   John Conteh   Atlantic City, NJ   w pts 15
WBC light-heavyweight championship

1980

29 Mar   John Conteh   Atlantic City, NJ   w tko 4
WBC light-heavyweight championship

13 May   Louis Pergaud   Halifax, NS, Canada   w tko 5
WBC light-heavyweight championship

13 Jul   Yaqui Lopez   McAfee, NJ   w tko 14
WBC light-heavyweight championship

28 Nov   Lottie Mwale   San Diego, CA   w ko 4
WBC light-heavyweight championship

1981

28 Feb   Vonzell Johnson   Atlantic City, NJ   w tko 11
WBC light-heavyweight championship

25 Apr   Murray Sutherland   Atlantic City, NJ   w ko 9
WBC light-heavyweight championship

26 Sep   Jerry Martin   Atlantic City, NJ   w tko 11
WBC light-heavyweight championship

19 Dec   Dwight Braxton   Atlantic City, NJ   l tko 10
WBC light-heavyweight championship

1982

7 Apr   Pete McIntyre   Atlantic City, NJ   w tko 2

17 Aug   Dwight Braxton   Philadelphia, PA   l tko 6
WBC light-heavyweight championship

1983

23 Mar	Eric Winbush	Atlantic City, NJ	l tko 3
9 Sep	Larry Davis	New York, NY	w tko 10

1984

11 Feb	Willie Edwards	Detroit, MI	l tko 11

1985

1986

10 Jan	Chris Wells	Hallendale, FL	w tko 6
21 Feb	Uriah Grant	Ft. Lauderdale, FL	l pts 10
15 Nov	Tomas Polo-Ruiz	Port of Spain, Trinidad	w pts 10

1987

30 Jan	Pat Strachan	Nassau, Bahamas	l pts 10
26 Jun	James Coakley	Nassau, Bahamas	w ko 3
4 Dec	Bobby Thomas	Weirton, WV	w pts 10

1988

8 Mar	Lee Harris	Richmond, VA	w ko 1
21 Oct	Frankie Swindell	Newark, NJ	l tko 1

1989

24 Oct	Kevin Wagstaff	Brisbane, Australia	d pts 8

1990

16 Feb	Markus Bott	Hamburg, Germany	l tko 3

1991

26 Feb	Ed Mack	Philadelphia, PA	l pts 8
9 May	Anton Josipovic	Novisad, Yugoslavia	l pts 8
15 Aug	Govonor Chavers	Marbella, Spain	w ko 1
5 Oct	Michael Green	Woodbridge, VA	l pts 8
29 Oct	Andrew Maynard	Washington, DC	l tko 3

1992

21 Mar	Jason Waller	Fredericksburg, VA	l ko 2

REFERENCES

Boxing News
The Ring
Big Book of Boxing
Boxing Illustrated
International Boxing Digest
Boxing Scene
Boxing Today
Fight Game
World Boxing

Newspapers.com
Philadelphia Inquirer
Philadelphia Bulletin
Atlantic City Press
New York Times

Ring of Deceit by Bruce Henderson and Dean Anderson, Bruce
    Henderson Books, 2014
I, Conteh, An autobiography, Harrop & Co, 1982
Boxing Confidential by Jim Brady, Milo Books, 2002
Thirty Dollars and a Cut Eye by Russell Peltz, 2021
Warrior in the Ring by Brian D'Ambrosio, Riverbend Publishing, 2014